# PROHIBITION

IN

# SOUTH DAKOTA

# PROHIBITION IN SOUTH DAKOTA

## Astride the White Mule

CHUCK CECIL

THE History PRESS

Published by The History Press
Charleston, SC
www.historypress.net



First published 2016

Manufactured in the United States

ISBN 978.1.46713.712.6

Library of Congress Control Number: 2016939309

# Contents

# Acknowledgements

Most of the information in this book was gleaned from records in the H.M. Briggs Library at South Dakota State University, so much of the thanks for helping make this all possible must go to the leadership and staff in that wonderful facility. A special thanks to Laura Plowman, who courteously responded each time I needed help during my three or four months of watching year after year of South Dakota history fly by my very tired old eyes as I stared down an unblinking microfilm machine.

The H.M. Briggs archives room was undergoing an expansive and deserving face-lift during my inquiries, but archivist Steven Van Buren, Crystal Gamradt and Kathie Gustafson were always most accommodating and helpful in tracking down information stored temporarily in a dozen nooks and crannies.

The Brookings Public Library staff also came to my rescue again and again in my archival searches.

Many others I met and asked for help during my quest deserve a tip of the hat. Gail DeYong, city administrator and municipal finance officer of Colton, South Dakota, dug out musty city records for me; Dan Flyger of Freeman put me on the trail of a bootlegger's daughter, author Leona V. Pietz of Parkston, and her daughter Sharon Schnabel of Tripp; Jim Fry and Clare Charlson of the South Dakota Research Council in Pierre always responded to my e-mails almost immediately, no matter what my scatterbrained question was, as did Kea Warne, South Dakota election supervisor in the secretary of state's office. Patsy Kringel of the state library in Pierre was most kind and very, very helpful.

Special thanks to Dick Smith of Brookings; Andy Howe, Clay County sheriff; Marty Stanwick, Brookings County sheriff; Bruce Blake of Sioux Falls; Matt Cecil of Brookings; Betty Foster of Sioux Falls; Lisa Studts, curator of collections, Siouxland Heritage Museums, Sioux Falls; Lisa Steenson of Brookings; editor Dan Bechtold of Winner; Brookings historian Barbara Behrend; Jim Lusk of Brookings; Chris Cozzo of San Bernardino, California; Betty Hochstetter of Brookings; Jerry Young of Brookings; and Laurie DeRouchey of Hoven.

A special thanks to my talented daughter, Amy Cecil Holm, who masterfully edits all of my outlandish ramblings and also works outlandishly cheap.

And finally, thanks to a high school friend whose name I've since forgotten who taught me how to skillfully and safely snap off the sealed cap of a bottle of low-point beer using only the shiny front bumper of my trusty, rusty 1936 Ford.

## CHAPTER 1

# Prohibition's Swinging Door

Deputy Sheriff Grant Haggerty took the phone call from Spink County sheriff Floyd Bradley at about 2:15 a.m. on a chilly South Dakota May 13, 1927. Haggerty thought the call was unusual because the sheriff had left three hours earlier to lead a four-man, all-night stakeout on the nearby farm of a bootlegger who had recently shot and seriously wounded a federal Prohibition agent. Sheriff Bradley had no radio in his car, so he was calling from another farm near the one being watched. He told Deputy Haggerty there had been more shootings at the Walter Chrisman farm, and two agents on the stakeout with him had been killed. Haggerty was told to call the night watchman at the Redfield Power Plant and tell him to immediately sound the city's siren using the prearranged emergency signal. Within a half hour of the siren's wail, nearly two hundred yawning and armed Redfield men were waiting for orders outside the courthouse.

The two dead federal Prohibition agents had been ambushed in and near the Chrisman barn east of Redfield. The killer was a wanted man even before he poked his shotgun through a small oat bin opening in his barn where he'd been hiding and fired point-blank at the agents. The hotheaded bootlegger, using the same shotgun, had severely wounded a state deputy sheriff near Redfield nine days earlier. He'd been on his desperate run since. Now he was even more anguished, wanted for double murder, and he was out there somewhere in the chilly morning darkness, armed and very dangerous.

The Redfield volunteers who were assembled at the courthouse were soon joined by about one hundred other men from nearby communities who had been alerted by telephone. Also gathering in Redfield were law enforcement officials from a wide area. Among the milling mass of early morning volunteers was United States senator Peter Norbeck, fifty-six, who was spending time away from Washington to be at home with his family. Senator Norbeck would be among volunteers assigned to guard a strategic bridge on a highway that police thought Chrisman might use if he attempted to leave the area. This wasn't the senator's first time working to enforce the law. As Darlington Township constable in Charles Mix County thirty-five years earlier, Norbeck had tracked down another bootlegger in the little town of Castalia, then six miles west and one mile north of today's Platte. Since then, Norbeck, a former South Dakota governor, had continued to fight for and help enact laws to strengthen Prohibition during his long and successful state and national political career.

The double murder in May 1927, to be discussed in more detail in another chapter, was the most abhorrent occurrence during the state's long Prohibition era. It was pivotal and seemed the apogee of the movement. Everyone—wets, drys and the slightly damp fence riders—was stunned by news of the barnyard murders. Surely there must be a better way to control the manufacture and unwise use of alcohol. With the killings, the Prohibition patina began to fade, even in the minds of some of the faithful dry advocates.

Since statehood in 1889, South Dakota had experimented with what many felt were draconian laws extracting personal choices and discouraging individual responsibility. Now after a decade of the war against liquor, and the killings near Redfield, more and more citizens felt an alternative to the madness had to be found. Even Senator Peter Norbeck, hunkered down in his heavy pheasant-hunting coat near the Spink County highway bridge, must have realized the nation's "noble experiment" simply wasn't working.

In South Dakota, there had always been an on-again, off-again relationship with Prohibition. The bobbing and weaving metamorphosis kept citizens, saloonkeepers, bootleggers and all the scofflaws and lawbreakers on tenterhooks, wondering what might come next. Not only was there the confusion because of the inconsistency of the state law, but South Dakota eventually became harnessed to the dual hitch of state Prohibition and a federal constitutional Prohibition amendment.

For more than forty years after frontiersmen established trade with the Native Americans in what is now South Dakota, no serious attempts were made to regulate the liquor traffic that became a part of a wide-open, unregulated wilderness commerce. White traders were well aware of firewater's influence during campfire negotiations for the valuable furs the Native Americans collected. John Barleycorn liquor generated one-way fair deals for the white man. It was only after trading became so inequitable to cause scandal that Congress in 1832 prohibited the transportation or use of alcohol in Indian country.

Lawmakers also endeavored to enforce the law and halt liquor in transit up the Missouri River by placing inspectors at Leavenworth. Shrewd traders, familiar with the territory's nuances, managed to evade these mandates by the use of one subtle subterfuge after another. Controlling the flow of liquor was ineffective to say the least, like stopping a flood with a finger in a yawning breach. Indian country was far too vast and much too wild for any semblance of control over what rolled out onto the immense, wild landscape in jugs, crocks, bottles and tins. Enforcement in the early days proved unsuccessful, according to a 1936 *Sioux Falls Argus Leader* interview with former state historian Doane Robinson.

The continued disruption of the values and traditions of Native American society was so aggravated by the use of liquor that other measures of control of its flow into Indian country had to be found. Volume 1 of the South Dakota Magazine Dakota History Collection explains how the government tried to make examples of the culpable. Among the first to be arrested in Dakota Territory was Black Hills pioneer Fritz Drogmund, who had a sleazy saloon in his small Custer hotel. The German immigrant was arrested in Custer in March 1876 by Deputy U.S. Marshal Ben C. Ash and charged with selling liquor to Indians. He was escorted back to Yankton a couple hundred miles east by Marshal Ash, tried and fined thirty dollars. It was a pittance considering Drogmund's financial successes and ruinous indiscretions at the expense of Native Americans. He told the Yankton judge he was broke and was therefore sent to jail until he could raise the fine money or work it off. Contributions by kindhearted Germans in Yankton soon set him free.

Released, he later boasted he'd walked from Yankton back to Custer in just fourteen days. Once back home, he soon decided to sell his Custer hotel and saloon and start anew in wide-open, anything-goes Deadwood, which was also under the government's no-liquor edict. Drogmund later claimed he made money in Deadwood "hand over fist," according to a *Sioux Falls Argus Leader* report. Watson Parker's *Deadwood: The Golden Years* indicates that by 1909, Deadwood had sixteen saloons for every 250 residents, most of them thirsty.

The federal Indian liquor laws were strengthened several times, but the efforts were ineffective. The first Yankton session of the Dakota Territorial

Legislature in 1862 adopted two liquor laws. One proscribed the licensing of liquor dealers, and another prohibited sale of intoxicants to Native Americans. At least eight other edicts dealing with liquor traffic were adopted up to the time South Dakota became a state in 1889. These included a county option law and several licensing amendments and regulations prohibiting the sale of liquor to habitual drunkards or its sale within three miles of state colleges or any fairgrounds.

South Dakota's early preference for statewide Prohibition began on September 9, 1885, when J.A. Owen of Kingsbury County stood up in the largest building in Dakota Territory at the time, the imposing Germania Hall at Ninth and Dakota in Sioux Falls, where the constitutional convention had convened. He requested a Prohibition committee be appointed to receive a resolution he wished to present on behalf of the citizens of his county. After consideration and debate of Owen's request, delegates opted to submit the Prohibition proposal as an amendment to the constitution because the majority feared a Prohibition clause in the constitution itself might turn the vote.

After a statewide vote in which both the constitution and Prohibition amendment passed, Congress on some minor technicality ordered a second vote. In that second 1889 statewide vote, 40,234 voted for the Prohibition amendment and 34,510 against. Thus, Prohibition became part of the state constitution. But the state, while admitted to the Union dry, had a constant, difficult time over the years keeping itself from being drenched wringing wet in white mule, otherwise known as alcohol that kicked like a mule. In 1895, citizens wished to squash prohibition and did so by a vote of 31,901 to 24,910. Liquor flowed once more, and saloons prospered. But the public saw the unfettered saloon system as encouraging drinking in excess and taking money away from workers' families. Saloons were not popular. So in 1898, another statewide vote was initiated, this time to create a "state dispensary system." It put the state into the liquor business. Supporters assumed such a system would

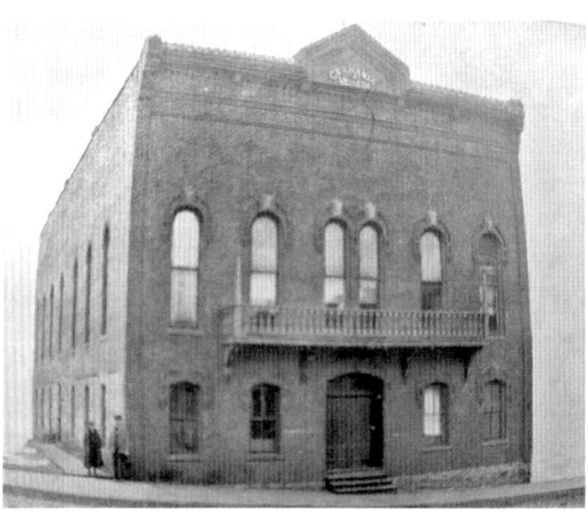

Germania Hall in Sioux Falls in the late 1800s when the state's first Prohibition law was inserted in the constitution. *Author's collection.*

provide more control compared with the wide-open, hated, liquor-by-the-drink saloon method of liquor distribution.

The people approved such a distribution plan 22,170 for and 20,755 against, leaving the administrative details up to the South Dakota legislature. Under the broad plan, the state would grant counties a certain number of state agents who would distribute liquor in containers and follow a strict set of rules, including having the buyer sign for the liquor, thereby ensuring as much as possible that no liquor was sold to alcoholics and providing authorities with a record of consumption by constant users. A dispensary system also set hours for selling liquor, according to a January 1897 *Argus Leader* report.

By 1899, however, before the legislature met to establish liquor dispensary rules and regulations in response to the public vote, the problems and shortcomings of a dispensary system became known, and the plan lost national favor. Aware of its many faults, the 1899 legislature, through various legislative maneuverings and probably even a smattering of back-room subterfuge, failed to write the enabling laws for the publicly voted on dispensary system. Instead, it set a date for another statewide vote to consider repealing Prohibition altogether.

So in 1900, South Dakota citizens returned to the polls once again and voted against Prohibition, 48,673 to 33,907. In his 1901 message to the legislature, Governor Andrew Lee scolded the 1899 legislators for bypassing the dispensary mandate. He said, "The revolutionary action of the last legislature in resubmitting the dispensary amendment by resort to an outrage upon parliamentary practice, after a pretended attempt to adopt a law putting the [dispensary] amendment in force, has been endorsed by the voters of the state by a most decisive majority. There can now be no further excuse for failure to correct the notorious errors in the present law."

Saloons, hated by even many dry supporters who were not averse to a now-and-then drink, were once again opened up, bars dusted off and the good times rolled. There was a slight bump in the wide-open, saloon by-the-drink road in 1914 when another state vote was initiated by state drys, but these temperance forces lost that one 38,000 votes for Prohibition to 51,779 against. Two years later, in 1916, another vote was called for. This time, the vote was 65,334 for Prohibition to 53,380 against. In response to the vote a few weeks before America entered World War I, the 1917 legislature enacted strict laws banning absolutely all beverages with any alcohol in them whatsoever, making South Dakota one of just fourteen states declaring

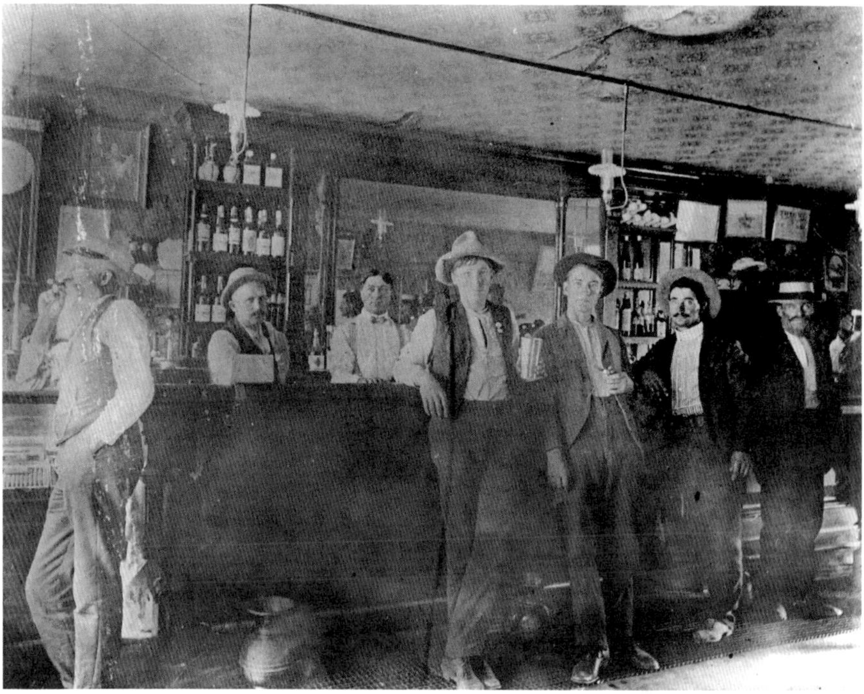

Spittoons, brass rails and customers are evident in this early 1900s, pre-Prohibition photograph of the interior of the Odermark and Brignali Saloon in the state capital of Pierre. *Courtesy of South Dakota Historical Society.*

intent to be completely arid, according to Dennis Cushman's *Prohibition: The Lie of the Land*. That bone-dry 1917 law remained on the books until 1935.

To this day, liquor issues pop up to either boost or reduce liquor sales, but mostly to boost sales. The 2010 South Dakota legislature, for example, considered more than twenty-five bills dealing with the sale of liquor. One lifted the long-standing ban on selling liquor on Sundays and on Memorial Day. It allowed municipalities to decide if liquor could be sold on these days. Originally, the bill included the allowing of liquor sales on Christmas Day, but this provision was amended out. Sale on those special days hadn't happened since the Roaring Twenties, when, with a phone call, a bootlegger would dutifully deliver a little extra Christmas cheer in the form of a bottle or tin of White Mule.

Prohibiting Sunday liquor sales then was similar to other laws that would be considered prudish today but that South Dakotans accepted in the early years. A 1907 edict, for example, forbid commercialized Sunday baseball games "and any tragedy, comedy, opera, ballet, farce, sparring contest, trial of strength and any motion picture of the same." Eight years earlier, the South Dakota legislature even took action on a law "to prohibit prostitution in covered wagons" and felt so strongly about what was apparently going on in covered wagons out on the prairie that it attached an emergency clause to the bill, according to 1899 Session Laws.

During Prohibition in South Dakota, it often seemed as if some people spent their days worrying more about everyone else's morals, or lack thereof, than their own. There was a puritanical attitude toward imbibing alcohol, as well as many other aspects of private life that now seem rather doltish. In Beresford in 1924, the city council outlawed Sunday baseball games, motion pictures and unlicensed pool halls, for example, as reported in the *Argus Leader*. Bridgewater banned spooning in automobiles. The town mayor urged parents to help enforce the edict by informing their children of the new ban. "These clandestine meetings in automobiles and other dark nooks of children of tender age must be stopped," Mayor Tachetter said in an *Argus Leader* interview.

In Sioux Falls in 1924, Minnehaha County sheriff Knewell proclaimed in an interview with the *Argus Leader* his abhorrence to "petting." He said he and his deputies would patrol roads and dark parking places looking for violators. Sheriff Knewell thought most of the petting in his county was by residents of other counties who came to the big city for parties where "everyone is neck and neck." Automobile dalliances were not only considered deleterious by Minnehaha County law enforcement officials, Sioux Falls police were ordered to watch for "neckers" in parks. Two special police patrolled Terrace Park and Sherman Park for just such violations. Special officer Soren Hanson, a former pool hall proprietor, was assigned to peek into parked car windows in Sherman Park; and H.S. Wilkinson, a former bookkeeper turned patrolman, did the same at Terrace Park, according to the *Argus Leader* of June 5, 1934.

In October 1931, a minor "tsk-tsking" scandal erupted after the *Sioux Falls Argus Leader* reported that Senator Peter Norbeck had kissed visiting Scottish opera singer and international star Mary Garden. Sponsors of the Rushmore National Memorial were honoring Miss Garden at a State Game Lodge banquet in the Black Hills when the peck on the cheek occurred. Senator Norbeck brushed off the incident, saying it must have originated in the "fertile brain of Walter (Speedy) Travis," who was a well-known, well-liked and highly respected Rapid City reporter.

Travis, who is honored with a reporter's chair in the State House of Representatives' press gallery and who later headed the state's American

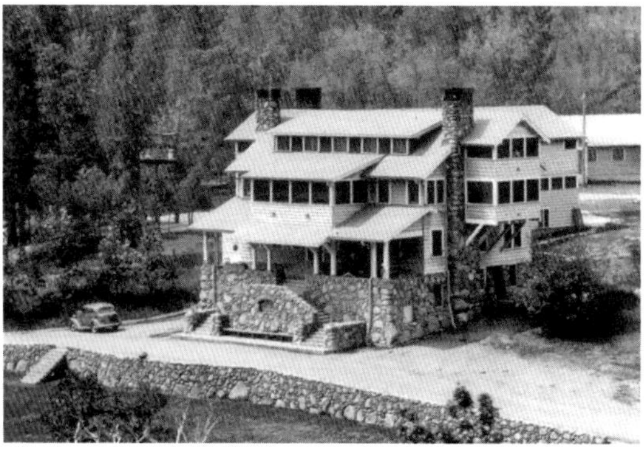

The State Game Lodge in the Black Hills, where in part of the summer of 1927, President Calvin Coolidge established his summer White House. *Author's collection.*

Legion organization headquartered in Watertown, stuck to his reportorial guns. He said the kiss took place after Doane Robinson of Pierre announced to the audience that the State Park Board, chaired by Senator Norbeck, had named a section of the new, scenic Iron Mountain Road the "Mary Garden Way." Miss Garden was obviously thrilled. She jumped from her chair and rushed, arms outstretched, to the startled senator. During a brief thank-you embrace, Norbeck gave her an innocent, fatherly kiss on the cheek. At the time, that was perilously close to scandalous, a 1931 issue of the *Argus Leader* reported.

The same puritanical electorate that was gasping over the Black Hills kiss also wasn't at all enamored by the decision of Aberdeen Parks superintendent S.H. Anderson, who, in June 1935, proclaimed men could henceforth mothball their long underwear–like bathing suits and wear bathing trunks in the Aberdeen swimming pool. He still personally favored the more old-fashioned kind, however. "Personally, I think swimmers are unduly burdened by the modern bathing suit," he said.

Other efforts to clean up the act were initiated by Sioux Falls police chief John Rooks, who in 1935 prohibited cursing in the police station. Officers and station visitors who swore on the premises were fined. A box was placed on the desk of Police Matron Lucy Wheeler, and each vulgar utterance would cost the "utteree" a nickel, according to a report in the *Sioux Falls Argus Leader*.

During the early years of Prohibition's on-again, off-again, long history in the state, two of the most resolute and adamant temperance advocates were cutting their teeth. Peter Norbeck and Edward L. Senn were good friends and were also very effective antagonists against liquor in the late 1800s, and they later became leaders during the final years of federal and state Prohibition in the early 1930s.

Senn was first a teacher and rancher in Charles Mix County and later became a crusading and extremely outspoken daily newspaper editor in Deadwood, perhaps the most unlikely of places at the time to crusade against just about anything that was then illegal. Norbeck had been closely allied with Senn since the very early days. Later, as a senator, Norbeck amassed great political popularity, power and influential contacts in the state and in Washington, where, with his influential contacts, he was able to help his old roommate and confidant Senn get the appointment as South Dakota's chief federal law enforcement officer in the fight against illegal liquor dealings in the state.

Senn's nearly decade-long tenure as Prohibition czar was exemplary. His selection for this enforcement task couldn't have been a better one. In the annals of Prohibition enforcement in South Dakota, he emerges as the superstar. He became South Dakota's Eliot Ness, albeit a less flamboyant one. Senn, like Ness of Chicago's famous Untouchables, was the real deal. He'd been involved in temperance since before South Dakota became a state. He'd been there when South Dakota's constitution was being drafted and the state Prohibition amendment was being debated. This period, and later years, brought the enigmatic Senn into close contact with the Norbeck family, and consequently, he became allied with one of the state's future most famous and effective political figures, Peter Norbeck.

In Senn's unpublished memoirs written a few years before his death in Deadwood in late 1951, and loaned to the author by Senn's granddaughter, Mrs. Laurie DeRouchey of Hoven, South Dakota, he writes of his pro-temperance adventures in South Dakota's early years. Here, in Senn's words, are some of the incidents he and young Norbeck experienced during those early times:

> *South Dakota was admitted to statehood in 1889. In voting on the proposed Constitution in 1888 there was a separate article providing for prohibition of traffic of intoxicating liquors. I had always been greatly interested in temperance work so took an active part in this fight. Though we were only a small frontier county, a campaign was organized and plans made to get speakers who were campaigning all over the state. At the time there were only two church buildings and no schoolhouses or public halls in Charles Mix County large enough to accommodate more than one hundred persons. In this campaign I served as a member of the state committee engineering the prohibition fight, having charge of three counties, Charles Mix, Douglas and Bon Homme.*

His three-county committee received use of a tent from the state committee and "traveled from point to point in the three counties and pitched our tent on the prairies." The Prohibitionists won, and South Dakota entered the union as a "dry" state. Later, Senn was hired as a teacher in a rural school about a mile north of the frontier village of Bloomington, thirty miles west of Armour, South Dakota. In Bloomington, the pastor of the Norwegian Lutheran Church was the Reverend George Norbeck, whom Senn had met during the Prohibition campaign. Norbeck had been president of the Charles Mix County Law Enforcement League, and Senn was its secretary. Both men were ardent in their temperance beliefs. Reverend Norbeck and his family came to Charles Mix County from Clay County, where son Peter was born in 1870. Senn and Peter met for the first time in 1890. Senn was married but lived a bachelor's life at the Norbeck home to be close to the school on weekdays. He and Peter became very close friends.

Norbeck was a rising star. He would serve as a state senator from 1908 to 1914; lieutenant governor from 1914 to 1916; governor from 1916 to 1920; and United States senator from 1920 (the year federal Prohibition started) until his untimely death in 1936, about a year after South Dakota's 1917 "bone-dry" Prohibition section became a part of the state constitution. The "bone-dry" reference spoke to the law's insistence that no beverage in the state could contain any alcohol. Federal Prohibition later added to the confusion in South Dakota by placing a limit on alcohol in beverages at .05 percent.

Senn said in his memoirs that the 1889 state Prohibition law was grossly violated in Charles Mix County and elsewhere in the state. One reason, he said, was because the drys had the law, but the wets elected most of the county sheriffs and other law enforcement officials, including the county state's attorneys. This is illustrated by an example Senn tells of a raid in which he participated with Peter Norbeck in the early years of Prohibition:

> *We had one notorious violator who refused to close his saloon in Castalia, then located six miles west and a mile south of Platte. We organized a county Law Enforcement League to help enforce the law. To further our efforts we elected Peter Norbeck, then of legal age* [he was twenty-two], *as a township constable of Darlington Township, making him eligible to serve legal papers anywhere in the county. C.I. Crawford, subsequently governor and U.S. Senator, was then Attorney General of South Dakota. I applied to him for assistance. He said that*

*though he was in hearty sympathy with the law and our efforts, his other obligations and limited force would not permit of giving us any assistance, except advice.*

*Our county state's attorney at that time was hostile to enforcement of prohibition. Therefore it was deemed advisable to not let him know of our intentions. We employed an able attorney, Judge V.V. Barnes at Yankton, to prepare a search warrant and advise as to its service. Also we employed an attorney at Wheeler, named Adam Grimes, to represent our League in court if we succeeded in getting a case there. To further our efforts we had elected a staunch prohibitionist, Frank Tomlinson, as our justice of the peace. Thus primed, Constable Norbeck and I headed one morning for the office of the State's Attorney at Edgerton, then three miles south of today's Platte. Pete drove a lumber wagon with an extra saddle horse. I came from another direction, brought by my wife, in a buggy.*

*Together we entered the state's attorney's office to face a crucial test. The search warrant had to have his signature before it could be legally served. I told him the purpose of our visit and ask*[ed] *him to sign the papers. He demurred and asked to delay action until he had time to examine the papers. I protested against this, telling him an abler attorney than he had prepared the paper, giving his name. Still he demurred, and I became outspoken, saying: "I want those papers signed before you leave this office, because if you go outside before doing so, you will tip off the raid and someone will go on horseback as fast as possible to Castalia," which was about ten miles distant, "to give the saloon keeper warning." Thus assailed and constrained, he signed the search warrant. Pete* [Norbeck] *took it and got on the horse and got to Castalia as soon as he could. I followed, driving the lumber wagon.*

*When I got to Castalia I drove up to the saloon and entered. Apparently it was in operation as usual. The saloon keeper's brother was behind the bar. A resident of the village was lounging on a pile of beer kegs. Several women were busily removing liquors from the shelves, taking them out the rear door. I said to the lounger, "Has Peter Norbeck been here?"*

*He said, "Yes, he has; he served a search warrant on the bartender, deputized me to take charge and went out to find the owner." I called his attention to the women removing the liquor and asked him to stop them and lock the doors, while I went to locate Pete. The village was small and I soon located him. He had not found the owner. We finally located him in a "wet" attorney's office, in a rear room out of sight. However, he finally came out in response to Pete's demands and submitted to arrest.*

> *All beer was then handled in wooden kegs. We seized nearly a wagon load of full kegs, and despite the activities of the women before my arrival, a considerable quantity of hard liquor in bottles. I drove this load to the home of Justice Tomlinson near Edgerton, with Pete and the prisoner and his attorney accompanying.*

A change in venue was requested by the Castalia saloonkeeper and granted by the judge. The new venue was presided over by an avowed wet judge. The defendant entered a plea of not guilty, followed by his attorney's request for dismissal. To this, Senn said the state's attorney "promptly acquiesced." The justice immediately ruled "case dismissed," and the trial was over in minutes.

Wrote Senn, "Though we appeared to be licked we refused to surrender the wagon load of seized liquor, and drove it to the Norbeck home. That night we stored it in our bedroom to prevent seizure by possible night visitors. As those kegs of beer had been hauled about twenty miles under the hot sun, there was much 'fizzing' during the night and we got little sleep."

The saloonkeeper eventually not only got his "fizzing" beer back, but he also sued Senn for damages for "spoiling his property." Senn lacked any defense, so his attorney advised him to pay the twenty-five-dollar fine to get the suit over with. "Thus ended the first and only official act of Constable Peter Norbeck," Senn concluded.

Senn said Norbeck was a determined fighter "yet a good diplomat." Norbeck once told Senn: "You and I are generally working to the same ends. The difference is when we come to a stone wall you try to butt through it and I try to work around it." Throughout their careers, these two special men in South Dakota history continued to plow through and work around the obstacles erected by opponents of Prohibition.

The first governor of South Dakota, Arthur Mellette of Watertown, concerned with the liquored-up lawlessness in the new state, asked the first legislature to set rules and regulations for a true liquor ban. He called for penalties "sufficiently severe and stringent to enforce a compliance with the provisions of the law and prevent its violation."

Dutifully responding, an enforcement law was approved by the legislature defining intoxicants as "all spirituous malt, vinous, fermented or other intoxication liquors or mixtures thereof, by what-so-ever name called, that will produce intoxication." South Dakota druggists, immersed in the often alcohol-laced patent-medicine business, were to be given permits by county judges to sell liquors when prescribed by physicians for "medicinal" purposes. Liquor was also legal if used for sacramental or scientific purposes.

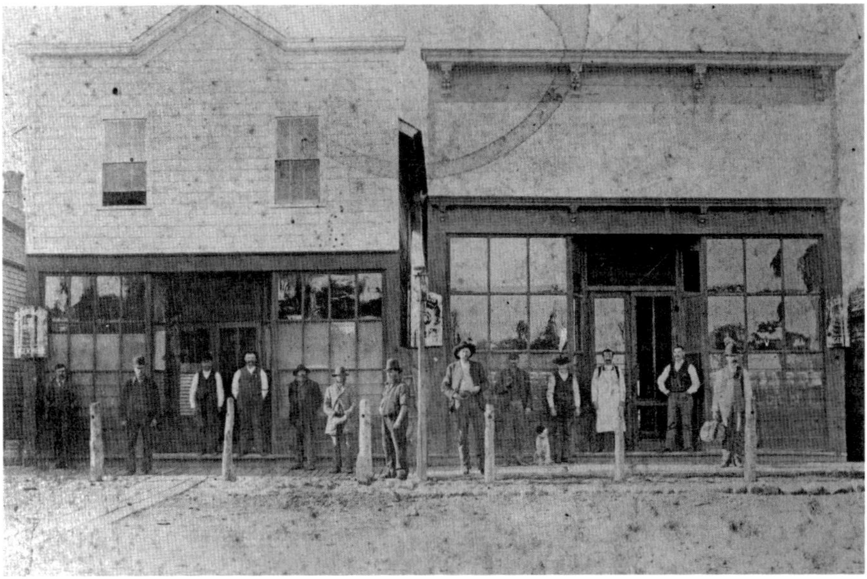

Saloon visitors in the early 1900s abided by an early photographer's request to pose on the wooden sidewalk in front of tying posts and two Arlington, South Dakota saloons that for obvious reasons both had front windows covered to hide inside occupants. *Courtesy of South Dakota Historical Society.*

Interestingly, county state's attorneys were mandated by the legislature to enforce the law. And as an indication of the wet or dry side taken by elected officials regardless of the law, the measure stated that if a state's attorney failed in the assignment, the South Dakota attorney general was authorized to step in to enforce the law.

Opponents of Prohibition, and those with an aversion to the government telling anyone what to do, especially in regard to personal habits, sought resubmission of a dry amendment during the second and third legislative sessions in Pierre, but the efforts were beaten back after energetic floor fights. In 1907, Governor Coe I. Crawford called for "measures further regulating the sale of intoxicating liquors and the number of licenses," which were at the time limited to one for every three hundred persons in a community. In 1909, Governor Robert S. Vessey requested a hospital be built for inebriates, to be paid from license fees. Governor Vessey believed "so long as the state permits the sale of intoxicating liquors, so long we stand doubly charged with the proper care of those unfortunates." No hospital for alcoholics was built.

As many political leaders were trying to shore up liquor barriers, one of the nation's most famous temperance speakers, Carrie Nation, who liked to have her first name spelled "Carry," visited South Dakota. Known as the Kansas saloon smasher because of her trademark axe that she carried with her and applied at random to the fancy accoutrements of bars and saloons, Nation spoke in Brookings in January 1910. The local newspaper reporter took a rather tongue-in-cheek approach to her visit and wrote that no one was present to greet her when she arrived in town by train from DeSmet. "After dinner at one of the local restaurants she took a leisurely survey of the town, but failed to run into any thirst emporiums much to her disgust," the January 11, 1910 *Brookings Register* said.

The paper described Nation as a "motherly-looking old lady of about sixty years of age and she does not look the part of a saloon smasher. In the evening she spoke at the opera house to a fairly large crowd there being about 250 people present at fifty cents a head....Some of the stage hands thought to have a little fun with her during the lecture and got busy with their pipes and cigars. She stopped her lecture and asked the stage manager to drive the jokers out into the night." Another popular temperance speaker who often visited South Dakota was lecturer William E. "Pussyfoot" Johnson of Nebraska.

Back on the state's political stage, Governor Vessey returned in 1909 to promote his hospital idea, telling legislators that "the respectable saloon is very much more dangerous to the average young man than is the squalid booze joint" and "the liquor traffic is the highest tax that is being paid by the common people of today and the heaviest drain upon their resources." Orators Nation and Johnson couldn't have agreed more.

In 1913, Governor Frank M. Byrne picked up the cudgel for more liquor law enforcement, asking the legislature for "strict regulation and control." This opinion from the state's chief executive intimating things were out of hand was reflected in the sentiment of the citizens. In 1915, the legislature again submitted an amendment to the state constitution calling for state Prohibition. In a statewide vote in 1916, Prohibition was back, becoming effective in South Dakota on July 1, 1917. After the state's giddy ride, the big "white mule" was again haltered and coaxed back in the barn by a vote of 65,334 to 53,380. Saloon owners were stunned. Some paid little attention to the ban, hoping to clear out their liquor stock over time and perhaps earn back some of their original investment. In a few cases, sympathetic, friendly law enforcement officials at the local level looked the other way.

With Prohibition again the law of the land in South Dakota, joyous officials of the state's Anti-Saloon League credited the victory to the general dissatisfaction of the public for the much despised saloon system, according

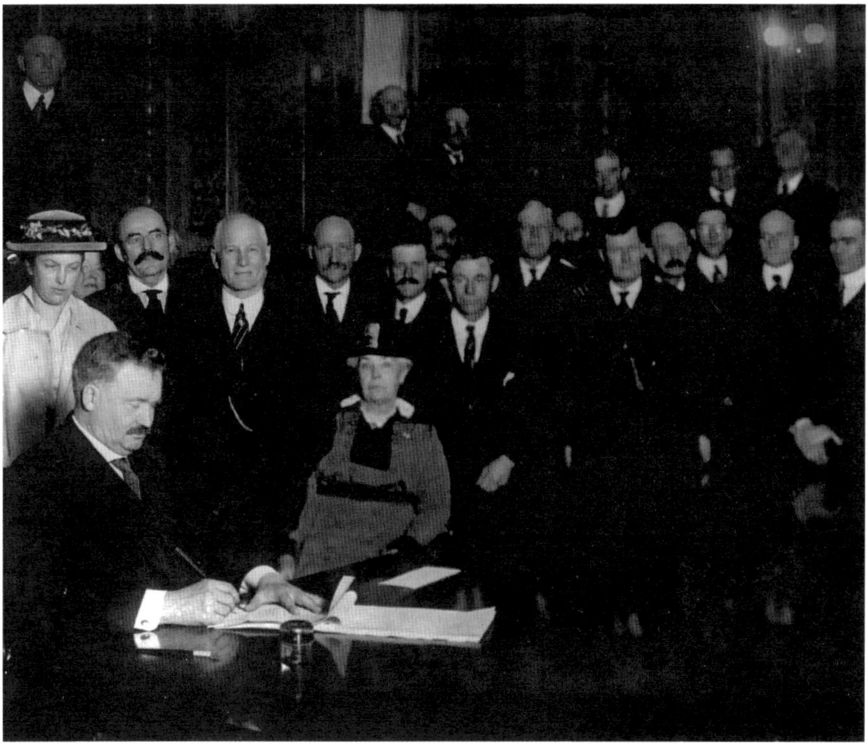

South Dakota governor Peter Norbeck signs the state's bone-dry Prohibition law in 1917. *Courtesy of South Dakota Historical Society.*

to the November 30, 1916 *Brookings Register.* Counties voting against Prohibition in 1916 were Aurora, Bon Homme, Brule, Campbell, Douglas, Edmunds, Faulk, Hughes, Lawrence, McPherson, Potter, Walworth and Yankton. McPherson County had 724 more wet votes than dry votes. Lawrence County voters just barely voted wet by 2 votes.

Of the counties voting for Prohibition, Brookings County had the largest dry majority by 851 votes. The smallest dry majority came from Carson County, by just 4 votes. The city giving Prohibition the largest majority was Brookings, by 438 dry votes. Mitchell was the next most favorable dry city, by 383 votes, with Watertown a close third with a 360 dry vote majority. No community with more than 1,500 population gave a wet or anti-Prohibition vote except Aberdeen, which voted wet by a few votes.

By 1916, former Darlington Township constable Peter Norbeck, South Dakota's new governor, took his turn. The personable and successful Redfield well driller/businessman called upon the 1917 legislature to transform the

1916 vote for Prohibition into rigorous and firm law. He thought the previous Prohibition efforts had failed "due to law enforcement." He said enforcement in the past Prohibition era had been weak because Prohibition was "largely optional with each community." Norbeck asked for the South Dakota attorney general to direct prosecution. He also wanted a state Prohibition commissioner to help enforce the law. Both his suggestions were adopted by the legislature. The prohibition commissioner was about to be named, but a second law passed later in the session changed the title to "state sheriff." The name change more adequately conveyed the intent to vigorously enforce state Prohibition laws. According to 1917 Session Laws, an appropriation of $3,000 was assigned to the new state sheriff's operations—hardly enough to do what was expected.

That year, and in subsequent years, legislators continued assigning more and more non-Prohibition enforcement responsibilities to the state sheriff. So numerous did the assigned tasks become—from tracking down cattle rustlers to car license checks, headlight tests and raiding midnight poker games—that it simply became too much for the undermanned, underfunded, understaffed state sheriff's office to handle.

By January 1919, forty-six of the forty-eight states had accepted the amendment. It was adopted after an arduous crusade by temperance groups, most notably the Woman's Christian Temperance Union (WCTU), the Anti-Saloon League and churches. On March 20, 1918, South Dakota became the tenth state to ratify the national amendment. Now South Dakotans, already saddled with their own extremely rigid Prohibition laws, had two masters governing liquor.

And so three years before the federal government endorsed ratification of the Fourteenth Amendment on October 19, 1919, for national Prohibition to begin on January 16, 1920, South Dakotans had already decided to set into law the moral standards for themselves. Only a month after the measure passed, one of South Dakota's most famous and nationally prominent temperance leaders died at his home in Highmore. Captain O.R VanEtten, eighty-six, a veteran of thirty-four Civil War battles, including Gettysburg, passed away on February 23, 1920. He had delivered over ten thousand temperance lectures during his active years and was a confidant of early national temperance leaders like Henry Ward Beecher, Harriet Beecher Stowe, Francis Murphy and Frances E. Willard. VanEtten was instrumental in the South Dakota temperance efforts and had been honored by Governor Peter Norbeck for his Prohibition work, according to the *Sioux Falls Argus Leader.*

By the time national Prohibition came along to lock up the bars and smash all the Lilliputian shot glasses and bulky beer mugs everywhere, the scofflaws and ne'er-do-wells and the good people who for generations had made their own home-brewed whiskey and beer in South Dakota were already moonshine experts, adept in making what many called white mule because of its juddering kick. Many called homemade brew lemon juice or vanilla extract because those flavors often were used to sweeten the alcohol. It had other euphemisms, such as scatter foot, barbed wire, John Barleycorn or just plain, unadulterated booze.

Store-bought stills were ordered, and homemade stills were retrieved from attics and haymows. They were soon turning out good, but not great, illegal moonshine by the thousands of gallons. The battle to impede this steady flow was never won and never lost. It became a stalemate. As one still was discovered and knocked down, another was fabricated. One illegal saloon would be closed, and another blind pig would open just down the road.

A small army of out-of-work and willing young rumrunners, or bootleggers, was available. As the law caught up with some, others seeking to make a few quick dollars took their place. Most freelanced, while some worked for large liquor wholesalers. Bootleggers, or "leggers," got their name from an earlier time for the practice of inserting bottles of booze into boot tops to carry around out of sight, from still to waiting customers. The odd-shaped, concave pint and half-pint booze bottles in use today were invented during Prohibition. They hugged the boot or body. Men and women looking to turn a buck by smuggling liquor into the country, or by selling the local product to their customers, wore specially made belts and vests with copious pockets to hide the flat pint bottles, perhaps as many as a dozen or more. Women sometimes concealed bottles in their bloomers, corsets and brassieres.

While much of the booze was made in small stills in the state, smuggling helped meet the demand. The routes for smuggling liquor from Canada were well mapped and scouted by the time the Eighteenth Amendment came along in 1920. For South Dakota, the quickest route and—because of the lonely, bleak geography and unpopulated miles—the easiest for smuggling Canadian booze was along the North Dakota border with Saskatchewan and Manitoba, the homes of premier whiskey maker Seagrams. The border crossing from Canada to Minot, North Dakota, was so popular it became known as "Whiskey Gap." Another source of liquor for South Dakotans was Chicago. The Windy City became such a busy bootlegging hub because of its location near Canadian smuggling routes and on to population centers to the east, south and west and because of the iron-fisted control of the flow of midwestern booze by Al Capone.

National Prohibition, of course, forbid the manufacture, sale or transportation of intoxicating liquors. It was necessary for the Eighteenth Amendment to be enforced, defined and backed up further by what became known as the Volstead Act, named for Minnesota lawmaker Andrew J. Volstead of Granite Falls, the unostentatious chairman of the House Judiciary Committee, which shepherded passage of the bill enforcing the Eighteenth Amendment. After ten terms, Congressman Volstead was defeated in 1922, probably because of low farm prices rather than for his Prohibition notoriety. He was given a political plum in the Eighth District Prohibition Enforcement Unit, occupying an obscure upper-floor office of the St. Paul, Minnesota Post Office. Volstead served as the district's legal advisor. As Prohibition ended, he was released on July 1, 1933.

Many of the ramifications and consequences of prohibition were unanticipated by Volstead or other temperance advocates. Its premise was wrong. The teetotalers and the freelancing morality police assumed that if the supply of alcohol were cut off, those who imbibed would simply quit drinking cold turkey. It didn't happen, of course, and the nation and its culture was forever changed because of this naïve hypothesis. Outlaws and gangsters found new opportunities and became national heroes. Internationally, America became known for shootouts, killings and the weapon of choice, the Thompson submachine gun, all of which ushered in America's "gun culture," still here today. Gangland leaders became wealthy, admired locally and revered by many. Al Capone and his ilk were aggrandized in movies, books and songs. Control of the illegal booze business in Chicago between Al Capone and Bugs Moran brought about a standard of violence exemplified by the St. Valentine Day Massacre on February 14, 1929.

Murder for hire became a well-paying vocation. The loosening of social mores during Prohibition included the beginnings of a drug culture. There developed a scorn and a disrespect for authority and the law. The cocktail and the cocktail party entered the nation's lexicon. The pace of American music and dance preferences shifted to an overdrive gear of frenzied, fast, wild, jerky machinations compared to the smooth and graceful waltz of more discreet times.

Some in law enforcement were corrupted by the money available from illegal manufacture and sale of liquor, gambling and prostitution or were intimidated into cooperation by gunmen such as the handsome, athletic former Beadle County sheriff, Verne Miller, who became America's most wanted hit man, until he was found in an Illinois ditch, his nude body wrapped in a blanket with his head bashed in and a .38-caliber slug in his brain for good measure.

The Roaring Twenties and Prohibition came at a time when millions of American young men were returning from the killing fields of Europe. The automobile was rolling off the assembly lines. Women's suffrage came to be. There was a mass migration from farm to big city. Charles Lindbergh's nonstop flight across the Atlantic captivated America's fancy and exemplified its daring and recklessness. Men and women sought to emulate Lindbergh's feat or set other aircraft records, and almost weekly, another mark entered the aircraft record books or daring pilots died trying. Electricity was lighting the dark corners of the farms and powering glowing neon signs that were alluring beacons to many.

Despite elaborate and expansive efforts by Prohibitionists, demands for liquor went largely unchecked. Much of the smuggling and bootlegging was controlled by powerful racketeers such as Capone and his Chicago and midwestern monopoly that became so well organized that the influence even reached into South Dakota. The appetite for liquor was insatiable, and the potential for liquor sales was tremendous. An army of imaginative entrepreneurs stepped in to help make and sell it, illegal or not. The Prohibition law, which sought the total abstinence of more than 122 million people who had been accustomed for decades to the consumption of two million gallons of liquor a year, was destined to fail.

What President Herbert Hoover hailed as a "great social and economic experiment, noble in motive," became a gigantic funnel, redirecting profits to the wrong people and the wrong causes. Prohibition, intended to usher in temperance for all, instead created opportunities for those who could find ways around it. Millions of creative people, including thousands in South Dakota, found the ways and means of obtaining alcohol through smuggling, turning industrial alcohol into drinkable alcohol, making home-brew, using medical prescriptions to obtain alcohol and strengthening the alcoholic content of what was known as "near beer."

With the enactment in 1917 of the state law on Prohibition, the office of the newly created state sheriff began to organize. Joining that small contingent later was a cadre of federal dry agents from the United States Department of the Treasury's Prohibition unit. The unit initially headquartered in Sioux Falls, then moved to Huron and later back to the federal building in Sioux Falls. Many of the federal agents had been trained at tracking down tax evaders and counterfeiters, and in some areas of the nation, dry agents were called "revenuers."

Also involved in the hunt for booze in South Dakota was the United States marshal's office. Counties had sheriffs and communities had local police forces, and they, too, were charged with enforcing Prohibition laws. There seemed never to be enough help, however. Federal dry agent numbers peaked at about twenty, and the state sheriff may have hired ten to fifteen from time to time.

It was a big job, possibly one that would have never ended without the later erasure of the law from the books. Good, dedicated men and women worked tirelessly for Prohibition. Some died trying, even in South Dakota, which was considered a nickel-and-dime, backwoods outpost by the big operators in the metropolitan areas.

Chapter 2

# Agents of Change

Edward Louis Senn, the last United States Prohibition administrator for South Dakota, who served until federal Prohibition ended in 1934, was one of the best in the nation.

He could also be a royal pain in the neck.

A fiery, crusading editor-publisher of the *Deadwood Daily Telegram* before his appointment to the state's top federal Prohibition post in 1925, Senn had a reputation for using a blunt hatchet when a sharp penknife would suffice. He told it like it was, and called 'em the way he saw 'em, with little concern for being what today is considered politically correct. He could have kept his disagreements private, but instead, he usually expressed his vitriol in public. Yet despite his faults, Senn epitomized the dedicated law enforcement officer of the day. He was otherwise perfect for the job: smart, articulate and unwavering in his temperance beliefs. He possessed an untiring zeal for what he believed needed to be done. Even with these admired talents, however, Senn couldn't seem to help himself when it came to rubbing people the wrong way. And that idiosyncrasy often got him into trouble.

Within ninety days of Senn's appointment to the highest federal Prohibition post in the state, he inserted his foot in his mouth. Perhaps remembering his experiences on the long-ago Castalia liquor raid with Peter Norbeck, the slim and balding federal agent took to task more than half of South Dakota's sixty-four county sheriffs. He called them "venal" and said they were guilty of hiding and even protecting lawbreakers. He advised voters to oust from office what he called "rogue sheriffs," confessing that when his office was

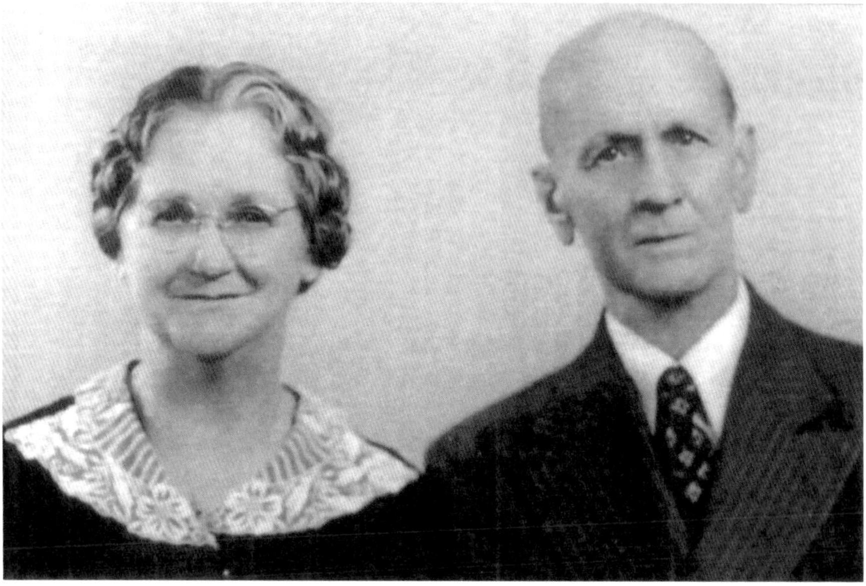

Edward Senn, federal Prohibition administrator for South Dakota, and his wife. *Courtesy of Patricia Senn Dewald, Bowdle, South Dakota.*

planning a raid to arrest Prohibition violators located in a rogue sheriff's county, he was hesitant to inform the local sheriff of his plans because he didn't trust him.

Senn wasn't particularly enamored with many of South Dakota's county state's attorneys either, saying an "aroused public sentiment" in the election of sheriffs and state's attorneys "was the solution to remedy the present condition" of lack of local enforcement of Prohibition. He said many local county officers refused to cooperate with him, so he avoided them when working in their localities, according to the *Sioux Falls Argus Leader*. Senn, a workaholic (he'd have hated the description so closely allied with the lexicon of liquor) in the battle against alcohol, and his comments about county sheriffs and state's attorneys didn't stop there. He also chastised community police forces. "Radical changes are necessary in police forces in seven cities in the state," he told a *Sioux Falls Argus Leader* reporter in 1926. Not surprisingly, these scathing comments got him into hot water with his superiors in the district Prohibition headquarters in Omaha. They, in turn, passed along word of his indiscretions to the nation's Prohibition leaders in Washington. Rumors were rampant. Senn, arguably one of the nation's best Prohibition administrators except for his public attacks, was a goner.

Even South Dakota governor Carl Gunderson wasn't happy with the lanky law officer who looked more the schoolteacher he had been than the boss of more than a dozen armed federal agents. The governor came to the defense of county law enforcement officials in a searing letter to Senn on January 20, 1926, which Governor Gunderson released to the press, just as Senn himself was accustomed to doing. The governor rightfully defended county sheriffs. Governors had the power to strip county sheriffs of their jobs, and Gunderson cynically suggested in his letter to Senn, "It seems strange that you have failed to furnish this office with evidence of failure on the part of county sheriffs to perform their duties as you were in possession of damaging evidence against thirty-three sheriffs."

Senn, despite his cavalier public criticisms, may have had a point in his reprimands of some law enforcement officials. Perhaps the look-the-other-way law enforcement tradition in Deadwood helped incise in his mind his uncomplimentary opinions of local law enforcement. He may have at times been insufferable, but he was often right. At the time, it was true that some of those sworn to uphold the law in South Dakota were indeed lax in their attention to the Prohibition edicts of the state and federal governments. Some sheriffs and local police were very lenient in enforcing liquor laws. They were reluctant to arrest longtime neighbors, friends and voting constituents for what they considered harmless indiscretions. A bottle of booze in the pantry or back pocket probably didn't seem to them to pose a serious threat to the state or national effort to control liquor's flow. Many law enforcement officials issued soft-spoken warnings and light wrist slaps, except when the violation was so egregious and so public that the sheriff or police had no choice but to take action.

In 1922, an effort was initiated by South Dakota attorney general Byron Payne to remove Tripp County sheriff Thomas Colman for failing to perform his duties. The complaint alleged the sheriff "delivered to John Holland, David Howard and others who were committed to the county jail intoxicating liquors while such persons were so committed to jail and said prisoners became intoxicated." The *Sioux Falls Argus Leader* in April 1922 reported that Colman was also charged with often being intoxicated himself while on duty in the county courthouse and on the streets of Winner. Sheriff Colman resigned his position before Governor William H. McMaster could take action on Attorney General Payne's damaging allegations and recommendation.

This temptation to wink at liquor laws by local law enforcement officers was mentioned during a community meeting in Sioux Falls in 1930, reported

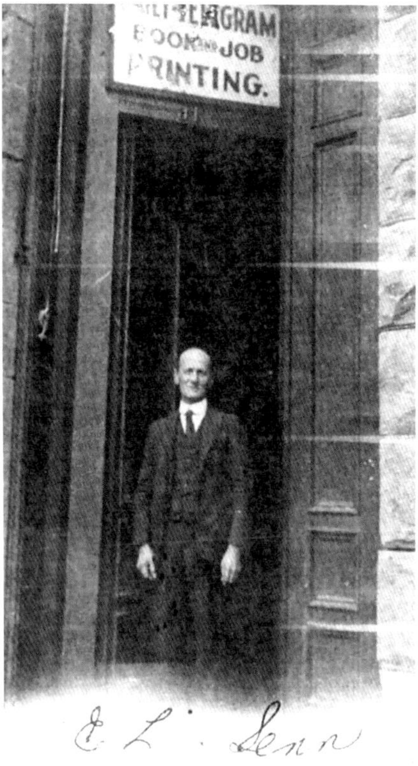


E.L. Senn, the fiery federal Prohibition administrator in South Dakota, was unhappy with what he felt was a lack of sharing of intelligence and planning surprise raids on moonshiners by the South Dakota state sheriff and his deputies and complained publicly to South Dakota's governor about the problem. *Courtesy of Patricia Senn Dewald, Bowdle, South Dakota.*

the *Sioux Falls Argus Leader*. Lawrence Green, Minnehaha County deputy sheriff, who was on the program with Senn, said, "If you think it is pleasant to take poor men and poor women with many children to jail because they have violated the liquor law you are wrong."

In many instances, the local police and county sheriff were well acquainted or perhaps even related to those who might violate a Prohibition law "a little." They also knew the bad guys who were capable of doing much worse than going on an infrequent rip and tear in town, and it was these scofflaws with whom the sheriff was primarily concerned. So the temptation to look the other way when liquor laws were broken just a little is somewhat understandable, although Senn would not have agreed. He had absolutely no time for the Prohibition lawbreakers, whether they were a relative, good friend or stranger.

A few days after Senn had the temerity to pillory his compatriots serving as chief law enforcement officers in thirty-three counties and seven large cites in the state, one of the chief South Dakota law enforcement officials, sensing a breakdown in the trust so necessary between enforcement agencies, came to Senn's defense, according to the *Sioux Falls Argus Leader*. State sheriff E.E. Gregory, a smiling, happy-go-lucky Bryant veterinarian and former United States marshal who had been appointed to the $3,000-a-year job by Governor Gunderson, called a meeting of the South Dakota constabulary in Pierre on January 29, 1926. It was the first gathering of its kind ever in the state, and it became the beginning of the South Dakota Peace Officers Association.

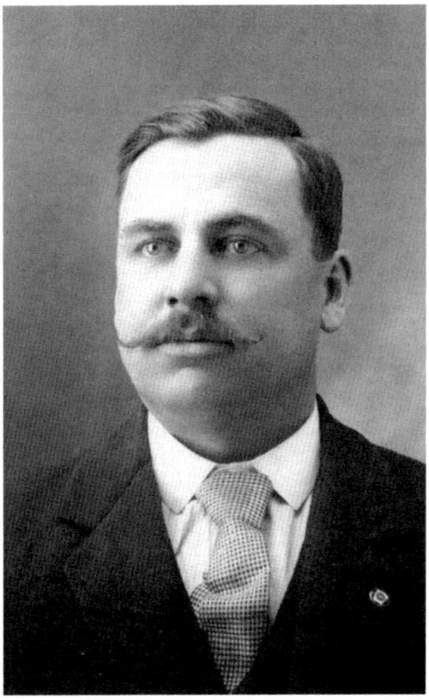
State sheriff E.E. Gregory. *Author's collection.*

Dr. Gregory did not mention Senn by name during his speech at the opening session of the state's law enforcement officials. He said his main reason for calling the session was to "exchange ideas and work out better plans for the apprehension of law violators to curb the acute crime conditions admitted on every hand." He told the audience composed of community police, county sheriffs and others that while they had nothing to do with the making of laws, "we have agreed to enforce them. Any officer who apologizes for enforcing law is a weakling and unfit to hold his position."

But even State Sheriff Gregory's admonitions did not satiate the maligned peace officers in their quest for Senn's blood. The organization sent a telegram to A.W. McCampbell, district Prohibition director in Omaha. It was in the form of a petition calling for him to relieve Senn. Director McCampbell claimed he had no authority to dismiss Senn but would pass along the resolution to his superiors in Washington, who subsequently ignored it. Rumors in South Dakota of Senn's impending firing persisted, however. A news item quoting Senn in the April 9, 1926 *Sioux Falls Argus Leader* certainly didn't help his cause. He arrogantly threatened to run as an Independent candidate against Governor Gunderson in the next gubernatorial election, challenging the governor to give him the "cooperation of the state sheriff in liquor law enforcement," the news report said. "E.L. Senn, deputy federal prohibition administrator for South Dakota, may himself seek the position of governor, he admitted today. He repeated charges that his work is being hampered by lack of cooperation."

In responding to press questions later, Senn dug the hole a little deeper by saying Governor Gunderson had not issued him the invitation he had requested to appear before the sheriffs' meeting at which the anti-Senn resolution was drafted. Even in this statement, Senn could not resist a subtle jab at the chief executive, intimating the meeting had been called and arranged for by Governor Gunderson. Probably the meeting had been called by State Sheriff Gregory, not by Governor Gunderson, who may not even have been aware it had been arranged.

Somehow, Senn managed to survive his public attack on county sheriffs, and he was reappointed to his federal post on July 1, 1930. But throughout his illustrious career, he continued to be volcanically vocal in his efforts to enforce the laws and inform the citizenry of liquor's frightful evils.

One day he might be with some of his dozen or more agents, declaring war on a targeted county or larger area and arresting those engaged in the making or transporting of liquor or possessing illegal liquor. The next day, Senn, an articulate speaker steadfast for temperance, might be talking to college and church youth groups, telling them how Prohibition would improve their lives and would move the nation forward. Senn may have had his foibles, but he was effective in enforcing the federal Prohibition mandates, and he was tireless in speaking out against what he considered liquor's devastating effects on individuals and the nation.

He often accompanied his agents on liquor raids, and the press loved it. Newspapers referred to the federal agents as Senn's Raiders. "Senn's Raiders in Union County Drive," an October 1929 *Sioux Falls Argus Leader* headline flashed. Others included, "Senn's Raiders Dry Up Mobridge" and "Senn's Raiders Busy at Pierre." Senn's activities made for good reading, and the public liked his somewhat "loose cannon" approach.

Senn served as chief enforcer of federal liquor laws in South Dakota for eight years, longer than any other state or federal Prohibition official. His job was finally finished in 1934 as Prohibition was on its way out and as the nation was reverting to the days of open drinking, clamorous saloons and the commercialization of intoxicating liquors. The news of this regression to the old saloon days must have broken his heart.

Senn was born on December 22, 1865, in Clinton, Iowa. In 1884, at age nineteen, five years before South Dakota became a state, he came with his parents to their homestead near Kimball. He taught school for three years and then enrolled in Valparaiso (Indiana) Normal School before returning to Kimball to resume teaching, according to the manuscript *E.L. Senn, Deadwood's Forgotten Fiery Crusader* by Denise Faehnrich. He later taught in rural schools in Charles Mix County and farmed and ranched on the side. He taught for seventeen years.

In 1901, when he was thirty-six, Senn moved to Lyman County, and while still ranching, he started his first newspaper, the *Iona Pioneer*, published initially on an old, clanking, claptrap of a heavy hand press weighting down a corner of his thin-lumbered claim shanty. He crusaded editorially, uniting homesteaders to combat cattle rustlers who terrorized him and his fellow ranchers. Unaware Senn had moved his print shop and family from the ranch to a home in Iona, up-in-arms rustlers burned his little ranch home to the ground early one morning, hoping to destroy his printing press and convince him to keep his mouth shut. Senn refused to be intimidated. He continued to editorialize against rustlers, and in the end, according to the Dakota History Conference report *Deadwood's Forgotten Fiery Crusader*, one of the largest cattle-rustling gangs in the area saddled up and left for less contentious neighborhoods.

As the state's West River area was opened to eager homesteaders after the Chicago and North Western Railroad bridge spanned the Missouri River, Senn followed along, establishing frontier newspapers at many of the new town sites. He became known as the "Final Proof King" because his newspapers' main source of income then was from the "final proofs," the legal public announcements homesteaders were required to place in newspapers to lay claim to the land. At one time, Senn owned thirty-five weekly newspapers in the West River area, and he later admitted he could not remember all of the West River towns in which he'd owned a newspaper.

In 1908, Senn, a progressive long before the state's progressive movement, was a delegate to the National Republican Convention in Chicago and a

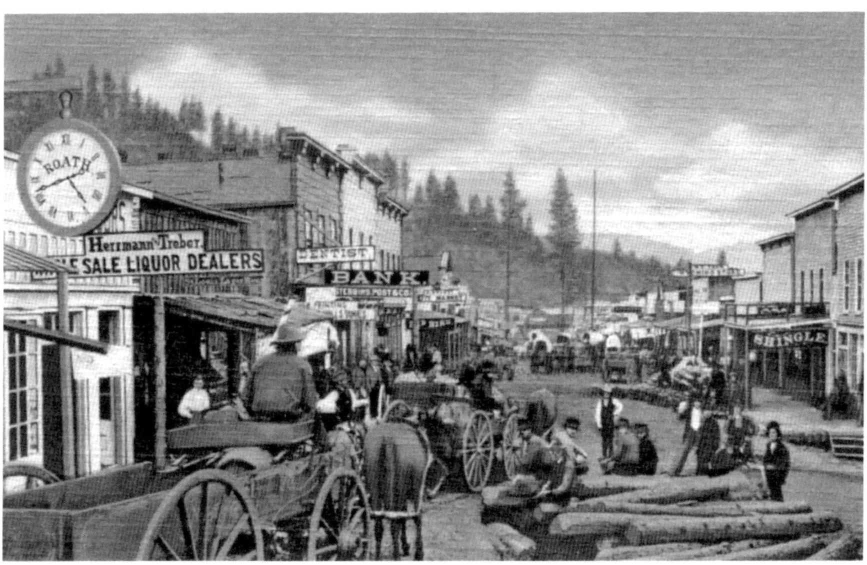


Even during the gold rush days in Deadwood, liquor was almost as good as gold and much more plentiful. *Author's collection.*

member of the Electoral College that nominated Howard Taft for president. By 1909, his bank account was sufficient for him to purchase his first daily newspaper, the *Deadwood Daily Telegram*. He soon took on the town's then-infamous industries of gambling, whiskey and prostitution and urged those who favored decency to join forces and elect law-abiding city officers. Watson Parker explains in *Deadwood: The Golden Years* that this was met with disdain by most of the citizenry, since a majority of them were dependent for their livelihood in one way or another on those three enterprises. Several large businesses boycotted his newspaper, refusing to advertise, and encouraged other businesses to do the same.

A financial supporter in those lean Deadwood years was his old friend from Charles Mix County Peter Norbeck. By then a successful, wealthy businessman heading a vast well-drilling enterprise headquartered in Redfield, Norbeck contributed financially to Senn's newspaper. To make ends meet as Deadwood advertisers boycotted his business, Senn also sold many of his weekly newspapers. The *Telegram* was soon operating in the red, slowly eating up Senn's small fortune, but he stubbornly refused to change his contentious ways.

On a Saturday night in early July 1911, Senn was brutally attacked by the owner of the Mansion, a popular bawdyhouse in Deadwood's red-light district. P.N. Carr, an influential Deadwood businessman, knocked Senn down, kicked him repeatedly and broke several of his ribs, according to the July 24, 1911 *Gate City Guide* in nearby Rapid City. Citizens throughout the state were sympathetic to Senn, but the Lawrence County state's attorney was indifferent. He said the editor of the *Telegram* might have expected what he got when he attacked the Mansion. The county lawman predicted if Senn didn't abandon his crusade, "he probably would get worse." He was right. Further violence against Senn and his *Telegram* occurred in October 1911. A gang broke into his shop and caused considerable fire damage. Senn still didn't flinch. He later editorialized against the new Deadwood mayor, Nathan E. Franklin, and in 1914, this precipitated another physical attack on Senn, this time by a friend of Mayor Franklin's, as reported in Senn's July 29, 1911 *Telegram*.

Gradually, Senn's persistent editorials gained traction. In 1916, when the state's citizens voted on state Prohibition, a majority of voters in Lawrence County were in favor of the liquor ban. Perhaps Senn's efforts had helped turn the tide. After the vote, a rejuvenated Senn said in the November 21, 1916 *Telegram* that he was "confident that in less than two years Deadwood will overthrow the corrupt and lawless influences which have dominated its

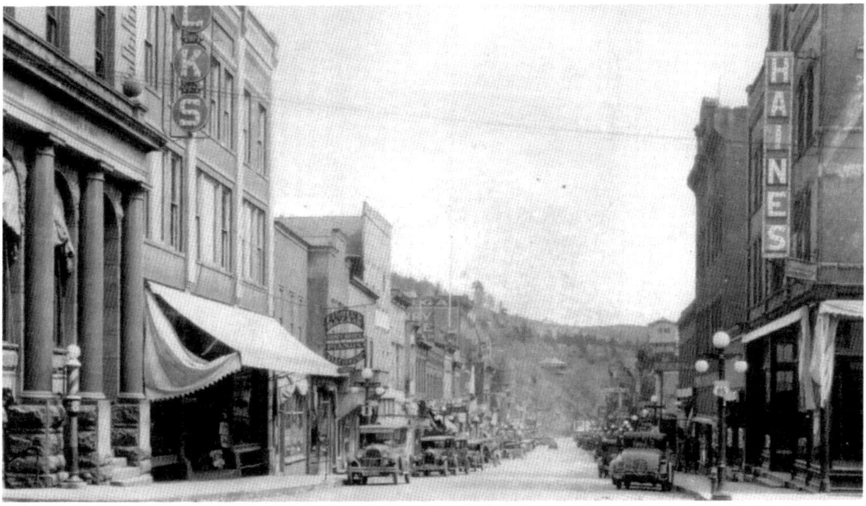


Deadwood's main street during Prohibition and long after was dotted with houses of ill repute, bawdy saloons and glitzy gambling dens. *Author's collection.*

elections and prevented enforcement of laws against prostitution, gambling and other evils."

Long after his Deadwood travails and outstanding federal service, in recognition of his long and successful newspaper career and his well-chronicled Deadwood battles, Senn was honored in 1950 by the South Dakota Press Association, which inducted him into its prestigious Newspaper Hall of Fame, located at South Dakota State University in Brookings.

Senn's appointment to the state's federal Prohibition post in the fall of 1925 must have caused some serious eye rolling, as well as cautious pause among the illegal liquor elements in the Deadwood area. They knew of his avowed disdain of booze and those who consumed or profited from it. As expected, one of Senn's first raids was in the Lead-Deadwood area in late 1926. He must have relished the opportunity to get back, in a perfectly legal way, at some of those who had demeaned him, ridiculed him, physically attacked him and caused him near financial ruin. He and his "raiders" returned to the area again at least once in 1927 and 1928, revisiting the community where he was so denigrated and viciously attacked. Many arrests resulted.

Senn, the outspoken free spirit, saved his second most controversial public accusation (after his attack on county sheriffs) for the city of Huron, where his unit's headquarters was then located. As he started his second full year on the job, he declared Huron the state's "wettest city," as reported in the

*Sioux Falls Argus Leader* on January 26, 1927. Huronites and their officials were apoplectic over Senn's public admonishment. Why not a quiet, private meeting with Huron officials to review his concerns for the city? Instead, Senn sent a letter to members of Huron's City Commission. In it he said, "Bootleggers are more numerous and booze can be purchased more easily and openly in Huron than in any other city in the state."

He charged Beadle County sheriff Lydia G. Larsen and Huron police chief Isaac Lachapelle with making little effort to enforce Prohibition laws. They, of course, vehemently denied the charge. "I am a Huron citizen and sheriff of this county and I will not allow anyone to discredit this city," a livid Sheriff Larsen said. If Senn had conferred with city and county officials, she said, "he probably would find conditions far different than he pictures them." Responded Police Chief Lachapelle: "This seems to me like an effort on the part of the prohibition director to create public sentiment so that he will be able to obtain funds to carry on work that the federal department in Washington has frowned upon."

A week later, Police Chief Lachapelle sent a letter to United States Prohibition director General Lincoln C. Andrews in Washington, D.C. He demanded an investigation of Senn and his charges against Huron. He said Senn had withheld from his department information on Prohibition law violators in Huron and had used the information as "propaganda to inflame citizens against police officers," as reported in the February 25, 1927 *Sioux Falls Argus Leader*.

The Huron police chief's letter continued:

> *Mr. Senn's attitude toward law enforcement officers has been of an antagonistic nature, so much so that the result is detrimental to the enforcement of prohibition. And I take the stand that it is unfair and unreasonable for a man holding the position that Mr. Senn does, to devote his time in gathering information from so-called undercover men, (as he claims he does) and take no further action against the offending bootleggers, but uses this information as propaganda to inflame citizens against police offices.*

Senn later said he had not intended his comments about Huron to be made public. But as an experienced newspaperman knowledgeable and aware of a hungry press during the era, he must have realized his letter to a group of elected city commissioners would eventually find its way to the public. To make matters worse, he also sent copies of the letter to members of the city's Citizens' Committee for Law Enforcement. The letter overkill is a good example of Senn's proclivity to use a dull hatchet when a sharp penknife would have sufficed.

Several weeks after Senn's allegations and the indignant responses by Huron officials, Police Chief Lachapelle resigned or was fired. Senn could not resist a final, subtle prod. In a press release published in the *Sioux Falls Argus Leader*, he stated with almost audible acuity: "Presumably the removal of Chief Lachapelle will have a bearing on the complaint he filed against me in Washington." It is not known nor is it clear if Lachapelle resigned or if, as Senn took the liberty to imply, he had been "removed."

Senn was relentless. A year after his 1927 assertion about Huron, he told the *Sioux Falls Argus Leader* he believed Huron and Beadle County had more than sixty active men and women selling illegal liquor. "Our directory shows more alcohol and moonshine located here [Huron] than in the cities of Sioux Falls, Aberdeen and Watertown combined." He added, "Our local directory of booze distributors shows that there are in Huron fully twice as many retailers to each 1,000 population as there are in any other city in the state."

It didn't help Senn's sagging popularity in Huron when, shortly thereafter, word got out of discussions to move the federal Prohibition offices from Huron back to Sioux Falls. The shoe finally dropped in early February 1929 when Huron officially got the bad news. Senn said the move to Sioux Falls would return the office to its original location. It had been moved to Huron at the behest of the previous Prohibition chief, Huron insurance executive J.H. Searls. When Searls moved the offices from Sioux Falls to Huron in February 1925, he said the move was due to "lack of space" in the Sioux Falls Federal Building. The Prohibition staff was "virtually a squatter in the building," he said. The rooms the dry force used included the grand jury room and the court's witness room. When court was in session, Prohibition personnel had to vacate the grand jury room.

Senn defended his unit's move back to Sioux Falls. He said with offices in Huron, his work was hampered by not having a legal advisor near at hand. An office in Sioux Falls would also lend itself to more efficiency, convenience and economy near the headquarters of all federal court officers. Huronites and the local chamber of commerce suspected other reasons for the office move. As a caveat to Huron, perhaps, Senn assigned Prohibition agent R.A. Labrie of Doland, who was then still recovering from severe wounds he had received in a liquor-related shooting incident near Redfield, to continue as chief of field forces out of the Huron office.

Throughout his tumultuous eight-year federal career of saying the wrong thing while doing his job right, Senn's loud and public admonishments of public and semipublic officials continued unabated. He took on the powerful and influential *Sioux Falls Argus Leader* and other South Dakota newspapers. He sparred in public with popular longtime Sioux Falls Municipal Court judge Ransom Gibbs; Sioux Falls mayor George Burnside; the Sioux Falls Police Department; most of the state's attorneys in most of the counties; the South Dakota Supreme Court; the South Dakota legislature; popular and distinguished national newspaper columnist Arthur Brisbane, whom Senn accused of taking kickbacks of millions of dollars from the nation's bootleg kings; the United States Chamber of Commerce; the assistant U.S. district attorney in South Dakota; his own superiors in this area; congressmen who espoused a wet philosophy; and dozens of others. Senn seemed displeased with everyone.

He even admonished South Dakota housewives for giving their children what he said were illegal intoxicants. He said fruit juice exposed to the air for more than two days would ferment, raising its alcohol level to in excess of even the federal standard of "non-alcoholic" (.05 percent) and the state's bone-dry law. "The dealer in cider who sells it after one or two days exposure to air is violating the state law, and the housewife who serves to her family a cider or fruit juice which has been exposed to the air for two or three days is violating the state law," he asserted.

He scolded the Woman's Christian Temperance Union and the Anti-Saloon League for opposing restrictions on cider or fruit juice when it was proven to be a source of alcohol, according to the February 17, 1927 *Sioux Falls Argus Leader*. Wine growers, most then located in California, placed large, inviting labels on their cans and jars of grape juice reading: "Warning: Will Ferment and turn into wine," but perhaps for marketing reasons, they did not explain how to prevent it from turning to wine, according to the website "Food Facts and Trivia: Prohibition." During the 1920s, the California grape industry grew by about 400 percent.

Despite his faults, as testament to Senn's effectiveness, he and his raiders made 540 arrests in 1928. The next year, 1929, Senn's Raiders were in on 416 arrests and, in 1930, 569. That year his raiders also seized seventeen stills and confiscated ten automobiles found to be transporting booze, reported the January 17, 1932 *Sioux Falls Argus Leader*.

Since federal Prohibition was initiated in early 1920, Senn was one of five men to serve as head of federal Prohibition operations in South Dakota. The first director was J.E. Pearson. He was with the Internal Revenue Service in Washington when appointed on July 1, 1920, because the Prohibition effort was placed under the auspices of the Department of the Treasury. Pearson served until 1922, when he became a federal agent in the South Dakota effort.

Pearson was succeeded by Wakonda attorney W.O. Knight, who served from March 1, 1922, to October 15, 1923. J.D. Taylor, another Washington Internal Revenue Service agent, then took over and served until Huron insurance man and justice of the peace J.H. Searls was hired on May 12, 1924. Searls's tenure was brief, and Senn was appointed on September 15, 1925, serving well and holding the job until federal Prohibition efforts ended in 1933.

Senn continued as a dedicated and active temperance advocate. In late 1933, he started a statewide newspaper, *Senn's Forum*, headquartered in Sioux Falls, that was devoted to temperance issues. Subscriptions were one dollar a year or single copies for seven cents, but it was not financially successful, and publication was soon discontinued. Among the stories he wrote during the paper's brief life was one about Sioux Falls nightclubs that he said "corrupted the city's young people." He also wrote about what a Sioux Falls lawyer's investigation revealed regarding the preference city officials gave to "vice and crime" in the city. One of his last articles was about how he said "hundreds of speakeasies" had paid for protection from federal offices during Prohibition. He died in Deadwood in 1951.

Even with federal Prohibition gone by 1933 and the acclaimed Senn's Raiders no longer on the Prohibition prowl, South Dakotans still lived under the impervious blanket of its own 1917 "bone-dry" Prohibition law. Enforcement of those ironclad mandates then became the sole responsibility of the underfunded state sheriff and his small staff of deputies.

They had their hands full.

## Chapter 3

# More "Dry" Troopers

After the question of Prohibition was approved in a state election in November 1916, three years before federal Prohibition laws on February 21, 1917, became a part of the mix, the South Dakota legislature passed what became known as the "bone-dry" Prohibition law, to take effect on July 1, 1917. The law ordered all saloons closed; prohibited alcohol in any beverage for human consumption; and banned the manufacture, sale, solicitation, advertising, transportation and receipt and possession of intoxicating liquors.

In the same session, to give the law teeth and to ensure all complied, the legislators created the state sheriff's position, with the sheriff to be appointed by the governor. The state sheriff was placed in charge of a state constabulary composed of county sheriffs and deputies. The state sheriff could also recommend, and the governor could then order, members of the constabulary to step forward to help avert criminal activity in return for a pay of five dollars a day.

The state sheriff's office was activated on March 18, 1917, and ordered to "take all steps necessary" for the enforcement of all the criminal laws of South Dakota, suppressing riots, preventing affrays, preserving and enforcing law and order throughout the state and supervising the state constabulary. It was an impossible job. With a budget its first year of just $3,000 to provide for a staff of three and the state sheriff, it was a big order.

Through the years, the state sheriff's department searched in vain for its law enforcement niche but never really found it. The office became just another arm of law enforcement in the state, filling in here and there where city police and county sheriffs could not or feared to tread. Its image was far less flamboyant than the one Ed Senn and other federal Prohibition agents enjoyed after federal Prohibition kicked in three years after state Prohibition started. Having the two agencies, one state and one federal, also often created confusion and jealousy. If an illegal still needed to be raided, who would do it? If a combined operation was called for, who would lead it? Usually, because it had more assets, more money and more people, the federal branch won out.

The state sheriff concept, attached as it was so closely to Prohibition, never really enjoyed wholehearted support from wet advocates, especially those serving in a cash-strapped legislature. Throughout its brief history, supporters of the state sheriff had to again and again remind antagonists and budget cutters about the amounts collected in fines by the state sheriff's actions. Those far exceeded the state appropriation for the office, according to the January 24, 1922 *Sioux Falls Argus Leader*.

Proponents of the state sheriff looked for new work and new assignments for the office. And over the years, until it was discontinued, the office was almost annually assigned new tasks as new laws were approved in Pierre. It was an easy matter for bill sponsors to plug enforcement responsibilities into the state sheriff's job description, usually with no corresponding increase in the sheriff's operating budget. Responsibilities assigned to it were often menial. For example, the state sheriff was asked to patrol county fairs, rodeos and other public gatherings, arresting palm readers, fortunetellers and other flimflam artists who charged a fee to predict the future.

By 1924, the office was funded sufficiently to employ nine deputies who were stationed throughout the state. Ed Glau was assigned to Aberdeen; Wood Smith, Mitchell; John Keegan, Watertown; G.W. Rector, Sioux Falls; Charles Peters, Mitchell; J.D. Hall, Avon; Fred Westgate, Sturgis; W.D. Oldfield, Pierre; and C.F. Wright, Hitchcock, according to the December 18, 1924 *Sioux Falls Argus Leader*. By 1932, funding had decreased so that only five deputies could be hired by the state sheriff.

The provision of the state constabulary section of the state sheriff law was soon put to the test. In August and September 1917, members of the Industrial Workers of the World (IWW), often referred to as Wobblies, congregated in Aberdeen. The first state sheriff, John Shanks, called them a "roving, wild, lawless, reckless class of individuals who gathered in such numbers as to cause alarm to the citizens of Aberdeen." The governor

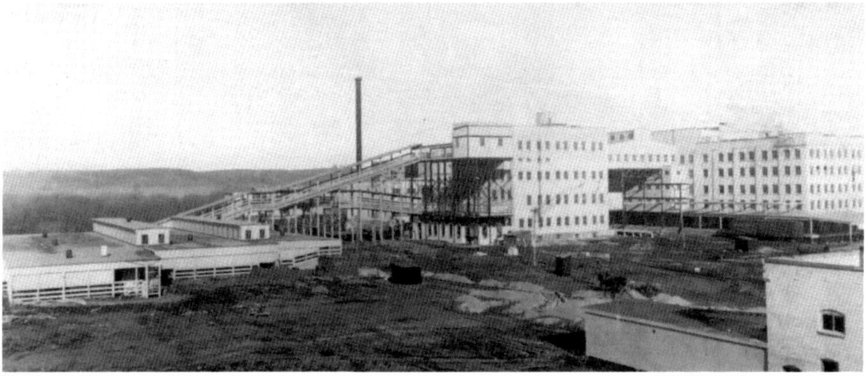

The sprawling John Morrell Packing Plant in Sioux Falls in 1912. *Author's collection.*

activated the constabulary, and the situation was brought under control without incident, according to the June 30, 1918 Report of State Sheriff.

Three years later, in March 1921, a constabulary of sheriffs and deputies from counties contiguous to Minnehaha County was organized a second time by Governor W.H. McMaster to help control unruly crowds during a labor strike at the John Morrell Packing Company in Sioux Falls.

The first seven annual reports of the state sheriff provide interesting insight into the office's activities. For reasons unknown, state archives do not have annual reports of the state sheriff's department for 1919, 1926 and 1929. Perhaps these were lost, never written because of the timing of appointments or not printed because of budget constraints.

In many of the fourteen published annual reports, every arrest made by the sheriff and deputies was recorded, including the date of arrest, the violator's name, county, offense and case disposition. Violations were primarily for liquor law infractions. These ranged from such minor transgressions as having a half pint of whiskey sloshing in a hip pocket to operating a vehicle loaded with hundreds of gallons of moonshine stashed in the rear seat or in a secret compartment. Every violation, major or minor, was recorded. For example, the first few listings in the first annual report covering part of 1917 when state Prohibition started and the first full year of 1918 are as follows:

> *April 13, 1917, Clark Winney, Hyde County, illegal sale of intoxicating liquor, bound over to the next term of circuit court; July 13, 1917, George Robertson, Stanley County, transporting intoxicating liquor, bound over to the next term of circuit court. Action dismissed because evidence was destroyed; August 13, 1917, Ed Debate, Minnehaha*

> *County, transporting intoxicating liquor, fined $75; Sept. 3, 1917, John White, Minnehaha County, transporting intoxicating liquor, fined $100; and Sept. 14, 1917, W.A. Billings, Beadle County, refusing to tell where he obtained liquor, acquitted.*

For the fiscal year 1917–18, State Sheriff John C. Shanks enhanced his report format, adding the names of the arresting officer and giving a detailed description of the items confiscated. For example, on November 4, 1918, W. Rightlaw of Brown County was arrested with a "trunk containing whisky." In June 1918, Sheriff Shanks arrested William Dwire of Tripp County and confiscated 244 quarts of "'Triner's Elixir of Bitter Wine,' turned over to the Tripp County State's Attorney and to the sheriff of Tripp County." The use of officers' names in the report was soon discontinued for obvious security reasons, and officers were thereafter identified by only a number.

The report also included the names of druggists and physicians who obtained liquor by virtue of their owning a special permit to do so, the liquor to be used for filling prescriptions ordered by physicians or for scientific or sacramental purposes. Then, many of the patent medicines legally sold in drugstores contained a good share of alcohol. In some cases, alcohol content reached more than 60 percent. Because these prepackaged concoctions were considered medicines, not beverages, they were exempt from federal law or the South Dakota bone-dry law. Six months after national Prohibition passed, more than fifteen thousand physicians and nearly six thousand pharmacists in the nation applied for licenses to legally sell alcohol for medicinal purposes, according to Sean Dennis Cushman's *Prohibition: The Lie of the Land.*

The inordinate amount of alcohol approved in 1918 for medicinal use in South Dakota—more than fifteen hundred gallons—seems excessive for the medical needs of just slightly more than the 600,000 people in the state at the time. Some of that booze may have satiated personal tastes of physicians or druggists, or some of it might have found its way out the store's back door in the dead of night for recreational rather than medicinal or health purposes. There were also instances in South Dakota of druggists and physicians arrested for illegal use of alcohol. In 1929, the South Dakota Woman's Christian Temperance Union voted to obtain liquor prescription lists kept at all county courthouses to review so the WCTU could be certain citizens were obtaining liquor for medicinal purposes only. The WCTU also pledged to have members at every liquor-related trial held in the state, according to the January 25, 1924 *Sioux Falls Argus Leader.*

The state sheriff's office was charged with monitoring permits for special uses of alcoholic beverages, but there was little follow-up to determine if the uses were as intended or recorded. In the 1920 state sheriff's report, wholesale druggists reported using slightly more than 2,727 gallons of alcohol, 102 gallons of brandy, 7,112 gallons of wine and more than 18 gallons of whiskey. It would be interesting to know what illness would cause an attending physician to write a prescription ordering a druggist to concoct a shot of brandy.

Through most of the 1920s, the listings of names and information on the arrests in the annual report were very detailed. State Sheriff Shank's report for the fiscal year ending June 30, 1920, contained names and information of nearly nine hundred South Dakotans apprehended. By then, the sheriff and his deputies were branching out in the enforcement of a plethora of state laws, including gambling, prostitution and cattle rustling, among others, and it is evident in the reports.

At that time, South Dakota was engaged in a major campaign to ensure proper lighting for automobiles. There was an ever-increasing number of vehicles on the road, but many were not properly lighted or licensed, and others were unsafe in other ways. Of the 900 state sheriff arrests in 1920, 602 were for automobile infractions, such as not having a license or operating a vehicle without proper "lenses," now called headlights. The third annual state sheriff's report also disclosed 193 arrests for liquor violations and 90 arrests for gambling.

While a review of the arrest records in the annual state sheriff's reports indicates most of the violations were related to alcohol or motor vehicle violations, there were other arrests for violations of dozens of state laws. For example, there is the arrest of Jack Fleming and Lee Fairchild of Brown County on Saturday, August 23, 1919, for "using obscene language during a ball game," and in October 1919, Sam Letcher of Davison County was bound over to circuit court on $300 bond for "advertising recipes for making intoxicating liquors."

Nineteen men in Butte County were snagged on a cold February Friday night happily engaged in a game of cards, probably poker. Agents arrested N.P. Lang, D.W. Hickey, C.P. Seward, L.A. Stearns, Phil Dale, W.A. Lash, Charles Lovinger, W.R. Arnold, J.C. Eccles, E.F. Morgan, Bert Kirkham, Charles Wilkinson, A.E. Pomeroy, Elmer Astin, C. Northey, Fay Roberts, L.P. Chuning, Fred Humphrey and Virgil Baxter. Each paid a $1.00 fine and $9.20 in costs.

Agents of the state sheriff's department hit the jackpot in a raid on a still in Lawrence County on October 1, 1920. The owner/operator wasn't found, but agents hauled from the site and inventoried "two complete stills, one nearly complete still, one and one-half barrels of wine, one pair of knucks [brass knuckles], $818.50 in cash, one gun, twelve cans condensed beer extract, twelve packages hops, three boxes raisins, twelve jugs which contained moonshine, three barrels mash for whiskey, two and one-half barrels of grape mash and two oil stoves."

Bootleggers and moonshiners in the Watertown area, and a few in Brookings, apparently had customers with a taste for California red grape juice. Over a two-week period in April 1920, state agents arrested Watertown resident S. Bellatti and confiscated ninety-seven gallons of his stock of California red grape juice; George Hipp, Fred Rosehke, Theodore Hall and Otto Luck, all found with thirty-two-gallon barrels of the West Coast juice; Andy Paulius, with three gallons of the red grape juice; Clarence Schulz, with three five-gallon kegs of California red grape juice; and George Maniotis, with twenty gallons of the special juice.

Brookings grape juice lovers were also entangled in the net. "Phillipson and Usletten" were arrested with one-half barrel (sixteen gallons) of juice, as was S.F. Baker of Brookings, with two gallons. Agents went from grape juice to candy the following year, arresting T. David of Spink County for "having and running a candy punch board." He pleaded guilty and paid a five-dollar fine.

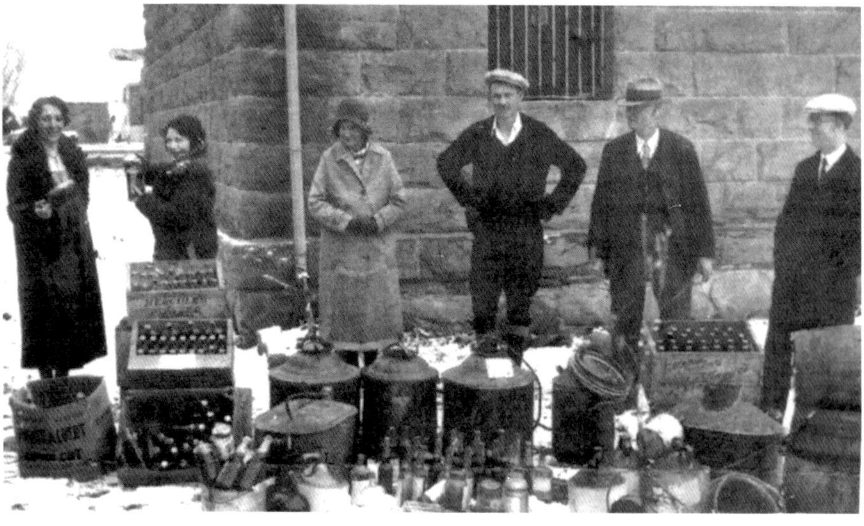

Butte County commissioners and county employees in Belle Fourche pose with the usual moonshiner supplies of bottles, bottle caps and stills. *Author's collection.*

Two entries in the sheriff's annual report for the fiscal year ending June 30, 1922, are especially intriguing. On July 22, 1922, agents apprehended George Korski and William Bossinger. The pair was charged with "criminal syndicalism." It was the first time syndication was mentioned in an official state report. Although most of the Prohibition crime in South Dakota was not gang or "syndicalism" related, there were many hints and indications through the years after that first 1922 mention of a connection with eastern racketeers, mainly in Al Capone's Chicago stomping ground. A small-town "syndicalism" was also discovered in Sioux Falls in the late 1920s led by Hank Kempel, and another gang was ferreted out in the Yankton area in the 1930s that was led by a young tough whom local police officers called "Little Dillinger." His exploits will be recounted in Chapter 6.

The "Kempel Gang" in Sioux Falls distributed illegal booze its members regularly hauled to South Dakota from the Chicago area. Kempel had ambitions to dominate bootlegging in Sioux Falls like Al Capone ran Chicago. Kempel was a regular customer of Capone's Chicago enterprises, according to the September 30, 1931 *Sioux Falls Argus Leader*. In fact, when Capone was defending himself for income tax evasion, Kempel's name was found on documents shown at the trial, and the Sioux Falls man was described as a Capone "associate."

Eastern gang connections were often suspected in other cases. For example, three Sioux Falls men were arrested in Galena, Illinois, in 1931. Chester and Earl Larson and Ben Mack paid $300 fines each in a Galena courtroom after they were arrested in their truck, which was loaded with three hundred one-gallon tins of alcohol. As the South Dakota trio drove through Freeport near Galena, one of those tins fell from the truck. A Freeport citizen retrieved the tin and took it to police. This led to the arrest of the Dakota trio. Aside from the fines, the men also lost their truck, a machine gun, a sawed-off shotgun and a revolver found by police in the vehicle, according to the May 2, 1931 *Sioux Falls Argus Leader*. That firepower would seem to indicate the Sioux Falls men were probably more than innocent draymen in the Land of Lincoln.

Other interesting listings in annual state sheriff's reports include the arrest on July 12, 1922, of Pastor George Perry of Lawrence County for bootlegging. The reverend paid a $100 fine and court costs. Biblical ministrations were used to defend the alcohol habit in another part of the state. After finding one hundred gallons of mash and several gallons of moonshine in Al Gutzner's basement in 1922, Deputy State Sheriffs Wood Smith and Charles Peters arrested Gutzner of Lane, South Dakota. Gutzner protested his arrest, saying the Bible told him making moonshine was acceptable. "The Bible says that wine and oil can be made and used," Gutzner said. Deputy Wood suggested he tell that to the judge. "I will," responded Gutzner, as reported in the March 25, 1922 *Sioux Falls Argus Leader*.

Dancing and booze seemed to go hand in hand. Fred Rapp in Bon Homme County had the temerity to "run a dance" on a late Sunday in June 1924, and John Becker in Brown County was arrested on July 25, 1924, for "running a dance on Sunday." July 25 in 1924 was a Saturday, so agents must have waited until midnight at a Saturday night dance and then moved in but recorded the date as July 25 rather than July 26.

As an example of the breadth and variety of criminality the state sheriff came up against, William Jennings and Bryan Guffy (an interesting convergence of names) were apprehended on August 26, 1924, in Meade County by state sheriff's deputies. There were charged with "selling beef without showing hides." Other than pursuing cattle rustling and hidebound cattle, state sheriff's deputies were also on the trail of many chicken thieves, a common and noisy crime of the era.

References to race or ancestry were usually left out of state sheriff annual reports. But the tenor of the times jumps out in a few listings, which included after the violator's name the word "colored" or "Mexican."

During the later part of the 1920s and into the 1930s, to save the precious money appropriated to it, the practice by the state sheriff of listing the names and details of every arrest was discontinued. Thereafter, only numerical summaries of arrests were published in annual reports.

While large liquor deliveries from backroom storerooms and the rear seats of bootleggers' vehicles made headlines in the state, the discovery of distilleries hidden hither and yon in backyards, fields, barns, homes and other creative and unbelievable locations also made the daily papers. The destruction of these distilleries, or "stills" as they were called, cut off the bootleggers' supply for a time. In 1927, the state sheriff destroyed fifty stills and poured out more than twelve thousand gallons of mash, the primary mixture for the production of alcohol. Augmenting South Dakota moonshine, smuggling from Canada also helped keep South Dakota liquor larders well supplied. Rumrunners, as they were called, who were making the long trip to the Canadian border, or to Chicago and other metropolitan areas, could turn a neat profit if they successfully made it through the gauntlet of roadblocks and sharp-eyed agents who watched for suspicious characters and the sagging rear ends of overloaded vehicles. Bootleggers often got around this telltale marker by installing special overload springs to their vehicles' rear axles.

Vehicles found as being part of a crime were confiscated and sold at auction. For a time, bootleggers thought stealing an automobile for delivery trips was a win-win situation, since the loss of a confiscated vehicle would be someone else's loss. There were numerous cases where innocent automobile owners had to hire lawyers and initiate lengthy court actions to retrieve their stolen vehicles.

The state sheriff's arrest reports and listings of the destruction of alcohol and alcohol-producing implements wasn't the entire picture of dry law enforcement work in the state. Federal Prohibition agents and their undercover informants were also arresting individuals for illegal liquor activity. Even as state sheriffs and federal agents were at work, local police forces and county sheriffs were also on the prowl, finding stills, destroying caches of liquor and making arrests. Officers of the United States marshal's office were also enforcing Prohibition laws. Sometimes, the entities worked hand in hand. Almost daily, the press reported successes by Prohibition enforcers, but probably only a fraction of the bootleggers, moonshiners and others involved in the nefarious trade in South Dakota were ever apprehended.

During the learning curve for law enforcement agencies, new investigative techniques were just coming into vogue. Fingerprinting was a new science being perfected. Faster cars and weapons with more firepower were in great demand to match or surpass what the criminal elements were able to obtain. Car radios and even adequate telephone communications were lacking. Because of this absence of mobile communications among law enforcement elements, it is safe to assume one arm of the law often did not know what the other was up to.

When it came to the cat-and-mouse game of hiding stills, the amended adage "where there's a still there's a way" certainly held true. Moonshiners were ingenious in coming up with ways to make, hide, transport and distribute liquor, as later chapters will show. Dry agents were forever challenged, but they, too, became more suspicious, cynical and curious when on a case. They questioned every nuance of what they heard, saw and even smelled during their investigation. They developed a sixth sense. At one time, there were suggestions to use bloodhounds to sniff out hidden stills and liquor caches, but human olfactory abilities were usually more than adequate to catch even a hint of the wafting moonshine miasmas.

One surprising tool of law enforcement was the employment of clandestine special agents or undercover men and women. Usually they were hired for brief periods to investigate a particular geographic area where they were not known. One of the common ploys for the federal undercover men was to pose as migrant farm workers, even taking jobs and pitching in at suspicious farms where agents believed stills were cooking up home-brew. They sought advanced intelligence that would be helpful in the approaching raids by dry agents. Use of undercover agents seemed a natural weapon for Prohibition since they had been effective weapons in conflicts for centuries. However, their work was loathed by many in and out of law enforcement. The state sheriff's office in particular did not subscribe to the use of what it called "spies" because it was not considered a fair fight when such tactics were employed.

Often when state and federal agents made combined raids, the state sheriff's deputies, who did not use undercover agents, were unaware of the clandestine contribution to the raid made by paid spies. Usually, a series of raids in a county or in a section of the state were planned to take place in rapid sequence thanks to information from undercover surveillance. Speed was invaluable in maximizing assets for a blitzkrieg on booze, so warnings could not be passed along from one moonshiner to the next.

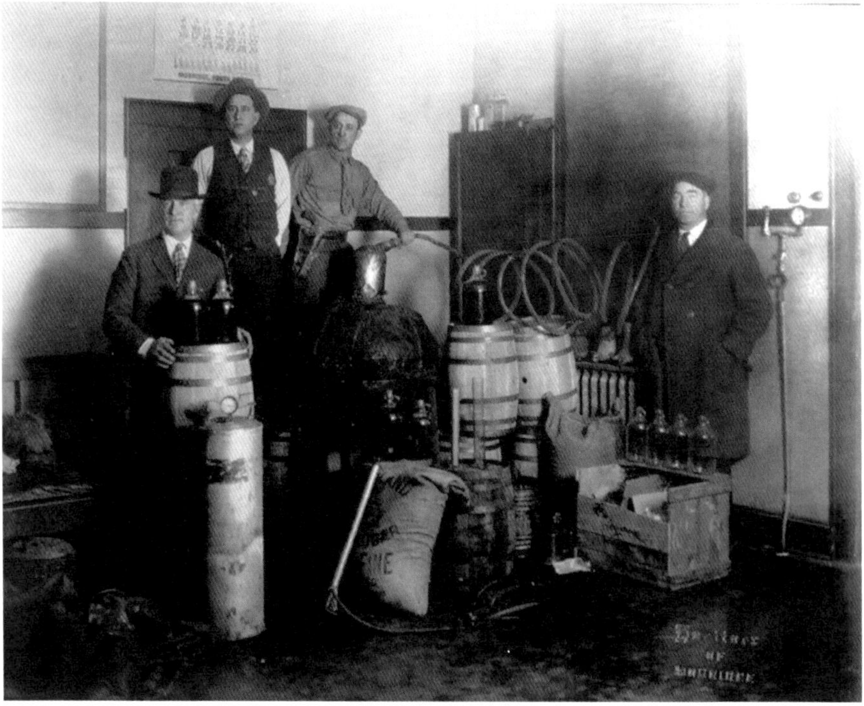

Proud lawmen in Mobridge, South Dakota, display the result of a raid on a Missouri River still. The two lawmen standing on chairs at left are packing heat. *Courtesy of South Dakota Historical Society.*

The first indication to the South Dakota public of the use of undercover agents "in the war against alcohol" was published in the *Sioux Falls Argus Leader* on May 25, 1922. The federal director of Prohibition in the district that included South Dakota, W.O. Knight, said that "undercover is to be the motto" of his department. Previously he had announced names of field agents, "but from now on we will not do so," he said. Throughout Prohibition, except for a brief period at the beginning, other than the heads of Prohibition in various law enforcement entities, men in the field and the special agents and undercover men were incognito, their names unknown and unpublished except in cases where they were injured or killed in the line of duty.

As mentioned, the use of undercover agents did not meet with everyone's approval. Some viewed the use of the undercover agent as an unfair advantage and a less-than-honorable method of apprehending criminals. The *Sioux Falls Argus Leader*, commenting on the debate in an editorial on January 31, 1927, had no problem when the undercover agent was in quest of what it called "the more important bootleggers." The state's largest newspaper was fearful, however, that the "small fries" would become the victims of zealous agents, who were themselves often novices at law enforcement. The newspaper worried about luring people into breaking the law for the agent's own aggrandizement.

"This paper has no fault to find with the legitimate undercover man who is honestly and conscientiously trying to bring about the capture and conviction of actual bootleggers; but it certainly has no respect for the type whose slogan is 'anything to make an arrest and get our pay.' And it feels that the best interests of prohibition can never be served by employing parasites of this stripe."

Fred Minier of Brookings, state sheriff in the late 1920s and early 1930s, had serious misgivings about the employment of undercover agents, according to the March 24, 1927 *Sioux Falls Argus Leader*. At a Pierre meeting of county sheriffs, to which federal Prohibition director E.L. Senn had also been invited but not alerted as to the meeting content, Minier said, "I do not believe the American people take kindly to a spy system and in my opinion if we take the work out of the hands of state officers and put it in the hands of undercover men, we might as well abolish the state sheriff's office. If a county sheriff can not enforce the law without undercover men, my frank opinion is that the county erred in selection of its sheriff."

His comments were counter to Senn's views. He employed undercover agents extensively. After hearing Minier's admonishments about the use of spies, Senn said Minier was entitled to his views on undercover work and other details of law enforcement, but Minier should also concede the same rights to him. "When the state sheriff or his deputies or local officers calls on federal officers for assistance," he said, "we will play the game as they want it played, and when we ask their help, we expect them to fall in with our plan."

The disagreement continued to be debated by the two men in public. This brief and telling news story was in the *Argus Leader* on April 7, 1927:

> *Loud language was heard in the lobby of the Lincoln Hotel today. It emanated from one corner, where Fred Minier, State Sheriff, and E.L. Senn, deputy federal prohibition administrator, were engaged in conversation. The hot argument was said to concern the differences of opinion on the part of the two officers as to methods of enforcing the prohibition law. An estrangement between the two enforcement officers is believed to have existed since it developed at the annual state gathering of sheriffs that Minier disagreed with Senn in the policy of using undercover men. Mr. Minier was reported to have left later for Sioux City where it is believed that he would lay complaints* [about using undercover agents] *before Mr. Senn's superior.*

A week later, Senn was asked by the *Argus Leader* to comment on Minier's anti–underground agent status. Senn, as always butting heads with everyone, responded by saying it was "regrettable that the state sheriff has taken the position that the use of undercover men is unnecessary and inadvisable. His invitation to me to speak on that topic [in Pierre] would have been declined had I known that he is so strongly opposed to undercover work, as I am desirous of avoiding friction."

Senn said many county sheriffs had asked his office for the assistance for undercover men. "In the discussion at Pierre," Senn said, "a considerable number of sheriffs testified of the effectiveness of such work in catching prohibition law violations." Senn mentioned the resolution presented at the Pierre meeting asking for condemnation of the use of undercover agents. County sheriffs voted it down sixteen to twelve. Senn declined to comment on the complaint Minier was said to have filed against Senn's use of undercover agents. If a grievance to Senn's superiors was in fact filed, it was set aside because Senn and his paid but unknown operatives continued to sniff out lawbreakers. A month after the Minier-Senn public disagreement, United States marshal Chet Leedom, addressing 750 ministers of the Methodist Church at a meeting in Vermillion, didn't mention Senn but defended his position, telling the churchmen that undercover work was necessary "to get hold of the real bootlegger," the *Sioux Falls Argus Leader* reported on May 23, 1927.

The state sheriff's department had seemed to be a necessary enforcement arm of the state in the teens after South Dakota enacted its bone-dry Prohibition laws in 1916. But when federal Prohibition was initiated on January 16, 1920, bringing with it a larger and better-funded federal Prohibition enforcement staff, support for the state sheriff's office began to wane. The office was considered to be duplicative of other law enforcement efforts in the state whose budgets were also strained. The wets in the state serving in the legislature found the state sheriff's office an easy target, arguing for its elimination as a budget-cutting measure.

In 1922, two years after federal Prohibition arrived, an unsuccessful statewide initiated law called for abolishing the state sheriff's office. Aligning with and defending the state sheriff's office were the WCTU, the South Dakota Anti-Saloon League and churches. In the November 1922 election, more than 30,000 South Dakotans defeated the initiated measure, 63,683 in favor of eliminating the office of state sheriff and 93,671 against. Also voted on that year was the matter of whether businesses should be required to close on Sundays. Citizens favored Sunday closing by a vote of 98,925 to 56,606.

Five years later, a bill was introduced in the 1927 state legislature again seeking to end the state sheriff's office, according to the January 28, 1927 *Sioux Falls Argus Leader*. Its sponsor, Representative Frank Glynn of Bon Homme County, said the office was costing the state $45,000 annually, but "the results obtained through the department are negligible." In most cases, he said, "the small bit of work that is done is really the work of the county sheriff." It was also his opinion the state sheriff's office was a "detriment to the county sheriffs in that the county sheriffs in many cases pass the buck to the state sheriff." He said the elimination of the office would be an economic benefit to the state, and it would also result in better county law enforcement by placing the responsibility entirely on the county sheriffs.

Again, support for keeping the state sheriff's office came from the Anti-Saloon League, the WCTU, churches, and this time, even from the well-known federal Prohibition man E.L. Senn himself. Fines the state received for liquor violations far exceeded state appropriations to fund the office. Senn cited figures showing, in addition to paying for itself, the state sheriff's office generated an additional $60,000 in fines a year, all of which went into the state school fund, according to the *Sioux Falls Argus Leader* of February 10, 1927.

The first state sheriff, Shanks, who was by then a field representative for the South Dakota Railway Commission, also entered the fray. He said the state sheriff's office had much to do and suggested the department could do even more, such as patrolling state highways, preventing cattle rustling and stopping the state's ubiquitous chicken thieves.

Support for the department prevailed, but its days were numbered. Those who wanted to end the department introduced another bill in the 1929 legislature. This time, the effort was not for the office to be abolished but instead that it become an arm of the South Dakota attorney general. The bill was an outgrowth of one advocated by West River ranchers who had intended to ask for retention of the state sheriff's office, but with its main emphasis to be rounding up cattle thieves rather than bootleggers. The stock growers and the attorney general reached an agreement acceptable to the ranchers concerning rustling enforcement, and the cattlemen backed off their plan to limit the sheriff's work to just preventing cattle rustling. They endorsed the idea of attaching the office to that of the attorney general. The proposal, however, failed to pass. Attempts to modify or end the department came up again in the 1931 legislative session, but they also got nowhere.

Ending the state sheriff's office had been supported during this campaign by budget-cutting governor Tom Berry. The newly elected governor had apparently borrowed an idea from Carrie Nation and campaigned with the pledge to put the axe to the state budget. Keeping with this theme, using an idea he perhaps got from Nation, he carried with him on the election campaign a small hatchet and was often photographed with it in hand. Between 1929 and 1933, as crops withered in the fields, total income in the state declined from $288 million annually to just $89 million, according to *Business Bureau Bulletin* 59 of November 1958. Finally, as the Great Depression's dark cloud put even more pressure on dwindling state budgets, and with only two opposing votes, the South Dakota Senate on January 24, 1933, voted to end the office, which that year had sought an appropriation of $56,700. The two naysayers were Senator James Kirk Jr., a Democrat from Avon, and B.U. Hestad, a Republican from Bryant. Later, the House agreed with the Senate majority, according to the January 24, 1933 issue of the *Sioux Falls Argus Leader*. The state attorney general took over most of the tasks previously under the auspices of the state sheriff.

Two years later, in 1935, Governor Berry proposed the creation of what was called the "Courtesy Patrol." The Courtesy Patrol, a spinoff of the former state sheriff's office, was a ten-member contingent, with each man assigned a patrol car that was called a "milk wagon" because it looked much like vehicles used then for neighborhood milk deliveries. The patrol traveled state highways not in quest of lawbreakers but to help stalled motorists. Each "milk wagon" was equipped with a tow chain, a gallon can of gas and a first-aid kit. It was the beginnings of what became today's South Dakota Highway Patrol.

The lifespan of the office of state sheriff was from 1917 to 1933. During those sixteen years, four men served as state sheriff. First was John C. Shanks, a native of Wisconsin. He was the former Centerville chief of police who later became a Turner County deputy sheriff before being elected county sheriff. He served until January 14, 1924, when Dr. Edward E. Gregory, a Bryant veterinarian, was appointed as state sheriff, according to the Bryant, South Dakota centennial book, 1886–1986.

Gregory was born in Durand, Wisconsin, in 1864. He was elected sheriff of Hamlin County in 1921 and in 1922 was appointed a United States marshal in Sioux Falls. During his tenure, he established for the first time in the state a rudimentary fingerprinting and filing system, according to a February 2, 1925 *Sioux Falls Argus Leader* report. After he retired as state sheriff, he moved in 1938 to San Bernardino, California, to live with his daughter, Mrs. Joyce Cuzzo. He died there in 1952.

Fred S. Minier of Brookings was a two-term sheriff in Brookings County. He was appointed state sheriff by Governor William Bulow in 1927 and served until 1930. Minier was reappointed to the office by Governor Tom Berry in 1933, and he had the dubious distinction of being the last state sheriff. Born in White in Brookings County, he was one of the first students at the newly launched Dakota Territory Agricultural College (South Dakota State University) in Brookings in 1884. He later entered the machinery and implement business. He claimed to have been the first Democrat ever to be elected to a county office in Brookings County. Minier died on May 29, 1944, at age seventy-seven in Brookings.

In 1927, State Sheriff Minier proposed having state motorcycle patrolmen in the Black Hills. His idea was partly inspired by what his office considered the strong possibility of an influx of criminals migrating to the hills during President Calvin Coolidge's summer vacation there. But Minier also hoped patrolmen could help reduce the number of accidents by the ever-increasing number of automobiles on the winding Black Hills roads. Governor Bulow approved his motorcycle plan, and five patrolmen were hired. Minier even arranged for their special uniforms, which were actually regular army uniforms. He supervised the purchase of the motorcycles and assigned one patrolman to the presidential guard at the State Game Lodge, where the president and his family stayed. The patrolman preceded the presidential car whenever President Coolidge or his wife or son were traveling to events, were on sightseeing trips or were traveling to or from the Summer White House established in Rapid City Central High School, according to the June 9, 1927 issue of the *Sioux Falls Argus Leader.*

Governor Warren Green appointed Bruce Barnes of Sturgis as state sheriff in 1931. He served until 1932. Barnes, a former rancher, was appointed because of his excellent work as a Meade County sheriff and for his knowledge and understanding of ranching and the rancher's nemesis: the cattle rustler. Barnes was a true visionary, and many of the advances in law enforcement in the state were his ideas or were initiated at his urgings.

He led a movement to have two-way radios installed in police vehicles, and according to the book *Law Enforcement: The SD Experience*, by Alan Clem and James Rombolz, he also helped establish a network to support radio communication. He helped organize the South Dakota Peace Officers Association in Sioux Falls in 1931 and served as its president after its first convention in Pierre in 1932. He was reelected president at the organization's second annual meeting in Deadwood in 1933. He was Meade County sheriff for four years, retired and then entered the automobile and implement business in Sturgis. In later life, Barnes remained active in law enforcement, serving as justice of the peace in Sturgis.

While Barnes was state sheriff, he also organized what he originally called "vigilantes" to aid in the capture of criminals. By August 1932, he had directed the enlistment of a force of nearly two thousand volunteers who could easily be called to action. Each county had approximately twenty-five of these volunteer minutemen, and Barnes directed their training, but there is no indication the minutemen, or vigilantes, were ever mobilized, the August 25, 1932 *Sioux Falls Argus Leader* reported.

CHAPTER 4

# Recipe for Excess

In South Dakota in 1932, one hundred pounds of sugar sold for five dollars. With that, all that was needed to make moonshine was water, grain and a little yeast. Another ingredient of the maker's choice might be added for taste, such as orange peelings or perhaps a ten-cent bottle of vanilla.

Many South Dakotans who used these ingredients were experts at the moonshining process long before laws were approved by the people, passed by the legislature or survived the arduous journey in Congress, all intended to halt the making of alcohol. Many first- and second-generation citizens who settled in South Dakota took alcoholic beverages for granted as a part of everyday life. Making and serving home-brew was a tradition and a part of their culture. The beverages they and others produced were used sparingly, brought out and dusted off for family gatherings and holidays, as a libation for occasional mealtime guests, for a toast to good health or for medicinal purposes.

In her book *Memories of a Bootlegger's Daughter*, Leona V. Pietz of Parkston, South Dakota, recounts the art of liquor making as practiced by her father, Adolph Schelske, whose German-Russian father homesteaded in the Parkston area in the 1880s. Because of the rich cultural tradition of farmers like Schelske, advocates of Prohibition nationally and in South Dakota soon discovered the difficulty of tampering with the symbiosis alcohol had with history, culture and family traditions.

Thousands of small-capacity stills were bubbling away in South Dakota even before the state passed its bone-dry law in February 1917. That was several years before the federal Volstead Act halted the making, transporting or selling of liquor nationally during Prohibition, so these local South Dakota producers of white mule competed with the big-time racketeers and their gigantic stills in Chicago, Minneapolis and Kansas City. Intricate big-city smuggling infrastructures sought to meet the demand in the rural markets, such as South Dakota and other midwestern states. Ships, including one with a South Dakota connection detailed in Chapter 10, wallowed to America's shores loaded with tons of liquor from across the waters to waiting bootleggers on the East and West Coasts. The foreign contraband in trucks and trains rattled to nondescript inland distribution warehouses where water might be added to cut alcoholic content and boost the bootleggers' profits.

Adding to this plethora of illegally imported inventory were the products of Dakota amateur manufacturers who took great pride in their private recipes passed down generation to generation. Even more local brewers made moonshine for the money. Time and again after arrests of moonshiners in South Dakota, they would tell officers they did it because there was more money to be made in moonshining than in farming or any other blue-collar job they could find.

One man who made good money in moonshining, and who manufactured some of the best booze produced in South Dakota, was Eleazer (Bert) Miller of Hill City in the Black Hills. He was considered one of the state's "master distillers," according to Carl West, Prohibition Enforcement Department chief chemist in Minneapolis. After an analysis of Miller's work, West concluded the Hill City moonshiner made an "excellent" product. West knew moonshining well. He'd been testing alcohol for thirty-seven years. While he praised Miller's brewing work, West was not impressed with the overall quality of the moonshine brewed in South Dakota. In an April 4, 1924 *Sioux Falls Argus Leader* interview, he told the reporter it was "a poor grade."

Master brewer Miller was arrested in late April 1929 while he was at work among swaying pine trees near Hill City. Officers also found a two-hundred-gallon still and other equipment. Miller had been in trouble with the law before but had always been a trustworthy prisoner. So when he asked to be allowed the privilege of going to a "certain place" (probably the outhouse), officers allowed him out of their sight for a few minutes. He never returned from his mission and was a fugitive until arrested by James McManus, deputy United States marshal, eight months later in Arizona, according to a December 31, 1929 *Argus Leader* report. Miller was sentenced to five years in prison for his alcohol and marketing talents.

At the time of his arrest at his well-appointed Black Hills still, officers found what they told the press were small "barrellettes," or kegs, suspended in the trees. It was the best "moonshine that ever swung lightly from tree branches," they joked. The small barrels were painted pine-needle green to blend with the surroundings, and they rocked gently from the trees during the moonshine's unique aging process. His coterie, left behind without their master chef, apparently didn't give up. While Miller was still incarcerated, federal agents in April 1931 returned to what they now called the "old Bert Miller ranch" and arrested Martin Swan at work on a one-hundred-gallon still as he attempted to emulate the talents of his cohort.

Recipes for a good batch of home-brew were easily available in magazine advertisements. Some of the published directions told how to make alcohol from apples, bananas, barley, corn, oats, watermelons and even potato peelings. Almost any ingredient would do. Mix some type of grain, such as cornmeal, a popular ingredient, with sugar, yeast and water in a large container; apply a smidgen of heat to hurry the process along; and let it ferment. In Pietz's book about her father's avocation, she told of her childhood job helping prepare the mash. "Each day while it was fermenting, each barrel would have to be stirred," she wrote. She had to be careful because gas bubbles in the mixture would rise to the surface if the stirring was too vigorous, and the mash would bubble up and spill over the sides of the barrels.

The mash was then transferred to other containers and heated to a point of vaporization, about 173 degrees Fahrenheit. Alcohol boils at a slightly lower temperature than water. The vapor rising off the mash was vented into coiled copper tubing, where it meandered around and condensation occurred in the cooler coil. The resulting liquid, which was the end product moonshine, dripped into an awaiting container. Often, by adding more sugar, the used mash remaining could be reprocessed to squeeze out more alcohol.

Moonshine got its name because the stills at one time were outdoors in isolated locations, under the moon, probably because of the need for wood fires. As heat sources improved and law enforcement officials became more adept at ferreting out illegal stills, the innovative brewers sought other places to put their stills. They came up with hundreds of locations and thousands of ways to hide their bubbling enterprise. Isolated South Dakota farms were ideal locations. The moonshiners were talented men who knew how to repair leather harnesses, weld broken machinery, solder water tanks, install crude plumbing, build a shed from scratch and fabricate distilling accoutrements out of practically anything, so building unique hiding spots came almost naturally to them. Despite the isolation of their farms and their abilities to hide their ingenious distilleries, the main problem they usually had were a few neighbors who were of the dry persuasion and were naturally nosy, inquisitive, talkative types.

Word had a way, sooner or later, of getting around along the neighborhood grapevine. Everyone was usually aware of what their neighbors were doing and when they were doing it. In South Dakota, dry and wet citizens were about equally divided. So in most neighborhoods, rural or urban dry neighbors who noticed unusual activity or sniffed out an aroma of alcohol wafting in the air if the wind was right often helped find the isolated, hidden supply bases. Moonshiners could never be sure who was a customer and who was a dry proponent or a snoopy undercover Prohibition agent.

Eventually, a federal agent, a state sheriff or a representative of local law heard about the stills. Further chapters will recount the record of discoveries, arrests and the violence that often ensued. Although thousands of stills were found and destroyed in South Dakota, the number was probably a drop in the mash barrel compared with the whiskey plants never found.

Another concern for the moonshiners was the professional bootleggers who came to their stills to acquire liquor in tins, jars, barrels or bottles and then hauled it to their markets or to middlemen. The booze maker could never be sure the law was not waiting down the road for the bootlegger and his filled-to-the-gills, custom-designed vehicle to roll up to a roadblock. A subsequent arrest might also include an offer of leniency in return for information on the source of the spirituous cargo.

Danger was also associated with the home-brewed distilling process. There was the possibility of liquor poison that could lead to paralysis, other ills or even death. Terms such as "swell head," "limber neck" or "jake paralysis" entered the vernacular because of some of the common liquor-poisoning symptoms. In some stills, lead pipes were used or lead-based solder connected and sealed some of the still parts, and some leeching could occur. Lead-laced booze was dangerous, made even more so because it was undetectable to the imbiber joyously swigging away until he dropped. Most of the moonshiners who were experts in their craft, such as Adolph Schelske of Parkston or Bert Miller of Hill City, took pride in their product and knew how to do it correctly. But others were amateurs who often experimented without knowing what they were doing. Quality control was not high on their list, and sanitation was often ignored.

Not only were they moonshine amateurs, but they were also guilty of placing their stills in unsanitary, unbelievable locations. It was not unusual for agents raiding stills and chemists determining a product's alcoholic content to find the crusty remains of insects and critters floating in the mash in various stages of decomposition. They became unwilling new ingredients in the recipe.

Newspapers in South Dakota reported on the many deaths attributable to alcohol consumption in South Dakota during Prohibition. Most were from overconsumption or from a fatal accident caused by alcohol-induced mental impairment. In 1922, according to the January 3, 1922 issue of the *Sioux Falls Argus Leader*, four residents of a farm in Independence Township near Webster were arrested for selling liquor to a young man from near Pierpont who died in an automobile accident after consuming booze the individuals had sold him.

One of the first reports of a South Dakotan drinking poisoned alcohol was in February 1922. Ben Regan, father of five and a prominent farmer near Mitchell, was found dead in what the press described as a "tumble-down shack" near the Omaha, Nebraska railroad tracks. John Baldwin, another occupant of the shack, was so intoxicated when police found them that he was unable to tell when, where or how Regan came to the place. Police took a few spoonfuls of booze in a bottle found near Regan, and tests revealed it was poisonous, said the February 7, 1922 *Sioux Falls Argus Leader*.

In March 1922, press reports from the prosperous Hand County town of Miller said police were searching for the person they believed was unknowingly manufacturing poisonous liquor. Several men in the area arrested for being drunk exhibited symptoms of having been poisoned, with "terrible stomach pains physicians said was a sure indication liquor containing poison of some kind," newspapers reported. A $100 reward was posted for information leading to the discovery of the still and the maker, according to the March 3, 1922 *Sioux Falls Argus Leader*.

In the wake of the numerous 1922 reports of poisonous liquor, federal agents published many of the reports to discourage consumption. The Prohibition director for South Dakota quoted the Prohibition office in Washington, saying because of its tainted nature, "liquor for beverage purposes is practically unavailable." The reports in the May 16, 1922 *Sioux Falls Argus Leader* also erroneously claimed the bootlegger market "was diminishing daily because of universal fear of their poisonous products" and that the home-brew fad was waning and moonshiners were on the run.

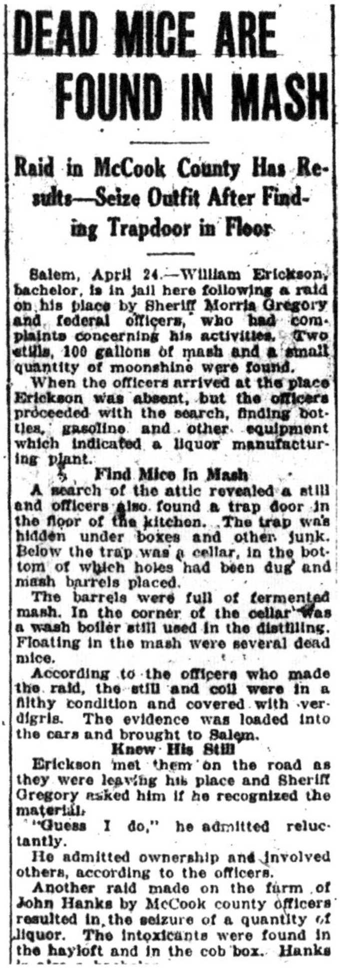

DEAD MICE ARE FOUND IN MASH

Raid in McCook County Has Results—Seize Outfit After Finding Trapdoor in Floor

Salem, April 24.—William Erickson, bachelor, is in jail here following a raid on his place by Sheriff Morris Gregory and federal officers, who had complaints concerning his activities. Two stills, 100 gallons of mash and a small quantity of moonshine were found.

When the officers arrived at the place Erickson was absent, but the officers proceeded with the search, finding bottles, gasoline and other equipment which indicated a liquor manufacturing plant.

Find Mice In Mash

A search of the attic revealed a still and officers also found a trap door in the floor of the kitchen. The trap was hidden under boxes and other junk. Below the trap was a cellar, in the bottom of which holes had been dug and mash barrels placed.

The barrels were full of fermented mash. In the corner of the cellar was a wash boiler still used in the distilling. Floating in the mash were several dead mice.

According to the officers who made the raid, the still and coil were in a filthy condition and covered with verdigris. The evidence was loaded into the cars and brought to Salem.

Knew His Still

Erickson met them on the road as they were leaving his place and Sheriff Gregory asked him if he recognized the material.

"Guess I do," he admitted reluctantly.

He admitted ownership and involved others, according to the officers.

Another raid made on the farm of John Hanks by McCook county officers resulted in the seizure of a quantity of liquor. The intoxicants were found in the hayloft and in the cob box. Hanks

*Sioux Falls Argus Leader*, April 24, 1925. *Author's collection.*

A month later, state sheriff deputies raided a farm near Lake City and arrested John Halbauer, nineteen, for manufacturing intoxicating liquors. They found him bedridden, and rather than escorting him to jail, they rushed him to the hospital because he was suffering from muscle paralysis on the left side of his body. They considered him to be so critically ill they doubted his recovery.

Physicians in Aberdeen determined the cause of the young man's extreme discomfort was tainted liquor. Later, checking his homemade still, police located the coil, often called the worm. Halbauer had used lead pipes rather than copper coils, and the result was lead poisoning. A report in the *Sioux Falls Argus Leader* on June 12, 1922, said officers believed the man had sold a considerable amount of his home-brew, and they were expecting more cases of lead poisoning to be reported in the area.

Two weeks later, James LaBell, a cook at a Huron café, went to the Huron Clinic suffering from alcohol poisoning. It was suspected LaBell's supply was part of the batch Halbauer had made at the Lake City still. Some months later, in Aberdeen, after reports of two more cases of nonfatal liquor poisoning, police arrested fifteen bootleggers in violation of liquor laws, hoping the remainder of Halbauer's alcohol would be among the booze confiscated. Aberdeen police also raided a number of what they called "soft drink" parlors and found two thirty-gallon stills in a dugout cave near the city. The underground factory was the largest distillery ever found in Brown County, police said.

In late January 1923, Fred Hossman, a Beadle County farmer, died after taking a few swallows of moonshine liquor. Witnesses said after he had swallowed the booze, he stretched out on his bed and died almost instantly, according to the January 29, 1923 *Sioux Falls Argus Leader*.

# Moonshine and Mash Found Hidden Under Hog Pens and Manure Piles

## Filthy Conditions of Manufacture Startling, Agents Report to Dry Chief Taylor—Chickens Found Roosting on Side of Uncovered Mash Barrels

All but the most confirmed of drinkers would stop violating the law, and there would be no prohibition problem, if drinkers could but see a bit of the filth which generally surrounds the making of monshine, in the opinion of J. D. Taylor, acting prohibition director for South Dakota.

Filth is one thing, and the chemical content of moonshine is another, he declared yesterday, commenting on the death of one man from alcoholism in East Sioux Falls last week, five the week before on a single party in Philadelphia, and upwards of 2,000 in the entire nation this year as a direct result of drinking poisonous liquor, according to records of the prohibition department. Innumerable living victims are paying the penalty with blindness, rotted minds, weakened bodies, and diseased organs, he declares.

Moonshiners conceal their mash and apparatus in places they think no one will penetrate, but have been sadly disappointed, according to the reports to Mr. Taylor by his agents.

### Under Cow Barn

On one farm recently the agents discovered two barrels of mash under the cow barn. There were boards and burlap over the barrels, covered by a foot and a half of manure. The boards dripped when lifted off, the agents said. The "kick" in the whole raid was that informants who had bought from this moonshiner bragged of the splendid flavor of his product. The agents expected to find an up-to-date scientific outfit on his premises.

On one raid early in the morning the agents found chickens roosting on the edge of the uncovered mash barrels. Numerous times have they found mash barrels and stills under chicken houses, with leaking floors above. They have found a great quantity of liquor hidden in farm toilets.

### Dripping From Hog Pen

One of the nastiest jobs the agents have struck was going into a hog pen to find the barrels. They took up planks which covered the floor and underneath found the mash. Dirt and liquids were dropping directly into the barrels.

One of the favorite hiding places for mash and the finished product is in manure piles, the agents say. The heat of the manure has the effect of more rapid fermentation. It's odor also conceals that of the mash and moon.

Flies are frequently found in the finished product. This is explained by the fact that the moonshine ferments and the cork pops off. Once the fly gets in the jug or bottle he dies, and his remains rot with the liquor. Huuman hair also is commonly found.

Alcohol which once was used to pickle hearts, appendices, and other parts of the human body on exhibit in a doctor's laboratory have been sold as beverage. Agents found bootleggers stole a quantity of their supply from a doctor's office.

That moonshine is poison with tremendous effect on whatever it comes in contact with is shown in the condition of copper stills, the agents say. Invariably stills are full of holes that have been resodered or plugged with rags, while the same copper receptacle might last a life time if used for a washtub.

There is also much zeal for huge profits and little care as to material used, the agents declare. They have found much liquor made with potatoes or potato peelings, dried apples, and even beets, besides the usual corn and rye. They estimate the average cost of manufacture as about $1.50 a barrel.

### A STORY MOTHER LIKED

Elsie—Mummy, do you like stories?

Mother—Yes, dear.

"Shall I tell you one?"

"Yes."

"Will you be interested?"

"Of course I shall, dear."

"Well, there was once a scent bottle—and I broke it!"—Pearson's Weekly (London).

### AN EDISON ACHIEVEMENT

Washington.—There are 700,000 incandescent lamps in use throughout the world today. And half of them, says "The History of the Electric Light," just issued by the Smithsonian institution, are in the United States. All embody the original features as outlined in the patent granted Thomas Edison in 1880.

*Sioux Falls Argus Leader*, December 8, 1923. *Author's collection.*

Lead poisoning wasn't the only danger. Moonshine ingredients ran the gamut. While lead poisoning from poorly designed stills caused considerable pain and some deaths in the state from 1917 to 1935, a poor business plan uncovered at the last minute may have saved others from death from another lethal mix. In March 1926, police raided the northern Black Hills ranch of Charles Miller. They not only found his still, but they also discovered he had been using discarded "cyanide of potassium" tin cans as containers for his mash. The chemical was commonly used in gold mining. So Miller lost some of his liquid gold because of his poisonous still and mash vats and was fined $250.00 plus $46.85 in costs. He also spent thirty days in Deadwood's Lawrence County jail, according to the March 12, 1926 *Sioux Falls Argus Leader*.

Drinking liquor that smelled of ether or chloroform sent a man and woman in Sioux Falls to the McKennan Hospital in July 1924. Answering a call on a Sunday night, police went to 1014½ East Eighth Street and found the couple writhing in agonizing convulsions and excruciating pain. Both were unconscious for several hours. Night police captain McMahon said an investigation revealed the two had been drinking a poor grade of moonshine smelling of ether or chloroform. Hospital personnel weren't sure if the patients would survive, according to the July 13, 1924 *Sioux Falls Argus Leader.*

In early 1931 in Huron, a citizen found twenty-six pints of liquor in a field at the edge of town. Beadle County state's attorney Leo Temmey huddled with federal agents and decided to have the booze tested. The liquor stashed in the field for later sale in Huron contained enough wood alcohol to cause death or blindness to anyone who drank it. Officers speculated it was probably a mixture of ordinary automobile radiator alcohol with a coloring solution added, according to the December 6, 1931 issue of the *Sioux Falls Argus Leader.*

In about 1900, a chemical mixture was developed in the industry as a fuel using denatured and jellied alcohol. It was called "canned heat." A similar canned fuel is now used to warm metal food containers at buffets and for camping uses. During Prohibition, it was a source of a cheap, popular drink with a big kick for the desperate and the poor. Methanol was added during its manufacture, intended to make it too toxic to drink, but many tried it as an intoxicant anyway. Although potentially lethal, there are no reports of deaths in South Dakota linked to the fast-burning concoction. Testimony in a case in Sioux Falls in January 1927 gave an indication of what a "canned heat" jag might be like. A North Dakotan, Robert Roberts, was in court for being intoxicated. He told Judge Ransom L. Gibbs he was on his way to his home in North Dakota from the Oklahoma oil fields when disaster struck. When he arrived in Kansas City, he was down to just sixty dollars. Then someone took his last dollar and his suitcase.

He somehow made his way to Sioux Falls. He said he went to the stockyards looking for work and helped a farmer who was unloading hogs chase down a runner who got away in the process. The grateful farmer offered him a ride to downtown Sioux Falls. On the way, the farmer also offered him a drink. He said the booze was so powerful he was in a "bad way" by the time the driver let him off.

Police, however, told Judge Gibbs a different story. They said Roberts had been drinking canned heat and even had spare cans in his pocket when arrested. Roberts told the judge he used the canned heat to warm his coffee, but the judge didn't buy it. He was fined twenty-five dollars. Since he had no money, he was given the option to either leave Sioux Falls or spend twenty days in jail. He elected to head north.

Because it was inexpensive, a cocktail of canned heat with other liquids was particularly popular with the bums, tramps, hoboes and others down on their luck. The canned heat contents were often strained through a rag or even loaves of bread to filter the mixture and supposedly strain out the poisonous methanol. On what was once Brookings Island, later known as Seney Island (now Kiwanis Park) on the Big Sioux River in Sioux Falls, police interrupted what the dazed men said was merely a friendly tea party on a chilly February 7, 1931. Nelson Young of Peoria, Illinois; John Bly of Omaha, Nebraska; and E.E. Lape of Sioux Falls were joyously sipping their "tea" elixir when officers arrived and arrested them on the well-wooded, popular island hideaway near the Milwaukee Railroad roundhouse. The "tea" was canned heat. Each man was sentenced to ten days in a warm Sioux Falls jail cell.

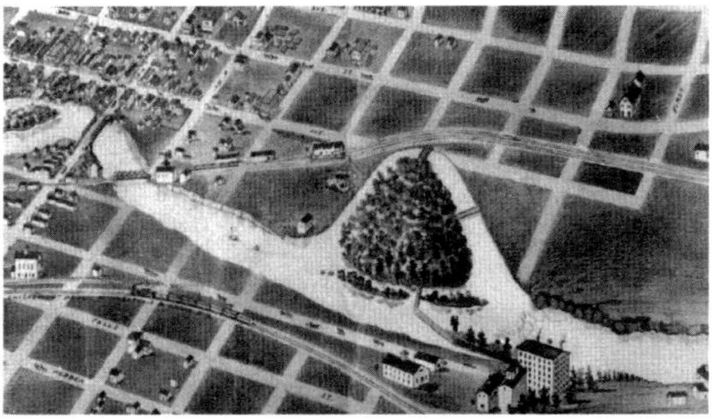

Seney Island on the Big Sioux River has become just another wooded riverbank, but in the early Sioux Falls days when this drawing illustrated the place, it was a popular camping ground for hobos where the manufacture of illegal booze was an art. *Courtesy of* Sioux Falls Argus Leader.

Canned heat containers originally came with a skull and crossbones printed on the label to warn users of the poisonous contents: ethanol, methanol and amphitricha oxide.

While these cheap substitutes for alcohol were readily available, so was the more expensive and reliable moonshine either smuggled to South Dakota by bootleggers or manufactured in city or town stills or hidden away on farms and in the vast South Dakota countryside. Law enforcement officials locating these hidden stills were constantly amazed where they were found.

Chapter 5

# A Little Maid in the Cellar

Relaxing after participating in a liquor raid north of Sturgis in the summer of 1923, Meade County deputy sheriff Fred Westgate told a reporter that alcohol stills were so prevalent in the vast West River country that "one can hardly put his foot down without stepping on one."

That same year, the Yankton County sheriff arrested a man in Bon Homme who said he knew of twenty moonshine stills operating in the county. Not only were illegal stills numerous in South Dakota, but law enforcement officers became quite creative in describing them. When dry agents raided the store and residence of Eli Raich in Lead, they waxed poetic, describing the product being manufactured at the still as having a "kick sufficient to make a regiment of Quakers go up against a division of heavyweight boxers like Jack Dempsey."

A popular Prohibition ditty went like this:

*You may have a fairy in your home*
*Or a miss in your car, but feller*
*Everyone nowadays surely has*
*A little maid in his cellar*

Distilleries large and small, dedicated to making moonshine whiskey, beer, wine and what have you, were almost as common during Prohibition from 1917 to 1935 in the state as hot, dry, windy days. From 1917 to 1920, they were bubbling away in violation of state laws in cellars, kitchens, bedrooms, hog houses, chicken sheds, barns and in the middle of nowhere. In 1920, federal Prohibition came along, but South Dakota had hit the ground running three years prior with its own set of Prohibition laws. Manufacturing of moonshine for evening nips, Christmas Eve tips and muggy Fourth of July rips had been part of the culture in South Dakota for years. Adjusting to the bone-dry ban imposed by the state legislature in 1917 and then to the myriad federal dry laws beginning in early 1920 caused a huge lifestyle shift for many who didn't feel they were breaking any law and others who knew they were but hoped to get away with it and make a few bucks to boot.

Eleven of fourteen South Dakota state sheriff's reports tell of hundreds of arrests for "manufacturing liquor." Although three of the annual reports are missing, the estimated number of arrests of moonshiners during state and federal Prohibition in South Dakota is in excess of 1,300. In 1923–24, state sheriff's deputies arrested 178 people with their hands on the still. The state sheriff's department, often working with local police and federal agents, found and decommissioned an average of about ninety to one hundred stills a year and also destroyed a few thousand bulky barrels of mash fermenting and waiting their turn over the stove. In addition to those arrested for manufacturing liquor, thousands more were apprehended for transporting, selling, keeping, storing, possessing and consuming white mule.

Besides the state sheriff and his deputies, other dry agents were also on the prowl, following up their own leads and hunches. Federal Prohibition officers, under the authority of the U.S. Treasury, were roaming the state and raiding other stills, as were local police, county sheriffs and agents of the United States marshal's office. The proliferation of law enforcement officials often snarled up the searches and jostled jealous egos, but more often than not, most of the appropriate entities cooperated on raids.

The number of raids on suspected stills declined each year during the winter months, when roads were impassable and it was too cold to inspect every foot of farmstead or tramp around in back alleys and isolated hills and vales. During a portion of the spring planting and fall harvest, farmhands were too busy to be engaged in liquor manufacturing. But in the late summer and early fall, it was gangbusters. Law enforcement officials worked overtime responding to tips received by letter, telephone and sly whispers from anonymous dry advocates. Valuable information also came to them from volunteer informants and intelligence gathered by paid undercover agents.

The peak Prohibition year for the discovery of stills was 1923, six years after South Dakota's Prohibition started and three years after the federal government joined the fray. State deputies and federal agents swooped down on 209 still operations that year. In 1922, 151 arrests for operating stills were made, and in 1924, officials arrested operators of 178 South Dakota stills. The number of arrests by state sheriff agents at still sites declined noticeably in the late 1920s and early 1930s, as Prohibition was nearing its end and there was less enthusiasm and less money to finance the cost of the raids.

The raiding of possible still sites usually resulted in agents easily finding and destroying or confiscating the equipment and arresting the "cook." But often, although odor and other clues were present, so cleverly were the stills hidden that they could not be found, even after thorough and repeated searches. When agents did find the evidence, the still owner not only faced stiff fines and sentences but also lost a considerable investment in equipment. For example, on July 9, 1920, a state sheriff's deputy, identified only as "No. 1" in the annual report, arrested William Hatwan, George Hatwan and J. King in Bon Homme County. Officers confiscated the following: "thirty bushels of corn mash, three bushels of ground corn, four pails, one can, one shovel, sixteen barrels, two gasoline stoves, two large wrenches, one iron pump, eighteen feet of pipe and thirty empty sacks." The *Sioux Falls Argus Leader* said the still was one of the most complete and by far the largest found in South Dakota to that time.

The illegal contraband taken from the Steven Hentges place in Yankton County on March 14, 1921, was even more varied and elaborate. Agents hauled away "two bottlers, twenty-seven cans of malt, thirty gallons of mash, fourteen bottles Evan's Beverage, two pints Blue Ribbon whiskey, one quart bottle, Willow Springs whiskey, three quart bottles Dublin whiskey, one 15-gallon keg grape wine, one hundred thirty-five quart bottles home brew, several kegs, jars, boilers and seven cases of empty bottles." Hentges was brewing up his own brand and also diluting, or "cutting," other whiskey brands, mixing and rebottling it for sale.

When agents of the state sheriff's department raided F.W. Schwenk's place in Yankton County on December 7, 1921, a small army of equipment gatherers and two trucks were needed to load and carry away the confiscated items inventoried in the department's annual report: "three testers, eight hundred quart cans of canned malt, one hundred gallons of malt in barrels, twelve quarts Primo, nine cases hops, two bales of hops, three dozen packages hops, twenty-one capping machines, one can sealers, one box hose holders, two gross cans, seven dozen packages gelatin, eight hundred pounds bottle caps, fifteen packages labels, seventy-eight packages rubber stoppers, two boxes siphon [*sic*], one hundred pounds iron shot [for cleaning especially dirty recycled bottles], six glasses beer, testing cups and five thousand quart jars." Schwenk was obviously heavy into the making of beer.

The next month, agents of the state sheriff's department visited a farm in Hutchinson County and arrested L.T. Kleinsasser, W.T. Warne and Peter Hofer. Agents seized "one stove and feed cooker, two sacks bottles, three hundred gallons mash, one sack rye, one cooler coil, six barrels, one milk can, one bushel basket, one copper cooker, one 15-gallon keg containing one-half gallon moonshine, one 15-gallon keg, one oxygen gas tank, one rubber hose ten foot, one three-hole gasoline stove, one lantern, one five-gallon battle, four samples mash, one bottle of liquor and one jug of wood alcohol."

Hiding stills from observant neighbors and marauding state and federal dry agents became an art form. The first rule in still location was to place it in the most undesirable and inaccessible location for law enforcement to reach, not out of the agents' concern for their safety but, rather, concern for their comfort and to avoid the dry-cleaning bills and the disruption of domestic tranquility after tracking pig manure or chicken droppings into his home's living room at the end of the day. Pigpens and chicken coops were among the most common hiding places.

At the home of Lon Vaught in Sioux Falls' Riverside Addition, a police report said officers found a still buried under his chicken house. Vaught denied owning the still and told police he regretted allowing a friend access to his chicken shed, implying his neighbor was the guilty party.

Agents became experts at literally sniffing out operating stills by following the alcohol bouquet. Moonshiners took pains to build exhaust systems to remove this miasmic weakness of confined concealment but never seemed to find a perfect system. Time and again in their reports, agents searching for stills said the odor was the tipoff that something was nearby and, at times, possibly underfoot.

What the press called caves were really more the dugout and storm cellar variety. They were favored by many whiskey makers. In the 1920s and 1930s, a storm cellar was common on farms. In the tornado alleys of the Plains States, especially, storm cellars were desired havens from vicious storms. They were also places for cool storage of sacks of potatoes, canned items or other foodstuffs that could be protected from the critters that also tended to congregate in these cool, underground hideaways.

In December 1924, Prohibition men were alerted to what appeared to be strange diggings in a partially harvested cornfield near Elk Point. In those days, corn was harvested by hand, so the harvesting might continue through most of the winter. Also, cornstalks were left standing, and these further screened the nefarious midfield activity.

With the Elk Point information in hand, agents in Sioux Falls left the warmth of their homes a few days before Christmas on December 22, 1924, the *Sioux Falls Argus Leader* reported, and headed south to the targeted cornfield. They proceeded to a Union County farm three miles east and seven miles south of town. No one was home, but officers decided to look around anyway. They found wagon tracks in the snow leading to the suspected cornfield. Sprinklings of manure had been spread out on the tracked road, presumably to indicate the wagon tracks were made while spreading manure on the field. Suspicious officers followed the manure trail.

The tracks led to what officers described as a "cave" but was really a hole dug into the field and then covered with boards and dirt. There were three small windows in the roof for light and ventilation. The underground plant was ten feet by forty feet. Inside, agents found a still of one-hundred-gallon capacity and forty barrels of mash nearly ready for distillation. There were thirty-two more spare barrels to be filled with mash later. The cave also had a six-burner stove, two pressure tanks of kerosene, a barrel of kerosene and supplies of sugar, rye and yeast. Officers were most impressed with the dugout's very own water well.

Agents ladled for evidence a sample of the mash into a fruit jar and took the vital and expensive worm, or copper coil pipe through which alcohol vapors from the heated mash passed and condensed. A barrel of kerosene found at the site was poured on the cave floor and on the roof, and the underground factor was set afire. The Elk Point underground still was then considered one of the largest and most elaborate found in the state, investigating officers said. Later during the Prohibition era as still capacity grew, the Union County still would be considered piddling small.

Three years earlier near Mobridge, one of the most difficult stills to find was finally located and destroyed. For years there were rumors floating around Mobridge of a still operating in the hills across the Missouri River. Locals said it had been turning out alcohol in a natural cave for three years. Law enforcement officials were eventually able to pinpoint the target across the river almost exactly opposite Mobridge. Finding where it was proved the easy part. Getting to it and arriving undetected were the challenges.

A special agent from the Sioux Falls Prohibition office, Dan Dougherty, and Special Indian Agent William Ahern secured a rowboat and waited until a dark March 1921 night when the river was relatively calm. A bridge over the Missouri River at Mobridge was still two years away. Reaching the west

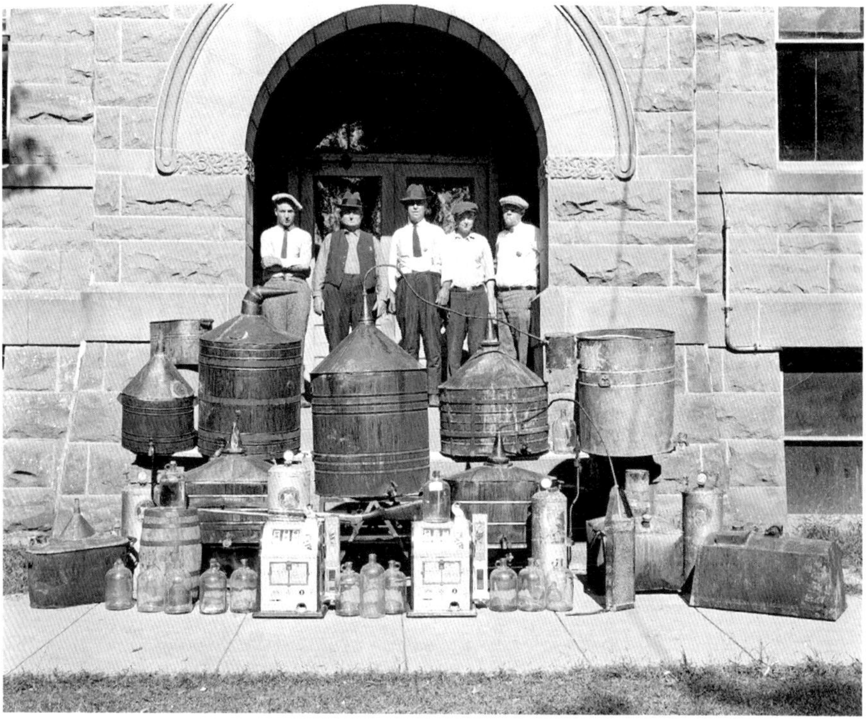

Union County sheriff E.E. Sherman of Elk Point, South Dakota (center) and some of his deputies watch over whiskey-making equipment on the steps of the Union County Courthouse after a raid on a moonshiner in the 1920s. *Courtesy of* South Dakota Magazine.

side of the wide Missouri, the agents were nearly exhausted after the long row. They rested for a few minutes and then embarked on the difficult task of scaling an almost vertical cliff to reach the cave. They pulled their way up and cautiously entered the cave. Inside they found the culprits working a twenty-five-gallon still. They arrested M. Robinson, Mike Otaman and James Cobie, all of Mobridge, ending what law enforcement officials said was one of the most difficult cases ever investigated and successfully concluded by men of the district Prohibition department.

West of Mobridge the same month, Perkins County sheriff Shelp and Deputy Rooks captured what they described as the "grandfather" of all liquor stills in South Dakota. It was on the farm of Henry Schuerle. The still's capacity of fifty gallons of moonshine an hour wasn't that unusual, however. They confiscated the still, three hundred gallons of what they said was "good quality" whiskey and wine and twenty large mash barrels, all hidden in a cave in the middle of a rutted, smelly, five-acre hog lot. The confiscated booze had an estimated value of $6,000, then a considerable amount. A new automobile at the time cost $500 or $600. The annual salary of the state sheriff was only $3,000. The large amount of product ready for market indicated a shipment had probably been imminent.

Information on another still's approximate whereabouts in Brookings County in 1925 was provided by a man named "Tex" Crawford who was arrested on a liquor charge and elected to cooperate with the law in hopes of a lesser sentence. Even with the information Crawford gave to Brookings County sheriff John Roberts, however, finding the still took several hours. When it finally was discovered, a truck was needed to haul the evidence away. That was because the still Crawford fingered turned out to be two stills with a combined capacity of 440 gallons. They were found in a cave near the Fred Bessler home north of Aurora, according to a report in the July 30, 1925 *Brookings County Press.*

Fall River County officials led a raid on a one-hundred-gallon still operated by Albert Doane and Tom Konrath in a southern Black Hills cave twelve miles west of Ardmore that, interestingly, was near a little town with

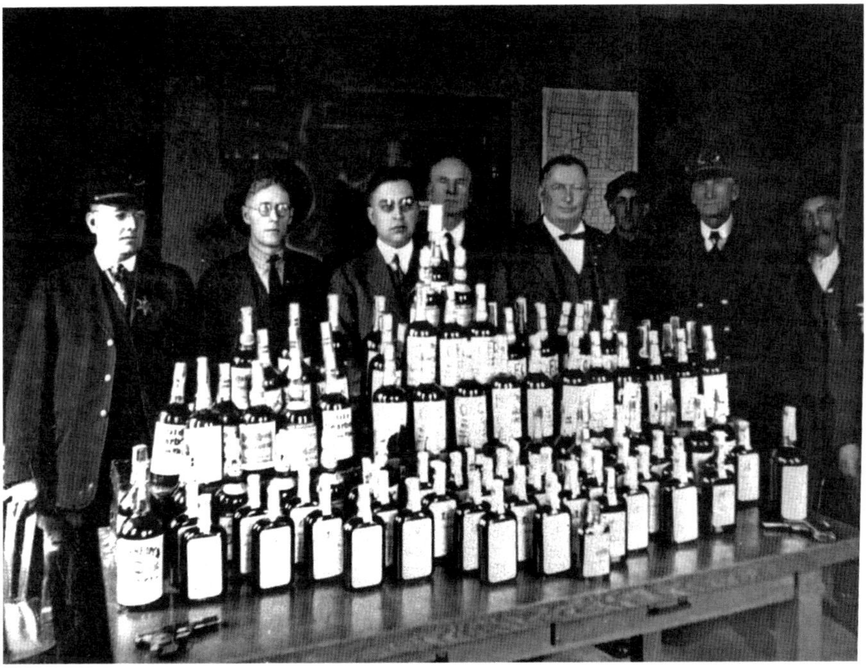

Proud law enforcement personnel in Brookings County display the results of several raids in the county that included confiscation of several firearms displayed at the corners of the table. *Author's collection.*

the intoxicating name of Rumford. The cave had a unique entrance. To get into the twenty-foot-square underground room, Fall River County sheriff R.L. Porter, Deputy George McCoy, Deputy State Sheriff Perry Moody and three federal agents climbed down a fifteen-foot ladder they lowered into a well. The cave entrance was hacked into one side of the well wall about halfway down. There were placid sheep grazing peacefully on a pasture over the cave "lending an air of innocence to the place," the *Argus Leader* reported on November 11, 1931.

A May 24, 1933 issue of the *Sioux Falls Argus Leader* tells of one of the most despicably unsanitary stills ever discovered. It was on the Henry Penningroth farm near Kimball. On May 19, 1923, state and federal Prohibition officers and the Kimball city marshal found it in a cave under the hog yard. Officers said the mash barrels in the cave were uncovered, so effluvium and drainage from above dripped into them. Penningroth's son, Elmer, and a hired man named Jones had been arrested earlier in Kimball when they unwittingly attempted to sell to the plainclothed officers six gallons of liquor made at the still. As a result, a raid on the Penningroth farm was planned for later in the evening. When agents found the still, the offensive odor in the cave was so putrid it was difficult for them to enter, they said later.

For a time, at the national level, to discourage alcohol consumption, Prohibition officials released gruesome stories of the filth they erroneously claimed was incumbent in the making of homemade brew everywhere. J.D. Taylor, district federal Prohibition director for South Dakota and two other states, said in late 1923: "Filth is one thing and the chemical content of moonshine is another." He quoted national figures showing nearly two thousand deaths in 1934 from drinking poisonous liquor. Others, he said, experience "blindness, rotted minds, weakened bodies and diseased organs."

Taylor told of mash in barrels found by agents in South Dakota with chickens roosting on the barrel edges. He mentioned mash hidden under pigpens and hog houses and said a favorite hiding place for moonshiners was a manure pile, where the heat generated by the decomposing manure helped speed the mash's fermentation. The smell of the manure also hid the odor of the moonshine and the mash. Taylor also said flies and human hair were commonly found in captured moonshine.

Dry officials in South Dakota and across the nation found many other moonshine operations in similar unsanitary locations. These "horror stories" became examples of what casual moonshine buyers might end up with when purchasing booze. At a conference of the nation's law enforcement officials in September 1922, federal Prohibition director William O. Haynes recounted many of the filthy conditions often a part of the manufacture of bootleg whiskey. "Vermin, maggots and dead animals of all kinds have been discovered in vats of mash," he said. His most revolting revelation was of thieves stealing alcohol from cadaver vats and specimen jars used in university laboratories and medical school classrooms. The contraband liquid was then bottled for resale.

No cadaver booze was drained off in South Dakota, but conditions found at some locations in the state were certainly horrendous. George Grater, who farmed near Clear Lake in Deuel County, picked what he thought was the ideal location for concealment of his still, but it wasn't exactly an exemplary site for the sanitary manufacture of moonshine or for anything. On a chilly March day in 1924, federal agents found 450 gallons of mash, some moonshine, 25 gallons of wine and a still in a cave under Garter's hog house, according to the October 30, 1924 issue of the *Sioux Falls Argus Leader*. One of the arresting officers said the location provided "fine drainage for the hog house, but questionable flavor for the liquor." Officers said the liquor stash on the Grater farm was the largest ever found in Deuel County.

At first, officers looking for a still on the Alvin Hamandberg farm two miles north of Harrisburg could only find an old, inoperative still gathering dust and mice in the Hamandberg haymow. But the aroma of alcohol was there, competing with the reek of a nearby malodorous manure pile. On a hunch, agents cleaned out a horse stable and swept straw from the floor beneath. They found a false door to a cave eight feet deep. The press reported that it contained seven barrels of mash, a large gasoline stove and six gallons of liquor.

Officers raiding the farm of William Erickson near Salem found two stills, plus one hundred gallons of mash and some other items, including several dead mice floating in the mash, and what the April 24, 1925 *Sioux Falls Argus Leader* reported officers described as a bright bluish-green encrustation on the coils of the filthy still.

Things were even worse earlier in the year when federal Prohibition officers, the Aurora County sheriff and deputies and members of the state sheriff's department parked their cars four miles from their targeted still and walked the rest of the way to what they later described in the February11, 1925 issue of the *Sioux Falls Argus Leader* as the filthiest of any still they'd seen. It was located on a farm near Plankinton. In the dead of night, in a low-slung hog house measuring about twenty by fifty feet, officers waded through slimy muck up to their shoe tops. They found a man clad in overalls, undershirt and boots working his still.

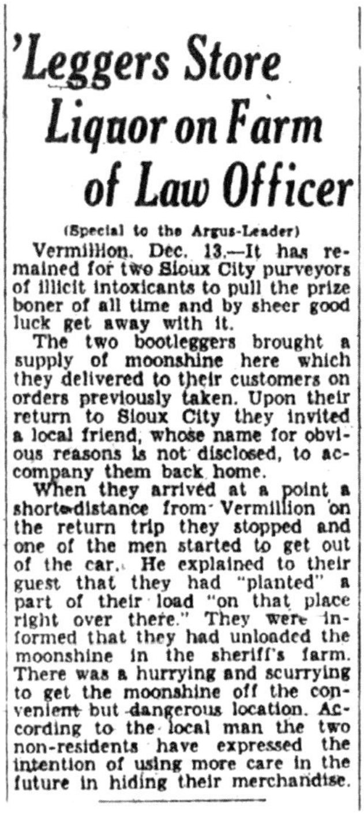
**'Leggers Store Liquor on Farm of Law Officer**

(Special to the Argus-Leader)

Vermillion, Dec. 13.—It has remained for two Sioux City purveyors of illicit intoxicants to pull the prize boner of all time and by sheer good luck get away with it.

The two bootleggers brought a supply of moonshine here which they delivered to their customers on orders previously taken. Upon their return to Sioux City they invited a local friend, whose name for obvious reasons is not disclosed, to accompany them back home.

When they arrived at a point a short distance from Vermillion on the return trip they stopped and one of the men started to get out of the car. He explained to their guest that they had "planted" a part of their load "on that place right over there." They were informed that they had unloaded the moonshine in the sheriff's farm. There was a hurrying and scurrying to get the moonshine off the convenient but dangerous location. According to the local man the two non-residents have expressed the intention of using more care in the future in hiding their merchandise.

*Sioux Falls Argus Leader*, December 12, 1930. *Author's collection.*

Near the still were five barrels of mash set into the dirt floor of the hog house. The barrels' uncovered tops were almost flush with the mucky ground. As one of the agents stepped near the barrels, filth oozed over into the mash. South Dakota Prohibition director Searls of Huron said he imagined curious hogs stepping near the barrels caused more than just mud to became part of the mash mixture. The stench of hogs in the shed was so powerful that the odor of alcohol could not be detected. Louis Broncho was the still operator. He told officers he'd been arrested twice before. He also assured them he never drank any of his product. Glancing about the filthy place, officers tended to believe him.

In October 1924, officers located a still and a stash of booze on a Missouri River sandbar in South Dakota near Sioux City. They also found barrels of mash partly buried in the ground and covered with a tarpaulin. That hadn't discouraged six mice and a large river rat from getting at the tempting fermenting mash. In their exuberance, they fell in and drowned to become part of the amalgam, according to a news story in the October 10, 1924 issue of the *Sioux Falls Argus Leader*.

An oat bin on the William Sibley farm near Mount Vernon held more than oats, Prohibition agents discovered during a raid in February 1923. Five agents, including Ike McCoun, who was still nursing a minor gunshot wound in the arm received in a raid on a Sioux Falls soft drink parlor a few weeks earlier, found a trapdoor in the bin. When opened, there was a drop of about six feet, then a passageway about five feet wide and six feet high extending ten feet to the north, then turning east for about twelve feet. There they found a still and 250 gallons of mash. Kerosene lanterns lighted the impressive labyrinth.

The *Argus Leader* on August 8, 1922, referred to an elaborate distiller's cave described by Sioux Falls police chief Charles T. Johnson as an "underground resort." An anonymous letter to the chief told of the still in the Hunter Grove section of Sioux Falls. He had long suspected something was amiss in that part of town because of an inordinate amount of moonshine available on the local market there. He searched the area where the still was supposed to be but found nothing. Then he noticed a small cleared section of ground. Near the edge of it was a metal pipe poking out. Looking closer, he found a small hole into which he was barely able to squeeze. It led into a long tunnel and then a room about the size of a common living room, the *Argus Leader* reported.

The chamber was empty, but Chief Johnson found another passageway leading to another good-sized space. There he found a simple fireplace and some boxes set into the wall as a storage cupboard. There were ventilating holes in the cave roof. He found a still and other moonshining paraphernalia. Leading from the second chamber was another tunnel to a ladder to a back door exit. No one was in or near the cave at the time, so no arrests were made, but the elaborate underground "resort" was permanently decommissioned.

Duck hunters bouncing along in their car near the edge of a small creek in Brown County suddenly felt an extra big jolt. Then their car wouldn't move. They'd driven over a part of an underground still, and one wheel had dropped into the excavation. They investigated and found equipment for making moonshine. Deputy State Sheriff Edward L. Glau retrieved the items and then jokingly invited the owners of the confiscated equipment to call him anytime to learn of their whereabouts. Of course, no one did, and the still and the other items joined others stored in a spare room by the state sheriff, eventually to be sold as scrap.

Lawrence County sheriff Lutey and Deputy Owen picked up a rumor from a usually reliable snitch about a still operating deep in the idle Golden Reward Gold Mine near Lead. For nearly an entire day, they stumbled and tromped around in the damp, cool air of the mine, checking every drift, stope, tunnel and shaft, but found nothing on their sixteen-mile hike. They emerged from the wild goose chase tired, mud-caked and disappointed, the newspapers reported.

Nearly a decade later, a still was discovered in an abandoned mine in Nevada Gulch in Lawrence County. Authorities found a 50-gallon still, 15 gallons of whisky and 250 gallons of mash in the old mine and arrested two men, L.B. Hamilton and Rodney Busby. Although abandoned mines offered many advantages as still sites, the need for heat and consequently the resulting need to vent the smoke was a major disadvantage when converting an old gold mine to a still site.

It became fashionable for the press and for Prohibition agents to rate the results of their raids and the stills they found, using adjectives like "the biggest" or "most elaborate" or attaching other measurable and usually dazzling terms to their capture. Examples of this "believed to be" hyperbole included the following:

April 1920: "What is believed to have been **THE LARGEST STILL** captured in South Dakota since state prohibition law became effective was brought to Sioux Falls by U.S. Marshal Bert V. Donahoe late Saturday night. The still, found in Yankton, was a sixty-gallon affair, small by later standards. It was somewhat unusual, equipped with a worm, or evaporation copper coil, twenty feet long, made of three-quarter inch pipe."

April 4, 1921: "What is termed the **SECOND LARGEST STILL RAID** ever made in South Dakota was found in a secluded cabin about thirty miles west of Rapid City. The liquor-making loot captured in the cabin required two automobiles and a truck to transport back to Rapid City."

March 15, 1923: "Under the cover of darkness while this section of the world slept, Deputy Sheriff David and Lee Brooks of Pennington County assisted by A.E. England, assisting officer from Rapid City, swooped quietly down upon a secluded cabin nestled in the hills twenty-five miles southwest of Rapid City near the Otho Mine of the Keystone vicinity, taking a mountain distillery, **THE LARGEST AND BEST EQUIPPED** of any yet captured in Pennington County."

July 25, 1923: "Claude Cline, a Milbank farmer, was taken into custody Wednesday by E.H. Glau, deputy state sheriff, and the sheriff of Grant County when a full-grown still and barrel of mash were found by officers in the kitchen of the house....The coil of the still was **THE LONGEST EVER SEEN** by the local officers." The lengthy copper coil was fifty feet long.

February 18, 1924: "Gerd Johnson and Harold Blunt, arrested when officers found a fifty gallon still in operation on the farm owned by Andy Johnson, which Blunt is renting near James, have both been convicted of manufacturing liquor. The still...was **THE LARGEST EVER FOUND IN BROWN COUNTY**, having a capacity of eighty gallons."

April 7, 1924: "**ONE OF THE BIGGEST LIQUOR RAIDS IN THE HISTORY** of Sioux Falls and Minnehaha County was made Tuesday night about 8:30 when a squad of officers arrested James Conley and R.F. Huntly at 1603 South Prairie and found sixty-seven gallons of moonshine, seven barrels of rye mash, three complete copper boiler stills and other paraphernalia."

May 28, 1924: "Near Deadwood, Federal prohibition agents subpoenaed for the federal court term at Deadwood did not spend their time in idleness waiting for certain cases to come up. They utilized their time and presence in making **ONE OF THE BIGGEST RAIDS IN THE WESTERN PART OF THE STATE**." They found a one-hundred-gallon still near the home of Gene Ferry forty miles southwest of Deadwood.

September 9, 1924: "Confiscation of **THE LARGEST STILL EVER FOUND IN BEADLE COUNTY** was reported today from the office of J.H. Searls, federal prohibition director." The still was found near Sand Creek about twenty-five miles from Huron on the third night of searching for it. It had just a sixty-gallon capacity.

July 4, 1925: "Only one arrest was the result of a visit by federal and state officers yesterday in Union County, which is declared the scene of **THE GREATEST DISTILLING OPERATION IN THE STATE**." On the farm of Felix Gerard south and west of Jefferson, the officers said they found five gallons of liquor, a thirty-gallon still and five hundred gallons of mash, along with other manufacturing material. The owner of the land denied the equipment was his, declaring they were left after a truck had broken down.

July 10, 1925: Federal Prohibition agents and a state sheriff's deputy discovered "**ONE OF THE LARGEST MOONSHINE MANUFACTURING** outfits in their careers." The trio penetrated a four-acre forest near the road a little more than a mile south of Jefferson and found a still house and a one-hundred-gallon still.

May 2, 1927: "Two weeks work of investigation around Kadoka resulted in **ONE OF THE BIGGEST PROHIBITION CLEANUPS** in several months," the *Sioux Falls Argus Leader* reported. Six people were arrested in raids there. A loaded Buick sedan was seized along with three stills, one of 65 gallons, one of 20 gallons and one of 15-gallon capacity, along with 225 gallons of "finished product."

July 5, 1934: County sheriff Floyd C. Short and Roy Dow, a federal agent, discovered "**THE LARGEST STILL EVER FOUND IN THAT PART OF THE STATE**" on the Willard Small farm five miles south of Chance.

Even children got into the act. Two young Hofer boys and two Hofer girls were credited with the arrest of James Bowen and Leo VanHoek of Bridgewater on September 25, 1922, for moonshining. The youngsters were driving down a narrow lane between two cornfields on their way to the Hofer potato patch to dig spuds. They saw two men a short distance away in the cornfield near what turned out to be a still under a roof made of a blanket suspended on poles. The curious youngsters thought something was amiss, so they drove back to Bridgewater for assistance. Mrs. Hofer returned to the field with them and drove to near where the still was located.

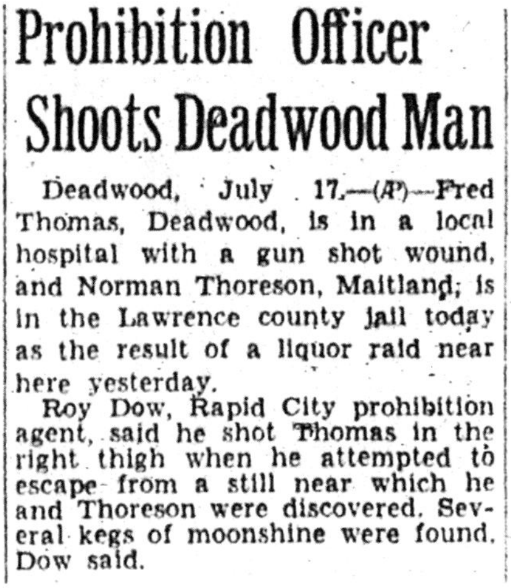

**Prohibition Officer Shoots Deadwood Man**

Deadwood, July 17.—(AP)—Fred Thomas, Deadwood, is in a local hospital with a gun shot wound, and Norman Thoreson, Maitland, is in the Lawrence county jail today as the result of a liquor raid near here yesterday.

Roy Dow, Rapid City prohibition agent, said he shot Thomas in the right thigh when he attempted to escape from a still near which he and Thoreson were discovered. Several kegs of moonshine were found, Dow said.

*Sioux Falls Argus Leader*, July 17, 1930. *Author's collection.*

This time, seeing the passing car, the two men ran away. The boys, each about fourteen years old, followed and soon overtook Bowen. The girls, about sixteen, ran after the other fleeing man, whom they recognized as VanHoek, but failed to catch him. Mrs. Hofer put Bowen in her car and left the two boys to guard the still while she and the girls headed for the Bridgewater police station, the September 25, 1922 *Sioux Falls Argus Leader* reported. At the trial, Bowen was convicted, but VanHoek's lawyer produced evidence showing his client was elsewhere at the time. After deliberating for twelve hours, the jury returned a verdict of not guilty for VanHoek.

On the western border of Minnehaha County, Prohibition agents, officers from the U.S. marshal's office and deputies of the county sheriff's department discovered a farmhouse with a distillery occupying the entire top floor of the seven-room house, according to a January 1925 issue of the *Sioux Falls Argus Leader.*

Thirteen was an unlucky number for Sioux Falls area farmer J.F. Christianson, who had a Hills, Minnesota mailing address. The July 2, 1929 issue of the *Sioux Falls Argus Leader* reported that agents raiding Christianson's place were astonished to find thirteen small stills. Four were in operation; nine were idle. All were illegal.

Minnehaha County sheriff George Broadman and a squad of deputies left warm hearths and homes on Christmas Eve in 1925 to raid a home on West Twenty-third Street near Augustana College in Sioux Falls. They found two stills and copper coils belonging to C.F. Nelson. Nelson said he was a novice at moonshining but proudly told officers his moonshine was a "quality" product made from pure raisin mash. Officers who had dipped fingers in the liquor for a taste to be sure the evidence was alcohol silently disagreed. It tasted terrible and was also "vile smelling stuff," they later told a reporter for the *Sioux Falls Argus Leader.*

Two days after Christmas in 1920, searching for a stash of moonshine on the Don Cockrell place in Platte, officers hoped to find the "white mule"

Cockrell was reportedly making to fill a $1,000 booze order. They finally located the still in an underground vault beneath a barn stall. The cave door was under a contented, cud-munching cow reclined on the fresh straw-strewn stall. Cockrell got a sixty-day sentence in the county jail, where he likely slept on a straw-filled mattress.

A solution of body rub available at any drugstore of the day was part of an unconventional 1924 distilling operation conducted by well-known Watertown character A.J. "Step-and-a-Half" Runyan, who lived near Lake Pelican. Codington County sheriff C.R. Goss, Deputy Sheriff Vincent Reilly and Watertown police officer D.W. Lattimer described the still to a *Watertown Public Opinion* reporter.

In the bottom pan of the still was a mixture of water and the alcohol body rub that contained a high percentage of the elixir of joy. Floating on this liquid was a slightly smaller pan into which the distilled alcohol dripped off as the rising vapors collected and then condensed on the bottom of another cool, water-filled pan hanging over the two containers. The booze dripped like rain back into the floating container. It was slow but effective.

One of the most unusual entries into a home in South Dakota in search of illegal booze was in August 1924 by Deputy State Sheriff Wood Smith. He and other officers were on a raid of F.L. Atkins's modern bungalow on the Missouri River lowlands west of Yankton. No one answered repeated knocks on the door. Deputy Smith noted the large stone chimney of the home and assumed it was part of an elaborate interior fireplace. He donned a pair of UnionAlls he had in his car for just such dirty work and then played Santa Claus. He entered the home by sliding down the chimney. Inside, the *Argus Leader* reported he and his compatriots found sixty-five gallons of beer, more than three hundred empty quart bottles, some jugs, hops and malt and bottling and capping devices.

In late 1926, federal agent Charles Bintliff and Deputy State Sheriff Smith captured Henry Rickgauer near Burke. Rickgauer was known by agents and local residents as the "Colome Island Liquor King." In an earlier confrontation with the "king" near his island still, he'd vowed to "start a cemetery" on the island the next time Prohibition agents came around. Agents Bintliff and Smith had heard it all many times before and were not intimidated, the *Sioux Falls Argus Leader* reported on November 11, 1926.

The oldest moonshiner arrested in South Dakota during Prohibition was found by accident. Federal officers arrested August C. Frohreich on his farm ten miles northeast of Yankton in March 1925. Finding his still and a stash of home-brewed beer and moonshine whiskey wasn't a part of the agents' original plan. They had earlier stopped at another suspected nearby farm and asked to buy beer. The man said he was fresh out and suggested they try the Frohreich place a few miles down the road. Agents did, and after purchasing some of Frohreich's product, they found a still in the barn and five hundred gallons of vegetable mash, a half gallon of moonshine, two hundred quarts of beer in the basement, a fifty-gallon keg of beer mash behind the kitchen stove and packages of malt and hops. Frohreich, seventy-three, pled guilty and was fined $100.

You never know who you'll run into—literally. Three men may have been reminded of that adage when their car collided with another a few miles west of Huron in May 1925. Unfortunately, the men in the other car were tired and testy dry agents returning home after a long day. When they looked into the offending vehicle, they found plenty of illegal booze and arrested the trio. At the time, driving while drunk was not an offense, so careless driving and transporting booze were the charges.

The famous Mule Head Ranch in Gregory County in 1930 was producing white mule worth much more per pound than the fat cattle roaming its vast acreage. Once owned by the Jackson brothers, the Mule Head was a cowhand legend in the state. It was raided by federal and county law enforcement officers on November 10, 1920. They found a small twenty-five-gallon still, four hundred gallons of mash and a small quantity of moonshine. While capacity of the still was disappointingly small, agents calculated thousands of gallons of Mule Head white mule had probably passed through the isolated ranch's gate over time, according to the November 11, 1930 *Sioux Falls Argus Leader*.

One of the last stills found in South Dakota before the state's bone-dry Prohibition ended was one dismantled in late April 1934. It was a $50,000 plant found on a ranch eleven miles northeast of Huron. Officers said it was the work of a gang from Wisconsin.

Officers in on the Huron raid arrested three men. Others were known to have been involved, but they managed to escape and were never found. The three arrested were Sam P.M Glanzer; his brother, Dave P. Glanzer; and their father, Paul P. Glanzer, the tenant of the ranch. Agents destroyed 25,000 gallons of mash and about 150 gallons of finished product, saving small samples for evidence in the trial to follow, according to the April 29, 1934 issue of the *Sioux Falls Argus Leader*.

Yankton County sheriff James Foley and others hit the 1926 jackpot in a raid near Lesterville. They seized 10,000 gallons of liquor mash, 960 gallons of finished whiskey, one 400-gallon capacity still complete with coil and a 400-gallon cooler, five 100-gallon steel tanks, two 1,000-gallon steel tanks, one 2,000-gallon wooden tank and an assortment of equipment valued at about $2,000, close to what Foley made in salary in a year. Julius Frank, J.E. Bruce, Henry Bollie and Henry Murphy, all of Sioux City, and Al Wyatt of Lesterville were arrested. Because of its size, the illegal operation was obviously planned and funded by an out-of-state cartel, but discovery of stills of even larger capacity in South Dakota was still to come.

While the average-sized still in operation in South Dakota during state and federal Prohibition was large enough to provide for personal or neighborhood needs, two industrial-sized stills were found in the state late in the Prohibition era. Why investors put money into these huge distilleries so late in the Prohibition game remains a mystery. The two big super stills weren't built until after national Prohibition had ended and during a time when nearly everyone was aware that the end of South Dakota's bone-dry law was in sight. The one incentive for illegal stills at this far end of the Prohibition years might have been the tax savings. As part of the repeal of national Prohibition in 1933, filing fees and stiff taxes on breweries and distilleries were initiated.

As will be seen in the next chapter, the giant stills in South Dakota required considerable construction efforts and the employment of skilled craftsmen, plus truckloads of product for the mash. Obviously, just the ebb and flow of truck traffic on a dusty rural South Dakota road would cause neighbors to become suspicious, and the more people involved in the construction of these two stills, the more likely word would eventually reach the long arm of the law.

Dry agents were aware of the stills as they were being built and did reach out and touch the two state champions, one in northern Clay County and the other in Minnehaha County, once they became operative. The stills rivaled even the largest plants hidden away in grungy suburbs and seemingly empty industrial plants in Chicago, Kansas City and New York. The two big stills in South Dakota were intended to serve the market needs of the four-state area of Minnesota, South Dakota, Iowa and Nebraska. But neither of the big plants worked out as planned.

## Chapter 6

# Super Stills

In December 1922, State Sheriff's Deputy Charles Peters and two federal Prohibition agents thought they'd found a history-making, record-setting moonshine factory near Freeman. The Freeman distillery was definitely considered king-sized among 1922 moonshine aficionados, and it was the size of the still that separated the men from the boys in the booze-making business. The Freeman site actually had four stills bubbling away. Within five years, even the combined capacity of the Freeman operation would be considered chicken feed.

Before discovering the big Freeman operation, state law officials in August 1921 arrested the man they said was the state's "King of Stills." They surprised Franklin Hines brewing a batch on his farm nine miles south of Cavour. The "king's" Cavour still was a relatively small affair, with a capacity of just twenty gallons. At the time, however, officers had seen nothing larger. Within a decade, a twenty-gallon still would be considered diminutive and commonplace.

That's why agents in on the Freeman raid in 1922 were impressed by the still size, and they also took special note of fifteen pounds of strategically placed dynamite in the distillery on the Henry Schaffer farm fourteen miles south of town. They assumed its purpose was to quickly destroy evidence should there be a need. The explosive was also indicative of the danger law enforcement officials faced. Some moonshiners and bootleggers held a deep hatred for them.

In fact, one of the young federal agents taking part in the raid, Charles Bintliff, who was twenty-two, was shot dead five years later while on a stakeout for an armed bootlegger near Redfield. In addition to the dynamite, Bintliff and his compatriots also found thirty barrels of mash and fifty gallons of finished moonshine. Helping Schaffer keep the four-still operation bubbling and humming were Emmanuel Ulmer, Emmanual Schaffer and Paul Hertz. What they were tending was nothing compared to what would be found a decade later at two super stills, one in Minnehaha County and one in northeast Clay County.

The story of the discovery of the Minnehaha County operation, at that time the largest still found in the state, began in Sioux City on Friday, October 5, 1928. Government agents may have publicly started investigating the case then, but the timing and the exact details of the undercover and detective investment in locating the still had probably started months or years earlier. That preliminary work will never be known because secrecy was the order of the day.

With the preliminary and surreptitious work leading to an Elk Point stakeout on October 5 completed, Nebraska federal Prohibition agent A.L. Mathwig and South Dakota federal Prohibition agent Charles Campbell waited in their car watching the highway traffic trundle by. They were looking for a particular northbound truck carrying a load of sugar that the driver had picked up only hours before in Sioux City. It soon passed by as expected. The agents' car slipped unobtrusively in behind it.

A few miles north of Elk Point, Fred Evans of Sioux Falls, the cautious truck driver, noticed the car following in his highway wake. Evans slowed down for a closer look at its occupants. Mathwig, the driver of the federal car with Nebraska license plates, had no choice but to pull out and pass the truck. He drove a few miles ahead of the truck and then turned off on a country road. The agents waited there out of sight until the truck had passed. They then pulled out and resumed tailing it.

Evans remained cautious. He again slowed. Mathwig repeated his ruse, speeding ahead, turning off and waiting. After slowing down, the truck tried to outdistance Mathwig, speeding up to put miles between the truck and the car. But Evans was only able to coax the heavily laden vehicle to about forty or forty-five miles an hour, according to a story in the October 9, 1928 *Sioux Falls Argus Leader*. Mathwig dropped back a few hundred yards to appease the worried driver's concerns. As the two-vehicle cavalcade neared Sioux Falls, the pursuit car faded back even more, intermingling with other traffic.

Once in Sioux Falls, the trailing agents watched from a distance as Evans stopped briefly at his home at 1409 West Twelfth Street. He soon returned to his truck and drove to a farm on a hill just off Highway 16, five miles west of Sioux Falls on the Ellis Road. By now, it was dark.

The owner of the farm was Garrett Hobbler. He'd bought the property earlier that year from Art France. Mathwig and Campbell parked their car a short distance away, out of sight of the farm. They crept up where they could observe the farmstead and the truck being unloaded at the barn. The agents settled in for a long reconnoiter through the night, mentally casing the place and becoming familiar with the layout and best approaches. About two o'clock on Saturday morning, they watched as the sugar truck, now empty, left the farm. They allowed it to leave, but the driver, Evans, had only a few more hours of freedom before being arrested in Elk Point that afternoon.

At about 9:00 a.m., Agents Mathwig and Campbell left their stakeout and returned to Sioux Falls to report what they had witnessed to their boss and other county law enforcement officials. Working with Minnehaha sheriff George Boardman and Deputies Carl Strass and Seth Adamson, the federal Prohibition unit planned out a raid on the farm. Sketching out the farm site layout, they decided on the best approach to the barn and what to do with the men they expected to find inside. They also assigned a team to simultaneously move in to apprehend any occupants in the farm home.

Sneaking onto the farmstead as best they could in the daylight hours, one of the teams entered the barn. Hearing them, farm owner Hobbler and his hired man, C.W. Peters, who were working in the barn, ran out. Shots were fired in the air in their direction. They stopped and were captured. At the same time, in the farmhouse, officers were as surprised as were the four middle-aged women having coffee at the kitchen table. It was later determined three of the ladies were innocent visitors who had picked the wrong day and time to visit their friend and neighbor Bessie Hobbler.

With everyone on the place handcuffed, arresting officers returned to the barn for a closer look. They were flabbergasted. Inside the barn was an enormous, elaborate, well-engineered and constructed still. The still and accoutrements filled the barn's entire first and second floors.

They marveled at a large, wooden, steam-heated still with a mash capacity of 1,700 gallons. A steam engine of about ten horsepower was ingeniously rigged to automatically activate paddles that stirred four wooden mash fermentation vats, each eight and a half feet high and the same in circumference. Each vat had a capacity of 3,600 gallons. Several large copper distilling domes extended to the barn's second floor to condense the vapors and convert them to alcohol. Also found were twenty sacks of corn sugar. On the second floor were forty-nine empty sugar sacks and sixteen large cardboard cartons, each containing one hundred new 1-gallon cans.

Some of the finished alcohol product was also located. Tests showed the newly manufactured alcohol was of very high quality, 168 proof. Near the barn, agents found four underground water reservoirs having a combined capacity of 100,000 gallons.

All of this was well disguised to appear from the outside as a typical, standard, well-built barn. Hiding the smoke generated by the burning fuel was always a problem for moonshiners. This super still's smoke flue extended from the boilers into the silo next to the barn. The roof of the silo had been raised slightly from the silo wall to allow the oven smoke from the coke fuel to escape through this narrow slit between the raised roof and silo walls around the entire circumference of the silo. Only close inspection revealed the smoke-blackened eaves under the silo roof, agents said.

An electric warning system from the farmhouse kitchen to the barn had also been rigged. A button in the kitchen activated a bell in the barn if trouble was spotted coming up the farm driveway.

At the trial of the perpetrators, farm owners Mr. and Mrs. Hobbler, hired hand Peters and truck driver John Evans all pled guilty on state charges having a maximum sentence of six months in the county jail and a $1,000 fine. The four received four months' jail time and $500 fines.

During the judicial proceedings before Sioux Falls municipal judge Ransom Gibbs, those arrested were represented by attorney Thomas H. Kirby of Kirby, Kirby & Kirby and W.J. Ellwood of the firm Ellwood & Knight. Minnehaha County state's attorney Lucius J. Wall handled the case for the state. It was brought out by Wall during the trial that the persons involved in the case might only be "fall guys" for a more powerful and well-financed liquor ring. It was intimated the super still might have connections to Chicago and Al Capone. According to documents agents confiscated at the farm, it was apparent there was some sort of a tie-in with "big interests" elsewhere. The extent of the outside influence remains a mystery, and it was never determined who paid to build the plant, estimated by federal agents to have cost from $10,000 to $25,000.

To add even more mobster fuel to the fire, authorities in Sioux City said bootleggers there reported they had heard via the grapevine about someone named "Al" who intended to "very soon" start hauling alcohol from South Dakota into Sioux City. Prohibition agents in Sioux City assisting in the case said it indeed might have been possible the Chicago gang was involved in the still. It was assumed the large plant had been in operation only a few weeks prior to the raid, and agents surmised the alcohol already made might have been taken to Sioux City for distribution from there over a wide area, according to the October 8, 1928 *Sioux Falls Argus Leader*.

Agents investigated a report of a telegraph form found at the Sioux City telegraph office believed to have been intended for Capone but said it contained no message, as though the person who had intended to send it had a sudden change of heart and unwittingly left the barely addressed telegraph blank on the counter. Prohibition agents said they also had information about a well-known bootlegger, dope peddler and stick-up man from Omaha who had been in the city on Monday, October 8.

Neighbors near the Hobbler farm whose telephones were on the party line with the farm told investigators of overhearing a telephone conversation between a man at the farm and someone in Rockford, Illinois. The person on the telephone at the farm, they said, told the Rockford party he wasn't "ready to start yet, the coils for the automobile haven't come." Authorities interpreted this to have some connection with the still because "coils" were an integral part of the process.

After the raid, the equipment in the barn was dismantled and the more innocuous items put up for auction. Throughout the investigation, trial and dismantling of the huge still, hundreds of curious passersby drove the short distance from Sioux Falls to see the farm and the infamous barn distillery. Cecil Byg of Sioux Falls, who was ninety-six when interviewed by this author in late 2009, was a teenager in 1927. He remembered being with his parents when they drove out to see the farm where the still was located. It was, Byg said, next to a sale barn at the corner of West Twelfth Street on what was Ellis Road. The cleverly refurbished silo used as the still's smokestack was of particular interest to him at the time, according to an interview by Bruce Blake of Sioux Falls with Byg's daughter Celia Benson in 2009.

John Foster of Sioux Falls was three years old when his parents, Harold and Mary, took him and his two older brothers, Don and Willard, to the farm on a Sunday open house affair held by proud law enforcement officials. Don Foster, who was eight, remembered there was a large crowd milling about in and around the barn. He recalled some of the mash drained from the vats in the barn had spilled onto the ground, and he retains the memory of pigs weaving unsteadily around the farm site, fighting over the last bits of the fermented mash. He can also remember his father, a kind Christian man opposed to drinking, pointing to the mean and ugly porkers, telling the children, "See boys. That's what happens when you drink." The oldest boy, Willard, who was ten at the time of his visit, is retired and continues to live on the Foster homestead about five miles north of the infamous still site, according to Betty Foster of Sioux Falls, wife of Donald Foster.

Almost to the day, six years later, the size of the illegal Sioux Falls distillery that so impressed the Foster boys would be topped by another even more modern and impressive alcohol factory discovered in northeastern Clay County near Beresford. Not only was the Beresford still the largest plant ever in South Dakota, but it, too, had hints of a Chicago crime connection. Further interest in the still arose with the intriguing arrest of the Russell brothers, William R. and George F. of Vermillion. William was the Clay County sheriff, and brother George was his deputy.

The gigantic still was found on the Thure A. Swanson farm in Garfield Township. It was raided in the late hours of Saturday and the early morning of Sunday, September 30, 1934, by more than a dozen state and federal agents. The raid was planned and executed by S.B. Qvale of St. Paul, Minnesota, who was District Fourteen supervisor of the Department of the Alcohol Tax Unit of the Internal Revenue Service. Qvale's division included Minnesota, North and South Dakota and the western half of Wisconsin. The Internal Revenue Service took the lead for the raid because after federal Prohibition ended in December 1933, a federal law was passed in 1934 requiring permits for distilleries and the levying of a tax on alcohol production.

Of course, the still proprietors in Clay County had not obtained the required federal permit or paid taxes on the few hundred gallons the plant had produced up to the time of the raid. Not only did the illegal still violate the federal tax laws, but South Dakota's bone-dry Prohibition law was also still in effect.

Why this huge and expensive still was built on an isolated farmstead in South Dakota so late in the Prohibition game is a mystery. Builders must have known the tendency of South Dakota voters by then pointed to voting out the bone-dry Prohibition law, then in its eighteenth year in the state. With Prohibition federally and in South Dakota soon to atrophy, illegal booze would have to compete with legal distillers. Perhaps the big-time bootleggers, men like Scarface Capone, George "Bugs" Moran and others, were confident their tax-free product could be sold even when competing with legitimate operations.

They may have also assumed their effective and far-reaching underworld marketing and delivery infrastructures were foolproof. The Clay County still's location was well situated geographically for the sale of the product in Sioux Falls, the rest of South Dakota, Sioux City markets in western Iowa and underworld outlets in Minnesota and eastern Nebraska. Further, in a low-population, rural state like South Dakota, the big-city boys unfamiliar with rural America may have assumed a still would be easy to hide and they could operate secretly, at least until their original investment had been recovered and a healthy profit was safely back in Chicago bank accounts. The "tax-free" opportunities were probably the motivating factors in building the big still.

Unknown to the racketeering financiers, however, federal undercover agents must have been well aware of plans for the Clay County plant almost from its beginning, although there are no details on just how this intelligence was gathered. After plans became known to federal officials, they decided to wait until it was actually producing product before moving in. Meanwhile, undercover agents maintained constant secret surveillance as the still was being constructed over a two- or three-month period. The secrecy of both the surveillance and the building of the still were equally impressive. Even neighbors of the farmstead who were interviewed later said they observed nothing suspicious. Agents kept a close watch, too, and were so familiar with the project they even knew about the 590 gallons of near-perfect 180-proof alcohol manufactured in the first runs that were trucked to Nebraska markets, according to the October 1, 1934 *Sioux Falls Argus Leader*.

Agents were aware the still had experienced difficulties when first fired up. The initial batch of mash had been overheated and burned. Federal agents also knew of early difficulties with the still's water supply and its five-hundred-foot well.

After the first small outputs of high-grade alcohol began to trickle out and the few hundred gallons of alcohol had been trucked to Nebraska markets, dry agents decided they had sufficient evidence. It was time to strike. The raid was planned for Saturday night, September 29, 1935, but because it was so massive, it carried over into Sunday. Eighteen state and federal agents, including John H. Johnson, deputy United States marshal, assembled in Sioux Falls to prepare for the top-secret mission. The agents drove to a point southwest of Beresford near the town of Dalesburg and then spread out and advanced silently to the farm site. During daylight hours, the farmstead had a good view of anyone approaching, but it was a dark night and agents kept to the shadows. The raiding party watched as a truck approached the farm gate, gave a blinking headlight signal and was waved in by a guard. When the truck was out of sight, the agents made their move.

Marshal Johnson and some of the officers entered the Swanson house while the others surrounded the barn. In the farmhouse, Johnson detained

Mrs. Swanson and Richard Reeves, the hired man. Farmer Swanson was not in the house but was soon taken into custody near what press reports described as "an outbuilding." As the farm home was being secured, other officers were entering the barn. They completely surprised the four men working inside, capturing them without incident.

Arrested in the sweep were Swanson, twenty-nine; his hired man, Reeves, thirty-seven; and the four men in the barn later determined to be low-level mob soldiers in the racketeering business. They were Jack E. Johnson, an electrical lineman who had lived in Sioux City for a number of years; Bennie DeRosa, thirty-two; Frank Marzella, thirty-seven; and Joe McCauley, forty-one. The latter three had moved to Sioux City only recently. In fact, McCauley told court officials later he was from Springfield, Illinois, and had been in Sioux City only a few days.

The resulting investigation implicated two others, Eddie West and John Naples, who were soon arrested in Chicago. The six men were believed to have connections with a Chicago crime ring "with plenty of money," Supervisor Qvale said. Bond of $8,000 for each man was set. All six remained in jail when no one came forward to meet the bond requirement. Later, the original four taken at the barn, the three in the farmhouse and the two Chicagoans were charged with six counts of operating a still in violation of federal liquor tax laws, including possession of a still, operating a still, manufacturing liquor, possession of mash, possession of unlicensed alcohol and conspiracy to violate United States laws by those acts.

One of the more intriguing aspects of the case was the arrest of Clay County's sheriff and his deputy brother. They were nabbed later that Sunday, not at the still site but in Vermillion. Sheriff William R. Russell, the personable former Vermillion grocery store manager and a married father of two, was arrested at the courthouse. His brother George was located at a Vermillion restaurant having breakfast and was arrested there. Both young men were former star baseball players who in 1927 played for the Sioux City Stockyards semipro ball club. They were charged with conspiracy to aid and abet. From the beginning, they maintained their innocence.

Prior knowledge by federal agents of the still as it was being built was the reason the Clay County sheriff and deputy were believed to have been involved in the cover-up. As the trial of the brothers later proved, they were very aware the still was being planned and built. They also thought they were a part of the federal agents' undercover work as the still took shape. They had visited often with federal undercover agents about the still and assumed they were part of the law enforcement effort to keep an eye on it. In an embarrassing misunderstanding, the St. Paul undercover agents working on the case assumed the sheriff and his deputy, rather than being part of the law enforcement team, were actually part of the group building the still, according to the March 25, 1935 *Sioux Falls Argus Leader*.

Looking over the $18,000 still after the operators had been arrested, agents were surprised to find ten three-thousand-gallon vats capable of turning out one thousand gallons of alcohol a day. The still and accompanying equipment were larger and more elaborate than the one found in the barn along Highway 16 near Sioux Falls in 1928. The Clay County still had one thousand gallons more mash capacity, had twice as many vats and could turn out product more quickly. Agents said the still was the only one of its kind outside Chicago "and the big places," the *Argus Leader* reported.

The barn on the Swanson farm measured forty by one hunderd feet. Cows occupied one end, while the larger end was exclusively for the alcohol operation from ground level to haymow. In the center of the barn, once used to stable Swanson's string of racehorses, was a driveway large enough to accommodate a trailer load of hay when the area was used for livestock. Now it housed two large steam boilers fired by coke fuel. The remainder of the wide barn alley was for storage of fuel and large boxes of yeast. Agents found more than five tons of granulated sugar, including the load the truck driver had unloaded at the barn only hours before.

Swanson's horse-racing interests may have put him in touch with a Midwest underworld element that subsequently sought him out for the distillery scheme, but this was never determined.

Agents also found a cooker into which steam was piped from the boilers. The alcohol vapors wafted off the ten vats into sixteen-foot copper columns and condensers in the loft. The alcohol the plant manufactured was of excellent quality, 188 proof, almost as good as could be achieved. The product could have been halved with water and sold as bootlegged alcohol or aged and treated with oak charcoal to sell as whiskey.

After the raid, Qvale immediately hired crews to dismantle the still, and workers were on the job early Monday morning after the Saturday night raid. The entire first day was taken up just emptying the ten wooden vats of mash. The rush to dismantle was because federal Prohibition leaders had reason to believe "a mob, possibly having a connection with the ring funding the still, might be assembling at Sioux City or some other place and try to make a raid on the barn to pillage articles of value to illegal still operators before government agents could render them useless," the *Argus Leader* reported on October 10, 1934.

The suspicion, as unlikely as it seems, was well founded. While the barn was under guard Sunday night after most of the raiding party had left with their prisoners and returned to Sioux Falls, a small group of unidentified men, who must have assumed the barn was empty and unguarded, entered through a barn window. Unknown to them, two federal agents left at the site sat hidden in the dark inside the barn. They listened as the men looked over the plant and discussed what should be looted. They talked of returning to the barn with more men to help dismantle intricate still parts and then left. They were not apprehended at the time by the two guards because they did not know how many men composed this late-night scout team.

The scouts, or a crew they supposedly went to enlist, never returned, possibly because of the alacrity of the dismantling crew at the site early Monday morning. It is possible the Sioux City looting crew had intended to return and approached the barn early Monday but changed their plans when they saw the dismantling activity at the barn.

Four of the six arrested after the raid—DeRosa, Johnson, West and Jackson—were sentenced to a year and a day in Leavenworth Prison in Kansas. Italian Frank Marzella, who had difficulty in court speaking or understanding English, received a sentence of nine months in the Minnehaha County Jail and eighteen months' probation. Swanson and his hired man, plus well-digger Gagnon, along with West and Napols from Chicago, received six months in the Minnehaha County Jail and eighteen months' probation.

Clay County sheriff Russell, who was at the time a Democratic candidate for reelection, and his brother George were released under $7,500 bond each and allowed to return to Vermillion, where they were needed to carry out their duties in the Clay County courtroom of circuit court judge Robert Tripp. The investigation, meanwhile, continued.

In early March 1935, the twelfth man, Jack Weimer, was arrested in Sioux City. Like lawmen William and George Russell of Vermillion, Weimer was charged with conspiracy for, among other activities, arranging for the still's well to be sunk and for paying many of the other construction bills. Like the two Vermillion law enforcement officers, Weimer pleaded not guilty. Thus, only three of the twelve arrested in the case entered not guilty pleas. The other nine had by then all entered pleas of guilty.

There was one jury for the trial of Weimer and the Russell brothers in federal court in Sioux Falls before Judge A. Lee Wyman. The Clay County brothers hired famous Sioux Falls lawyer Tom Kirby and Everett Bogue of Parker. Coincidentally, Kirby had been involved in the trial of some of those arrested in the big 1928 Sioux Falls super still raid. Representing Sioux City resident Weimer was Sioux City attorney Weir Murphy, who had earlier represented the others who were believed to have been part of a Chicago gang.

Kirby and Bogue argued the innocence of the two Clay County lawmen who believed they had been working surreptitiously with federal agents as the still took shape. If the two Vermillion men had been involved in the illegal scheme, would not they have alerted those working on the still that the federal agents knew about it? Weimer's attorney claimed the same for his client. The jury hearing these arguments included Clarence Harmon of Mount Vernon, who was elected foreman; S.C. Hatch, McLoughlin; Dave Radack, Avon; F.H. Adams, Norbeck; Louis N. Aaseth, Gayville; J.M. McDonnell, Montrose; Roy O. Fletcher, Reliance; M.L. Hancock, Okobojo; Clarence Horton, Sisseton; Fred Brishin, Fulton; E.A. Tilgner, Humbolt; and Louie Dubbe, Hartford.

When the trial ended, Clay County sheriff William Russell and his deputy, George Russell, were acquitted of all charges, but Weimer was found guilty and sentenced to three years in the penitentiary at Leavenworth. The Russell brothers' popularity in the Clay County community did not wane because of their arrests. In fact, Sheriff William Russell was reelected to a second term, and then his brother George won election as sheriff and served two terms, until 1940.

The super stills at Sioux Falls and near Beresford were the only large operations having fairly good indications of mobster connections. With federal Prohibition gone from the books, and with South Dakota's Prohibition soon to be voted out by citizens, these huge distilling operations helped put an emphatic ending to a remarkable era in South Dakota's history, or nearly so.

There remained a rather amateurish South Dakota syndicate of sorts in operation even after Prohibition ended at the federal level in 1933. This time, agents for the Internal Revenue Service moved in after a two-month investigation in the summer of 1934 and arrested ten Yankton County men on the charge of conspiracy to defraud the government with liquor tax evasion.

Arrested as part of what the revenue men called "a moonshine and alcohol syndicate" in a well-timed raid on July 26, 1934, were Nick Ternes, Lesterville; James Syrovatka, Tabor; Harry Feffar, Utica; Joe Bhensky Sr. and Joe Bhensky Jr., Utica; and Leo Machak, Lesterville. Ringleader Joe Syrovatka, twenty-three, known locally as "Little Dillinger," avoided the

July 26 raid, but he and another man, Donald Fuks, gave themselves up to the United States district commissioner, V.S. Vaughan of Yankton, on August 8, 1934. Also later arrested were Albert Fuks of Janousek and Gust Barkel of Lesterville.

Revenue service agents said the syndicate was the largest ever in South Dakota in terms of individuals involved and territory covered. Liquor produced by the syndicate, they said, supplied Sioux Falls, Mitchell and much of southeastern South Dakota, plus other small towns in Nebraska and Iowa. Taken as evidence in the July 20 raid were several stills, a truck and its load of sugar and several hundred gallons of moonshine.

"Little Dillinger" Joe Syrovatka and his brother James were both sentenced to two years in Leavenworth Prison. James was also sentenced to two years for transporting liquor, but the sentence was to be served concurrently with the other. Gust Barkel received a one-year prison sentence. Nick Ternes was fined $100, and the others all received eighteen months' probation.

With the shutting down of this South Dakota liquor syndicate, the Prohibition era in the state came to an end.

CHAPTER 7

# Good Men, Bad Apples

During the fast-paced, helter-skelter war and postwar Prohibition years from 1917 to 1935 in South Dakota and the nation, most of those who swore to uphold the law did so admirably. For lawmen, maintaining the public trust was often difficult, especially enforcing Prohibition laws. Many lawmen in South Dakota did not believe deep down in what the state and national leaders had proscribed. Arresting lifelong friends or neighbors for having an afternoon drink on the front porch, hoisting a proud and happy toast to a newly wedded daughter or sipping a glass of wine in a salute to the joy of Christmas was not a crime in their minds, but Prohibition made it so. Dedicated lawmen had to set aside the friendships and the innocence of it all, bang loudly on front doors, click on the handcuffs and escort the offenders to jail.

To their credit, only a handful of officials violated citizens' sacred trust. Few were tempted to look the other way or accept a few dollars slipped into a palm or pocket when no one was looking. Still, bribes and offenses of this nature did occur, and as a consequence, a lack of respect for the law and those charged with enforcement was rather common.

The deputy sheriff and his postmaster friend in Scenic in 1924 were stocking up for a Christmas celebration. Deputy sheriffs and postmasters should be community role models, but the Pennington County sheriff journeyed to the windy, sage-brushed little town after receiving a tip that one of his deputies and the town postmaster were involved in bootlegging. The sheriff failed to find the liquor supply he was told would be shipped to the two suspects through the mail. He did find a half gallon of moonshine belonging to postmaster F.A. Bartlett and three quarts of booze belonging to Pennington County deputy sheriff C.C. Rush, so the long trip wasn't all for naught.

In Deuel County, on the eastern border of South Dakota, Deuel County judge L.A. Burns was busy by day handing down fines and sentences to scofflaws of one kind or another. Evenings, when he had the time and the inclination, he was buying and then downing illicit booze. He was fined $200 and sentenced to thirty days in jail in Deuel County Circuit Court on February 18, 1922, charged with transporting liquor, according to the *Sioux Falls Argus Leader*.

Charles Kaiser, chief of the Verdon, South Dakota police force, pleaded guilty in early December 1922 to operating an illegal lottery. He was arrested by State Deputy Sheriff Ed Glau after the office received numerous complaints from citizens claiming the little town of Verdon, south of Groton, was often the scene of "liquor escapades and poker games." The *Sioux Falls Argus Leader* reported that Kaiser pleaded guilty and paid a twenty-five-dollar fine.

While these indiscretions were certainly not in keeping with the traditions of good law enforcement, they were minor compared with two cases that dominated the news and conversations among South Dakota citizens.

One involved Robert B. Leady, the man assigned by the federal government's Prohibition Department to lead the South Dakota effort enforcing the Volstead Act and the Eighteenth Amendment. Another very bad apple, Verne Miller, started out as a respected war hero and was then a trusted and popular patrolman on the Huron Police Department who was soon elected Beadle County sheriff. Something snapped, and he evolved into a small-time bootlegger and then a big-time hit man immersed in the gangland battles for supremacy in the big bootlegging leagues of Chicago, Kansas City and elsewhere. He was for a time the nation's most wanted man.

Robert B. Leady had a promising future ahead of him. He arrived in South Dakota as group Prohibition chief for the state a few months after national Prohibition laws became effective on January 16, 1920. It was a good, well-paying job. Leady had cut his Prohibition teeth working for the federal government in Denver, Colorado. Once settled in Sioux Falls on April 15, 1920, he was out in the field almost immediately. In mid-May, he made one of his first arrests at Geddes, taking John Flegram into custody and confiscating twenty-five gallons of wine. With him was his loyal assistant,

Theodore Musgjerd. Leady and Musgjerd followed up the Geddes raid with other successful raids and arrests. They were rising stars in the South Dakota temperance movement.

Leady's small cadre of federal agents was as surprised as anyone a few months later when F.D. Keller, director of Prohibition operations for the northwest district, announced Leady was being transferred to North Dakota. No one but possibly his assistant Musgjerd knew Leady requested to be reassigned to North Dakota. It turned out he wanted the North Dakota job because of easier access to smuggled Canadian booze he could then sell in this country, the *Fargo Forum* reported on March 11, 1921.

Still considered a noble public servant when he left South Dakota, Leady drew gushing praise as a fighter against those who violated federal liquor laws. The *Sioux Falls Argus Leader* had this to say: "During his six months [*sic*] of service to South Dakota Leady has been feared by all moonshiners and bootleggers....Leady has caused grief to many a moonshiner of 'spirits,' and records at the Federal Building show that he has brought many in the illegal liquor practice to justice." Within a month of the *Argus Leader*'s rapturous ballyhoo of Leady, the federal officer was arrested for attempting to do what he was hired to prevent. He was caught dealing in liquor.

The official charges were violation of Prohibition laws and conspiracy to commit a crime against the United States. The case broke after the arrest in early October 1920 of his former assistant Musgjerd in South Dakota. Musgjerd had resigned his Sioux Falls job when Leady left for North Dakota, followed his former boss to North Dakota and was soon hired as Leady's clerk in the North Dakota office.

Theodore Musgjerd, alias Andres Hanson, and another man, Peter Olson, whose real name was E.O. Haugen, were nabbed in Sioux Falls with a big load of Canadian liquor. Olson, aka Haugen, was proprietor of the Allen Hotel in Moorhead, Minnesota, where the smuggled Canadian whiskey was apparently stored until it could be sold and shipped.

The scandal broke when Ike L. McCoun, a Sioux Falls private detective and later a policeman who had worked on various bootlegging cases with Leady, turned on his old friend, setting up an elaborate scheme to implicate the federal officer. In doing so, McCoun hoped to gain favor and improve his chances of being hired as a federal Prohibition agent in South Dakota. Interviewed by reporters from the *Sioux Falls Argus Leader* and the Associated Press in October 1920, McCoun told the following story:

> *One month before Leady had been reassigned* [to North Dakota] *he came to me and said he had five barrels of whiskey to sell and asked me if I could help him dispose of it. At the time I had an application in for appointment to a position as a federal prohibition agent. After consideration I believed it would be a big step toward obtaining an appointment if I could get the goods on a government agent. I told him I would see what I could do. Later Leady came to me and said he couldn't deliver the goods in this case. Just before he left for North Dakota Leady asked me if I could assist him in disposing of whiskey on the local market. I told him that I might be able to.*
>
> *The first I heard of actually carrying out of his end of the affair was last night. About 6 o'clock I had a telephone call from Musgjerd, who was at Dell Rapids* [about twenty miles away]. *He said he had some "good stuff" for me. He cautioned me that it was "confidential" and asked if I could help him swing the deal. I told him to come ahead. About 9 o'clock he called again, this time from downtown* [Sioux Falls]. *I told him to come right out to my house at 1812 East Eighth Street. He came out in a taxi cab. I faked a telephone call downtown to a patron and told him that the stuff was to be delivered. Musgjerd fell for the scheme and agreed to deliver the whiskey to my house where the sale was to be made. He wanted $3,000 for the load of ten cases. Musgjerd left for downtown to get the car and I left just afterwards in a taxi cab for police headquarters.*
>
> *Following a hasty conference, we decided that Coonan, a police chauffeur, should be the buyer. Not having the money, we borrowed a check book from Mayor Burnside who happened to be in the station at that time. Several policemen accompanied us to my home. Coonan and I went into the house while the policemen were stationed at convenient points around the premises. Soon Musgjerd and his partner arrived. I introduced Coonan as the buyer. Musgjerd said that I and his partner should unload the stuff into the basement while he talked business with Coonan. Coonan then demanded to see the whiskey before a deal was made. Musgjerd opened the top of the back seat.* [The car carrying the 120 quarts of whiskey was a Jordon roadster. A roadster was what today's convertible was called.] *The whiskey was there, and Coonan immediately informed the man that they were under arrest as policemen approached and surrounded the car.*

After the arrest of Musgjerd and Haugen, they were each fined $100 on city charges and then rearrested to face state charges. Federal charges were also pending against them. In municipal court, it was learned the cutting of the $3,000 liquor sale pie was to have former agent Leady receiving $1,000, the provider of the liquor getting $1,000 and Musgjerd and Haugen $500 each.

After the Sioux Falls trial, Musgjerd, Haugen and Ike McCoun went immediately to North Dakota to be present at Leady's hearing in Fargo on Monday, October 11, 1920. At Leady's indictment, M.A. Hildreth, United States district attorney, described Leady to Judge Amidon as an "arch actor" in a "devilish plot to beat the government in the enforcement of the prohibition act," according to the October 14, 1920 *Sioux Falls Argus Leader*. The next day, Leady pleaded not guilty and was released on $2,000 bond to await trial.

At his trial in March 1921, McCoun was the principal witness for the government. He had by then, as he had hoped, been hired by the new head of South Dakota's federal Prohibition office, J.E. Pearson. Leady's trial was brief. A jury needed just thirty minutes on March 12, 1921, to find the former dry agent guilty as charged, along with the two co-defendants who brought the booze to Sioux Falls, according to the March 12, 1921 *Fargo Forum* of North Dakota. Judge J.W. Woodrough sentenced Leady to one year and a day in Leavenworth Federal Prison. Musgjerd got a six-month sentence in the Cass County Jail, five months of which he had already served. Haugen got thirty days in the county jail and was fined $100. Leady got off relatively easy. The maximum penalty for conspiracy, first count and first offense, was a $10,000 fine or two years in prison, or both.

A sidelight in the trial was an envelope found by Sioux Falls detectives in Musgjerd's booze car on which Leady had written the names of four potential Sioux Falls customers for the liquor. McCoun was one of the four listed, along with John Boyd, a retired Sioux Falls farmer; John McKenna, a Sioux Falls real estate agent; and a man whose last name was Paula, who was a Sioux Falls grain buyer. Leady denied any knowledge of the list, but J.H. Davis of Duluth, Minnesota, a penmanship expert, said the writing matched Leady's. The four assumed Sioux Falls buyers were never implicated in any way. Retired farmer Boyd testified at the North Dakota trial, saying Leady and his wife had stayed at his farm when Leady first arrived at his new federal job in Sioux Falls and was in need of temporary housing, a March 11, 1921 story in the *Fargo Forum* revealed.

A more tragic South Dakota story, through which is woven the tapestry of massive national illegal liquor profits, is of a swashbuckling war hero from the little town of Kimball who became Beadle County's sheriff and moved into high crime as a bootlegger, bank robber and, in the end, killer.

Vernon C. Miller was a handsome, athletic seventeen-year-old when he left his Kimball, South Dakota home for a job as an auto mechanic in Huron in 1914. At the age of nineteen, he joined the army and was a member of the South Dakota Mexican Expedition, pursuing desperados who were raiding border towns and harassing ranchers along the Rio Grande. After America entered World War I, Miller continued his army service. He got his baptism of fire in France with the Eighteenth Infantry Regiment. Miller was popular with his fellow soldiers and advanced to the honored position of sergeant of the color guard, carrying the American flag for his regiment and for his country in parades and special ceremonies. He was also decorated for valor and bravery under fire.

Miller was discharged honorably in 1918 after the war ended and returned to Huron a hero. He joined the city's police force. Because of his notoriety, personality and heroic credentials, he made many friends in the city and the surrounding area. He was a natural politician, and some of his influential friends convinced him to run for Beadle County sheriff. He was the successful candidate in 1920. With South Dakota's bone-dry Prohibition law in its third year by the time he took office, enforcing those laws in the county was one of his many responsibilities.

In June 1922, Sheriff Miller was incensed when he was told about Huron police justice R.B. Hatfield's comments regarding a known moonshine operation in the county. Hatfield said Sheriff Miller and his department were purposely overlooking the illegal operation and allowing the still to continue producing moonshine, implying a payoff of some kind. When Miller learned of this accusation, he confronted Hatfield and demanded to know the still's location. With Hatfield in tow, Sheriff Miller and Deputy Bid Roberts, whose later exploits in bank robberies in other states resulted in a twenty-year prison sentence in Indiana, obtained a search warrant and drove to the Will Melsenhelder farm seven miles south of Huron. There they found the largest still then in Beadle County, according to the June 20, 1922 *Huronite*. They arrested Melsenhelder and seized his still, three gallons of mash and thirty-seven pint bottles of beer.

It was never known if Sheriff Miller was being paid off to ignore the big Melsenhelder still he had just raided. But for unexplained reasons, something changed in the mind of the handsome, promising young law enforcement officer. Less than a month after the liquor raid, on July 14, 1922, Miller left town with $4,771.09 in Beadle County funds. The amount included $2,556.79 in taxes his office had collected but had not yet turned over to the county, $2,178.30 in trust funds deposited with the sheriff on execution and

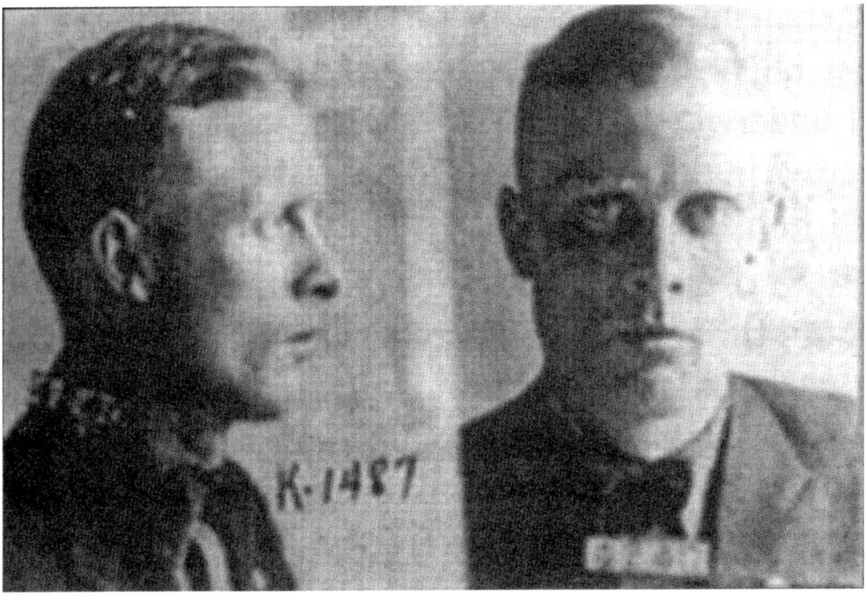


Former South Dakota sheriff and FBI's most wanted Verne Miller. *Author's collection.*

some other funds. On August 9, the Beadle County Commission declared a vacancy existed in the office of sheriff, reported the *Huronite*.

Perhaps Miller's unlawful withdrawal of what was then a large amount of money had something to do with his wife's serious illness and her expensive medical bills, or maybe Miller was merely taking one more step into the criminal underworld. Within a year, the former sheriff was tracked down and arrested in the Twin Cities. On April 4, 1923, a Beadle County jury convicted him of embezzlement. He was sentenced to the South Dakota Penitentiary, where he became a model prisoner and was even trusted to serve as the warden's personal chauffeur. Miller was granted parole and discharged from the Sioux Falls prison on December 4, 1924. He returned to St. Paul, Minnesota, and soon became involved with bootlegging operations there, making an underworld reputation for himself and making underworld friends, as well.

He was back in the South Dakota news in March 1926 when Aurora County sheriff George Boardman announced Miller had been arrested by the Stickney City marshal. Stickney is thirty miles from Miller's hometown of Kimball. Miller's new Studebaker car was found loaded with thirty gallons of liquor. At the time, it was also learned Miller had been arrested in Sioux Falls in October 1925 on a federal Prohibition charge of possession of liquor. After his release from the penitentiary and his 1926 arrest in Stickney, it was learned he had acquired a drug habit and was also dealing with the effects of syphilis.

Several months after the March arrest near Stickney, federal judge James D. Elliott of Sioux Falls, for the first time in South Dakota, issued a "personal injunction" against Miller. It was a new tool in the nation's Prohibition efforts. Under the special injunction, the defendant was required to refrain from violating any law for a period of one year. Failure to do so would result in a fine of $500 to $1,000 and prison for one year in addition to penalties normally given for the crime committed. Miller was one of five serial Prohibition lawbreakers in South Dakota at the time. The others who were issued personal injunctions were Don King of Huron, Evan Evanson of Brookings, James Murphy of Huron and Theodore Kerr of Turton. Federal Prohibition director E.L. Senn praised the personal injunction instrument in the war against bootleggers whom, he said, "had the money to hire a lawyer and delay the customary form of prosecution for months," according to the July 28, 1926 *Sioux Falls Argus Leader*. He said he had a thick file in his office with the names of one hundred violators against whom injunctions may be sought.

Drug use and his venereal disease began to dramatically change Miller's personality. Friends said he became increasingly unstable and had unpredictable bursts of violence. On February 3, 1928, friends and family living in the Kimball, Huron and White Lake areas were shocked to read of his indictment for the murder of a Minneapolis police officer and the assault of another. Lack of evidence in the case, however, resulted in his release.

By now, powerful bootleggers and racketeers knew of Verne Miller's reputation. He was on the unwritten list of freelance gunmen for hire in the Midwest. Many gang leaders and racketeers sought out his deadly service. In 1930, after one of his close friends, Eugene "Red" McLaughlin, was killed by members of Al Capone's Chicago gang, Miller, either on his own or in concert with others, tracked down three of the gang suspected to have been involved. He found them at a Fox Lake, Illinois resort, a popular underworld hangout. On June 1, 1930, in an ambush, he shot and killed all three. The crime made national headlines and became known in the underworld and to law enforcement everywhere as the Fox Lake Massacre.

As the end of national Prohibition approached, gangs, big-time bootleggers and racketeers cast about for other nefarious opportunities. Bank robberies became the crime of choice. Banks then had lax security measures, and the automobile provided thugs with the mobility for quick escapes to distant hideouts. In 1927, South Dakota Penitentiary warden George T. Jameson declared the automobile, not Prohibition, as the reason the penitentiary's population had risen to about 460 prisoners. "A lot of people are driving automobiles when they ought to be driving a pair of mules," he said. "They find they can't keep up, and so they steal to make up the difference between their incomes and their scale of living," Jameson said in the August 7, 1926 *Sioux Falls Argus Leader*.

On July 15, 1930, Miller took up armed robbery. He teamed with seven buddies, including George "Machine Gun" Kelly, to stage a daylight raid on the bank in Wilmar, Minnesota, leaving with $70,000 under their arms. About thirty days later, in an argument about a "double cross" over the Wilmar robbery, Miller shot and killed Frank "Weinie" Colman, Mike Rusick and Sammy "Jew" Stein and dumped their bodies at White Bear Lake, according to press reports.

Still in good graces with Machine Gun Kelly and the two others who participated in the Wilmar bank heist, the gang next targeted the bank at Ottumwa, Iowa, and walked out with $40,000 in cash. Then on April 8, 1931, Miller, Machine Gun Kelly and others robbed the bank in Sherman, Texas, leaving with another $40,000.

After the Texas robbery, Miller seemed to become weary of bank robbery as a vocation and graduated to become a gangland hit man. Chicago mobster Louis Stacci contacted Miller and paid him to try to free one of Stacci's men, Frank Nash, who was also one of Miller's friends and cohorts in the Texas bank adventures. Nash was then in federal custody and scheduled for transfer to Leavenworth Federal Penitentiary. On June 17, 1933, Miller and several other gunmen who had been hired by Stacci waited for Nash and the federal agents escorting him to Leavenworth. When Nash and the agents arrived at Union Station in Kansas City, Missouri, Miller and the others were waiting, and there was a violent gun battle. Nash was killed in the mêlée, as were four law enforcement officers. Two other lawmen were wounded, but Miller and his gang escaped unscathed. One of the gunmen with Miller was identified by the Federal Bureau of Investigation as Charles "Pretty Boy" Floyd of Oklahoma.

The deadly confrontation in Kansas City, incidentally, was the one incident more than any other that helped provide impetus for J. Edgar Hoover of the Federal Bureau of Investigation to lobby for federal money to beef up and modernize law enforcement agencies. The FBI was changed largely because of Miller's escapade in Missouri.

Miller, by now one of the country's most wanted criminals, went to New Jersey, where he stayed with mobster Abner "Longy" Zwillman. While there, it is said, Miller argued with a Zwillman gunman and shot him to death. After the incident, police described Miller as "the most dangerous criminal at large in the country," reported the November 15, 1933 *Huronite.* Miller was next located in Chicago staying with a girlfriend. Police learned of his presence and raided the woman's apartment, but Miller was able to shoot his way to freedom once again and became the object of a nationwide manhunt, according to the November 11, 1933 *Huronite.*

On November 29, 1933, Miller's enemies finally caught up with him. Police found his body naked and trundled in two mangy blankets bound by wire in a roadside ditch outside Detroit, Michigan. He'd been shot, and his head had been bashed in for good measure, reported the *Huronite* in December 1933. It had all the earmarks of a typical gangland slaying, police said. Scores of mobsters and gangsters had reason to snuff out Miller, but his killer or killers were never found. Some in law enforcement speculated it was the work of New Jersey mobster Zwillman. Others pointed the finger at Stacci, who was not happy with the botched outcome of the Nash rescue attempt in Kansas City. Perhaps Miller's death was a Capone-inspired retribution for the Fox Lake murders.

A day after his body was found, word of the gangster's death reached his father, Charles Miller, in White Lake, and others in Beadle County. The father, two of Verne's sisters, three half sisters, three half brothers and Miller's stepmother had last seen the wayward son in September 1932, when Miller slipped into South Dakota and managed to spend a few hours with them. There was also a rumor Miller had been seen in Aberdeen a few weeks before his death, according to the December 2, 1933 *Sioux Falls Argus Leader*. The newspaper said Aberdeen police were adamant, claiming Miller was seen with a female companion in the downtown area of the community driving a Stutz coup with an Illinois license plate.

As funeral arrangements were being made in Huron by Miller's family, the father of the notorious killer asked the William Reaves Post No. 7 of the American Legion to be in charge of a military funeral. The Huron post membership voted unanimously not to participate either at the funeral or the grave site because the deceased's life of disobeying the nation's laws was in violation of the American Legion's national preamble. In a morning memorial service at the home of Miller's father in White Lake, on the same day as the Huron funeral, the small White Lake Gores American Legion Post No. 96 did participate in the ceremony. Uniformed White Lake post members also accompanied the body to Huron, according to L.W. Barnes, a White Lake funeral director.

More than one thousand people, some of whom were mourners and some of whom were just curious, attended Miller's funeral. Services were conducted by Reverend F.E. Lochridge, pastor of the Methodist Episcopal church. An American flag was draped over the casket in what was described in the press as a "simple" ceremony at the Welter Funeral Home. A few flower bouquets surrounded the casket, including one from an unidentified out-of-area source. It was a floral spray with the note: "Our Pal," which had a "goodfellas" ring to it. Mourners filled the chapel to capacity, and many could not get in, so Huron Police guided traffic around the viewers who spilled out into the street.

Because so many well-wishers and the curious were unable to view the body in the funeral chapel, the casket was opened after the services to allow all who wished to file by. Some who viewed the body and knew Miller well said they were not sure they recognized their old friend. Cosmetics and other means had been used to hide to some extent the extreme injuries to his head. L.W. Barnes said relatives confirmed the body was their son and brother, according to the *Sioux Falls Argus Leader*. Miller was buried in Huron's Riverside Cemetery.

The Reverend Lochridge, in his eulogy for Miller, recounted the gangster's brave and unselfish service during the war. He also mentioned his public service as a former sheriff in Beadle County, but he did not further embellish his praise. He asked mourners to remember Miller by his virtues rather than his sins and then ended his eulogy, saying: "We draw a curtain at this point."

An earlier murder case in Pukwana, later dismissed, had an interesting Verne Miller connection. Farmer James Conley was planning a barn dance at his place north of Pukwana for Saturday night, September 5, 1931. At about 2:00 a.m. on Sunday, a fight broke out at the dance, and Conley, sensing more trouble from drunken celebrants, called Brule County sheriff Clarendon D. Miller, who was an uncle of Verne Miller. At the time of his speedy trip to the Pukwana barn dance, where it was estimated eight out of ten people were intoxicated, Sheriff Miller, sixty-nine, was the oldest active county sheriff in the state.

Sheriff Miller and a deputy arrived at the Conley farm and broke up the fight. When Miller and deputy moved in to quell another nearby disturbance sparked by the original fight, those involved in what was later described as a free-for-all drunken riot attacked the sheriff, who died during the mêlée. A coroner's jury determined Miller had died from a blow to his left temple.

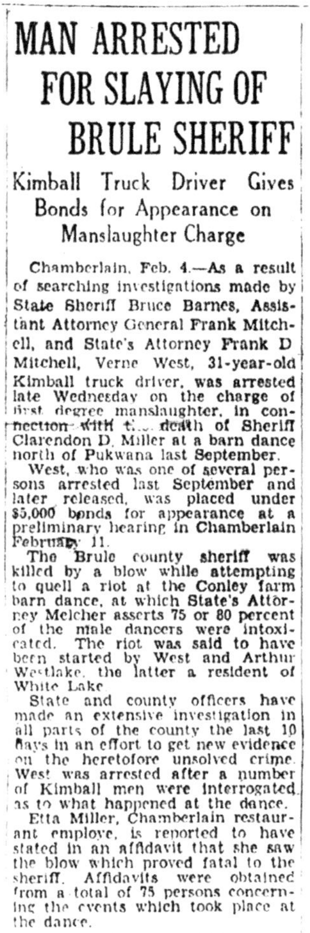

MAN ARRESTED FOR SLAYING OF BRULE SHERIFF

Kimball Truck Driver Gives Bonds for Appearance on Manslaughter Charge

Chamberlain, Feb. 4.—As a result of searching investigations made by State Sheriff Bruce Barnes, Assistant Attorney General Frank Mitchell, and State's Attorney Frank D Mitchell, Verne West, 31-year-old Kimball truck driver, was arrested late Wednesday on the charge of first degree manslaughter, in connection with the death of Sheriff Clarendon D. Miller at a barn dance north of Pukwana last September.

West, who was one of several persons arrested last September and later released, was placed under $5,000 bonds for appearance at a preliminary hearing in Chamberlain February 11.

The Brule county sheriff was killed by a blow while attempting to quell a riot at the Conley farm barn dance, at which State's Attorney Melcher asserts 75 or 80 percent of the male dancers were intoxicated. The riot was said to have been started by West and Arthur Westlake, the latter a resident of White Lake.

State and county officers have made an extensive investigation in all parts of the county the last 10 days in an effort to get new evidence on the heretofore unsolved crime. West was arrested after a number of Kimball men were interrogated as to what happened at the dance.

Etta Miller, Chamberlain restaurant employe, is reported to have stated in an affidavit that she saw the blow which proved fatal to the sheriff. Affidavits were obtained from a total of 75 persons concerning the events which took place at the dance.

*Sioux Falls Argus Leader*, February 4, 1932. *Author's collection.*

When his body was examined at the scene, his blackjack was missing. It was assumed to have been the weapon.

State Sheriff Bruce Barnes and lawyers from the attorney's general office investigated the incident. Verne West, a thirty-one-year-old Kimball truck driver, was soon arrested on a charge of manslaughter. A.D. Brooks of Pukwana, floor manager at the dance, testified that he had asked West after the mêlée who had hit the sheriff, and West said he did, although at the time West was not aware the man was the county sheriff. On September 8, three days after the incident and after Sheriff Miller had been buried in Kimball's Pleasant Grove Cemetery, Brule County state's attorney H.V. Melcher ordered an autopsy. The body was exhumed and an autopsy conducted by Dr. E.W. Jones of Mitchell, Dr. J.L. Bettag of Pukwana and Dr. O. Charles Erickson of Sioux Falls. They determined death had not resulted from a blow to the head but was caused by a heart attack from artery hardening. The accused assailant was released.

As an aftermath of the death of the state's oldest sheriff, his son, I.K. Miller, was appointed by the Brule County Commission to succeed his father. At twenty-six, he became South Dakota's youngest county sheriff. In the 1932 general election, young Sheriff Miller was elected by a larger plurality than his father had garnered in the 1930 election. In fact, the Brule County turnout was the largest to date by more than four hundred votes, an indication of voters' respect for the deceased Clarendon Miller and his son.

CHAPTER 8

# Bottling Up Bootleggers

During Prohibition, the division of labor in the illegal whiskey business went like this: moonshiners were the manufacturers, and there were plenty of them at work in their homemade, out-of-sight factories in South Dakota. Down a rung on the illegal liquor ladder were the bootleggers, who were the wholesalers. They obtained, transported and sold the product. There were by far more bootleggers than moonshiners in South Dakota. A subdivision within the bootlegger ranks were the apprentices, who hadn't moved up to become route purveyors with their own fancy cars and little black customer books. These beginners plied the dimly lit dance hall parking lots, rodeo grounds, pool halls, seedy restaurants and back alleys.

There were also neighborhood bootleggers whose customers left money in a fruit jar on their back porches and during the dark of night received another jar of moonshine in return, much like the milkman made house deliveries. The moonshine left on the porch was then shared with friends in the neighborhood who had preordered and prepaid.

There were also the hip-pocket bootleggers at the ladder's lower rung who walked their rounds hoping for a sale. They were everywhere, carrying their meager and well-diluted supply in a hip or vest pocket.

Abe Jampolsky of Aberdeen was arrested in 1922 for bootlegging, but his trip with illegal booze was brief. He traveled only from his back porch to a backyard chicken coop because when police knocked on his front door in April 1922, Jampolsky took off out his back door with an armload of whiskey, intending to hide it among some nearby cackling chickens.

Police caught him halfway to the chicken shed and charged him with transporting liquor. His attorney said his client had carried the liquor from one place to another on his own property so he had not violated the law. However, it was discovered the chicken shed was on a neighbor's lot, and Jampolsky's armload of booze had therefore traveled approximately sixteen feet beyond his property, according to a report in the April 22, 1922 *Sioux Falls Argus Leader*.

John Burbeck of Avon was a successful booze runner. He was, literally, a bum-legged "rum jobber," the Canadian term for bootlegger. Burbeck was spiriting illegal booze from Canada into South Dakota and making a small fortune doing it. During his career as a bootlegger in South Dakota and as a smuggler of Canadian booze, he'd earned the title among law enforcement officials as South Dakota's "Prince of Bootleggers."

By January 1922, his luck changed. He was arrested and in the Sioux Falls jail awaiting extradition to Canada for his escapades there. Canada's extradition request was denied by Washington, D.C. officials, and he was set free. This was a rather surprising turn of events. His freedom, it was learned later, was in exchange for him agreeing to become a federal Prohibition snitch. After his extradition was denied, but before he left jail, he was interviewed by a reporter for the *Sioux Falls Argus Leader*.

"Boy, you can tell the world I'm going straight," he told the reporter from his jail cell, where he'd just heard the good news. His first stop after his release, he said, was to have his lame leg amputated. He'd injured it in a non-combat accident at an army camp years ago. It never healed and was slowly getting worse. That injury was indirectly responsible for his bootlegging adventures. Medication to dull the pain was expensive and habit-forming. He needed money to buy the drugs, and bootlegging paid handsomely and put him in touch with drug dealers. He acknowledged he was an addict and said he intended to whip the dependency once the leg pain was gone.

He said that after he was fitted with an artificial leg he'd probably start a ranch on land his father owned in the short grass country west of the Missouri River. But he never had his leg fixed, and he never poked cattle on his father's land.

As his future life unfolded after his close call with Canada, the "Prince of Bootleggers" begin proving he was also the prince of con men. He failed to go straight as he'd sworn to do in his Sioux Falls jail cell avowal. Almost a year after his newspaper interview in 1923, he was in trouble, nabbed in Murdo for auto theft. The Nash car he was driving, perhaps as inexpensive transportation for his trip out to inspect his father's ranch land, was stolen from the Tri-State Livestock Commission in Sioux Falls, the January 12, 1922 *Sioux Falls Argus Leader* reported. He was sentenced to two years in Leavenworth.

After his release in September 1925, the law again caught up with him a mile west of Pumpkin Center near Sioux Falls. He was a passenger in a big, new Dodge driven by Sol Berg, known to South Dakota dry agents as "the millionaire bootlegger from St. Paul, Minnesota." In the car were ten cases of imported scotch and bourbon whiskey, including Haig & Haig, bourbon and Three-Star Hennessey, according to Minnehaha County sheriff George Broadman.

Burbeck limped into court and claimed he was an innocent passenger in the car. Berg's attorney, N.B. Bartlett, claimed Burbeck was a paid "stool pigeon" for the sheriff's office and had informed authorities about the contraband in Berg's car. At this time, it was probably simply a hunch by the attorney, with no verification coming from the county or federal officials, which is understandable. Burbeck was not sentenced for his part in the Pumpkin Center caper.

His painful leg still demanding regular doses of "pain killer," Burbeck was soon back in the news in May 1926. He had found another car to his liking and was arrested in Sioux City, Iowa, for car theft. After this arrest, his suspected undercover life became known. As the attorney in the Sioux Falls trial had guessed, Burbeck had, indeed, been working undercover. He was not on the Minnehaha County sheriff office's payroll but was an undercover agent for E.L. Senn, head of the federal Prohibition effort in South Dakota.

Car theft exceeded undercover demands of Prohibition sleuthing, and he got no help from Senn. He was sentenced to another stint in Leavenworth. Once out, he apparently limped off into obscurity, never to be heard from again, the May 8, 1926 *Argus Leader* reported.

Just as most of the citizens in most of the state's communities and rural neighborhoods knew the bootleggers who served the area and were aware of the places where booze was made and sold, law enforcement officials also compared notes on their knowledge of who was dealing and delivering. Over time, some of the state's bootleggers became well known by officers and gained statewide or area-wide notoriety. In Rapid City in 1923, Harry "Shorty" Beamer was a busy bootlegger whom officers dubbed the "king of bootlegging."

South of Rapid City in 1924, officers called John Konrath "the biggest bootlegger in Fall River County." Appropriately, Konrath was from the town of Rumford, a name befitting his profession.

In 1924, Albert Johnston of Sioux Falls was apprehended for having two quarts of moonshine concealed in his vest and two more bottles in his hip pockets. It was a relatively minor offense, but unfortunately, Johnston was driving a nice Essex car when he was stopped, and both Johnston's whiskey larder and his expensive car were confiscated, the *Sioux Falls Argus Leader* reported.

Hip-pocket bootleggers were ubiquitous. On the low rung of the ladder, their freelance marketing plans were simple and similar. They bought a small quantity of alcohol, perhaps a gallon or two, from other bootleggers who were dealing in larger quantities. They would then "cut" their meager supply with tap water, perhaps doubling the amount of the original purchase, and therefore were able to more than double their original investment. With one or a few pints or quarts of watered-down hooch tucked away, they made the rounds, hawking their goods to likely buyers. If the bootlegger was having a good day, he would return to restock his baggy coat or pants pockets with more booze. The flat shape of today's pint and half-pint bottles originated in those days so the bottles could hide comfortably in the hip or coat pocket.

LeRoy Capps and his daughter, Violet, were stopped by Sioux Falls police who were standing outside the Jewell Theater in January 1927. Capps and his daughter were about to enter a building across the street at 118½ Phillips Avenue. When they were hailed by a nearby patrolman, the daughter tried to flee. She was carrying a package containing ten half pints of whiskey. When police searched her father, they found ten more half pints in his pockets and "about his clothes," the press reported. It turned out to be a family business. The investigation revealed Capps and his daughter had arrived in downtown Sioux Falls in a car driven by Capp's son, Clifford, the *Sioux Falls Argus Leader* reported in its January 24, 1924 issue.

Small-time hip-pocket bootlegger Orville Peters of Clark changed his delivery manner from hip pocket to arm because of the size of the order he was filling. He was making his "run" in broad daylight. As he scurried along, it wasn't a case of the police finding him but of him actually physically bumping into them. A *Sioux Falls Argus Leader* story on March 20, 1933, indicated Peters was delivering a tin of alcohol carried under his arm on Clark Street when he passed by and accidentally bumped into a deputy sheriff. The deputy apologized and then asked him what he had under his arm. Peters told him it was "just a bit of old iron and nothing more." The deputy accepted the "iron" admission but questioned the "nothing more" and arrested Peters.

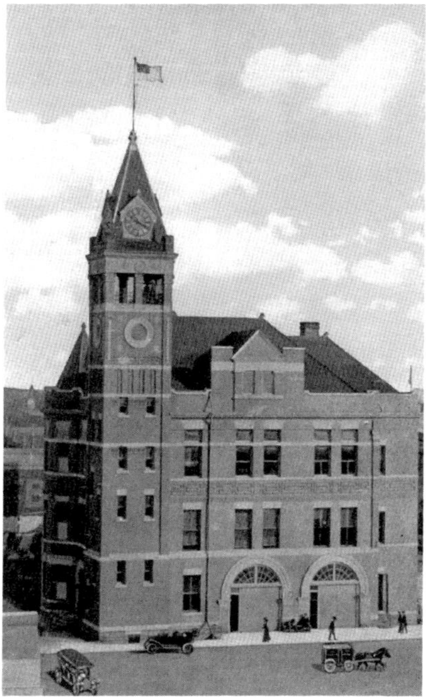

Watertown City Hall, which housed the busy Watertown Police Department during the Prohibition years from 1917 to 1935. *Author's collection.*

When George Stanley was arrested, his cargo wasn't under his arm. It was in his hip pocket. Stanley stopped by Watertown City Hall to transact business. He also needed to make a phone call and knocked on the open door of Police Chief Johnson, asking permission to use his telephone. Johnson nodded, waved him in and pointed to the phone on a shelf behind his chair. As Stanley was leaning over a corner of the chief's desk talking on the phone, the chief's keen ears detected a gurgling sound. After the phone call, Chief Johnson inquired about the gurgle. Stanley confessed to his illegal stash. Officers later searched the home of Stanley's brother, Edward. They found four half pints in a bureau drawer and one in the baby carriage, plus twenty-four pints in various other locations in the home. Stanley was fined forty dollars in municipal court for his illegal, noisy cargo, but he had no money, so he served time in jail, each day worth two dollars off his forty-dollar fine, the January 18, 1933 *Sioux Falls Argus Leader* reported.

The hard luck story of the year happened in Rapid City on June 16, 1922. Fred Powell called attention to himself as he was walking past the police department because his bottle of booze slipped from his pocket and loudly shattered on the sidewalk. He was immediately arrested.

With improved highways, mass production of the automobile early in the last century and its further perfection in the 1920s when Prohibition was at its zenith, many bootleggers who dealt in larger supplies of liquor emerged. They could move liquor over a larger geographic area faster than bootleggers of an earlier horse-and-buggy time who served only small neighborhoods. The telephone, too, was a wonderful aide to motorized bootleggers who received liquor orders from customers miles away.

Often, bootleggers had other primary professions, and their liquor sales meshed with the selling of liquor to bring in extra money. Two Minnesota men in a big, fancy car were stopped in Groton the night of May 16, 1931, newspapers reported, and officers seized one hundred gallons of alcohol and a .38-caliber pistol from the vehicle. The bootleggers were stockbroker Alexander Beaton and cosmetic salesman C.F. Scheller.

By March 1932, 99,194 automobiles and 13,032 trucks were registered in South Dakota, according to state records. Even as early as 1924, the first state sheriff, John Shanks, mentioned in his annual report to the governor the difficulties law enforcement officials faced because of the "combination of improved highways and the general use of motor vehicles."

In 1932, police in Aberdeen arrested William Tietz of rural Mansfield for intoxication and fined him twenty dollars. He was immediately rearrested on a state charge of transporting liquor. He may have gotten away with both the local and state charge, but he'd been drinking, and he fell asleep at the feet of his team of horses at a downtown Aberdeen intersection. Officers believe Tietz's wagon—in which they found eleven quarts of moonshine in small bottles and fruit jars nestled in straw in the wagon box—broke down at the intersection. Tietz alighted from the wagon seat to fix the problem but fell asleep near the faithful horses' pie tin–sized hooves. The team remained calm until police were called to remove their keeper from his somewhat perilous resting place, the *Argus Leader* reported in its March 10, 1932 issue.

The automobiles used by bootleggers were usually new or nearly so because reliable transportation was necessary and could be the difference between business success and failure. Stock cars and eventually the popular NASCAR (National Association of Stock Car Racing) are products of the Prohibition era. Bootleggers were skilled at what was called "souping up" their car motor's performance for the extra power to outrun government cars. Many of the vehicles used by bootleggers were also reworked to provide more room for booze, such as removal of the rear seat for storage of bottles or tins.

The imagination of skilled craftsmen was evident in the manners in which the interiors of cars were altered to carry out-of-sight hooch. Vehicles for transporting heavy loads were also fitted with overload springs because law enforcement officials had learned to be suspicious of vehicles with sagging rear ends. Many bootleggers' cars also were equipped with oversized gas tanks to reduce stops for gasoline and the chance gas station attendants might see the load of booze as the gas tank was filled. Spotlights, needed to locate a customer's house address at night, were also a standard on bootleggers' cars, according to the April 2, 1921 *Sioux Falls Argus Leader*.

Tin containers for booze were popular because their rectangular shape made them easier to stack, thus saving space. They were also ideal because they withstood the bumps and bounces of an automobile trip on washboarded, loose-graveled, undulating 1920s roads.

For a time, many bootleggers stole automobiles to transport their expensive caches. Because the government confiscated vehicles used in transport liquor, bootleggers soon learned that finding and stealing one to their liking allowed them to save their own vehicle for non-bootlegging uses. For a while, the stolen cars were confiscated, but judges became less enamored with holding these stolen cars, many often being purchased on time by the real owners. It was often the dealer or lender, not the owner, who suffered more from the loss. Over time, car owners also became more conscious of where they parked their vehicles and locked them or kept them in garages to discourage auto theft.

The largest liquor cargo ever found in an automobile in South Dakota was captured near Huron. The car with the massive load also had some ingenious devices for use during high-speed chases.

The confrontation happened west of Huron on Sunday night, July 11, 1932. Federal agents Palmer Gullickson and J.H. Sinclair tailed a known Huron bootlegger out of town. The bootlegger parked his car along Highway 16, twelve miles west of Huron, at about 9:30 p.m. Federal agents pulled up and detained the man but found no liquor in his car. They then assumed he was waiting for a supply of liquor, so he was handcuffed and held to await his supplier. About thirty minutes later, a big eight-cylinder 1932 Buick five-passenger coupe arrived at the rendezvous. Gullickson and Sinclair quickly moved in and trapped the driver they identified as Bernard "Bud" Bruns of Wessington. As Agent Sinclair grabbed a .45-caliber pistol from Bruns's belt, Bruns lunged out of the car's left front door, knocking the agent to the ground. Bruns ran into a cornfield, eluding agents who lost sight of him and returned to the captured car. A manhunt was later initiated, and Bruns was apprehended.

In searching Bruns's car, the agents found a set of Wisconsin license plates that officers presumed were switched from time to time with the South Dakota plates to confuse law enforcement observation. The agents also found two glass jars on the Buick's floor within reach of the driver. The jars were filled with tacks and roofing nails, like tiny grenades to be thrown from the car to break and spread glass and nails in the path of a following vehicle. Officers also found a device to activate a brief smoke screen out of the car's exhaust to slow down a pursuing vehicle.

But the unusual load of liquor in Bruns's car was their biggest surprise. The vehicle was loaded with 228 one-gallon tins of alcohol packed solidly in

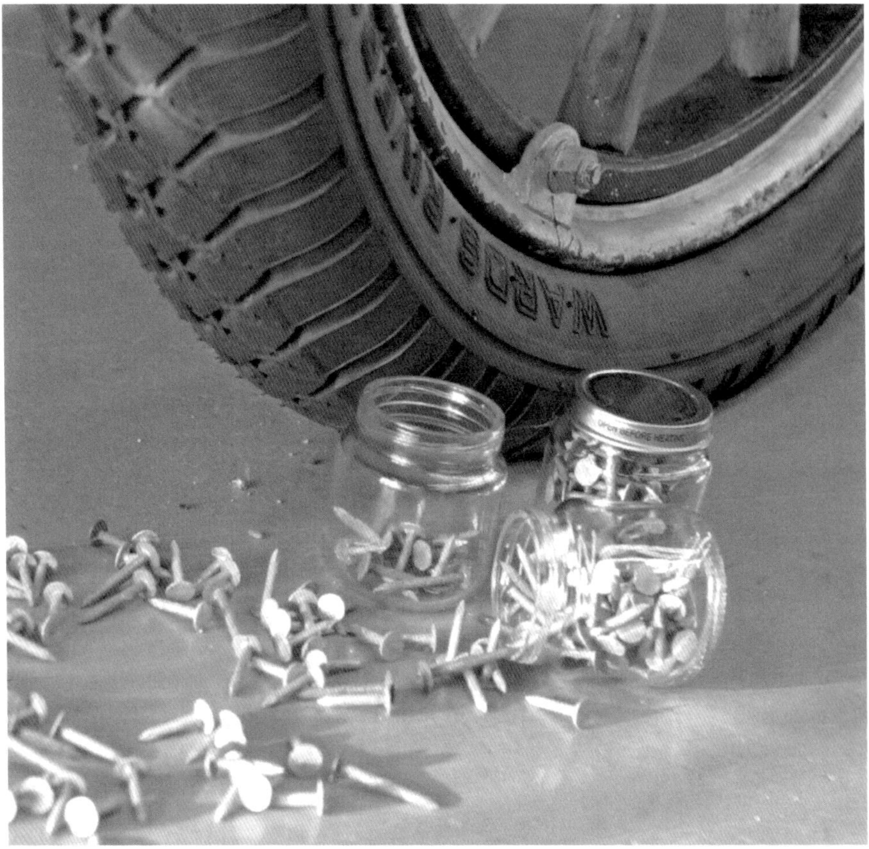

Bootleggers in cars loaded with booze also carried small glass jars similar to these that were filled with roofing nails to pierce tires of lawmakers' cars in pursuit. The jar "hand grenades" were tossed from bootleggers' cars to end the chase in favor of the bootlegger. *Author's collection.*

a space from just behind the front seat to the extreme end of the turtleback body. The rear seat had been removed, as well as the interior portion of the car behind the rear seat. Officers estimated the street value of the alcohol at about $5,000, the July 11, 1932 *Sioux Falls Argus Leader* reported.

They found a book with addresses hidden behind the car's dashboard that contained names of clients in Cicero and Wilmette, suburbs of Chicago, and Evanston, Illinois. Cicero was known as a stronghold of gangster Al Capone, and agents believed the liquor found in the car originated there. The book also contained the names and addresses of about fifty Chicago citizens. The book was also filled with coding. For example, it mentioned "hogs" and "sows" and so many of one or the other per day for a period of ten days. Agents guessed the coding was probably names for liquor types and quantities. A dated receipt folded in the book revealed the car had crossed the new Blackhawk toll bridge in Lansing, Iowa, on July 4, six days before the South Dakota confrontation.

The Huron apprehension wasn't the first time a Chicago connection was suggested by the evidence police found. In 1929, James Krumri, manager of the Sioux Falls Cataract Pool Rooms, and Frank Quigley, a Sioux Falls barber, were apprehended on Saturday night, August 10, in Winner with thirty gallons of alcohol. The two told Tripp County sheriff R.D. Gammon they obtained the booze in Sioux Falls but it had been brought to South Dakota from Chicago. They claimed it had been trucked all the way from the Windy City under the protection of the Chicago police. The men said they were in Winner "on vacation" and had brought along the booze to sell on the way to help pay for their expenses. The vacation didn't work out as planned. They were both fined $350 and their Ford coach was confiscated, the *Argus Leader* reported.

From time to time, police hit the jackpot, finding illegal booze and delivery lists in bootleggers' cars. In December 1923, Sioux Falls police staked out a local auto repair garage where traveling bootleggers always rented space for their loaded cars to be parked at night for security reasons. When owner Carl Schmahl of Lake Benton, Minnesota, showed up in

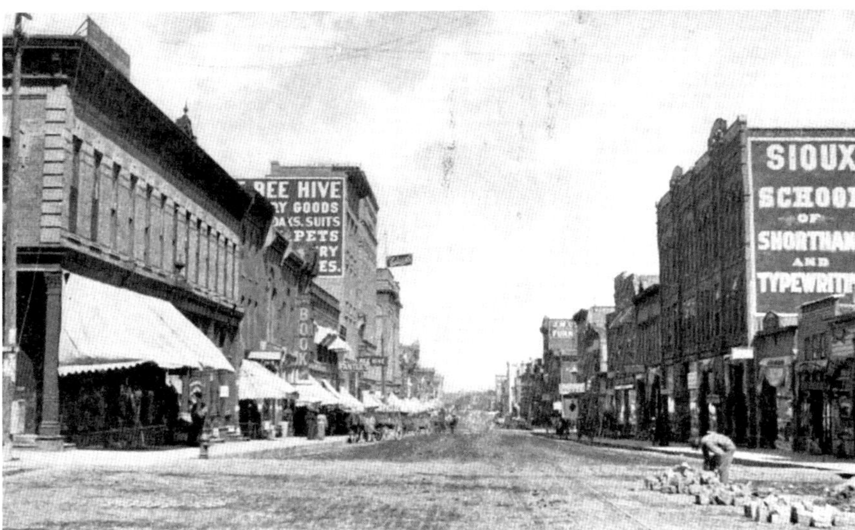


Late in South Dakota's eighteen years of bone-dry Prohibition, Sioux Falls, on the eastern edge of the state, became a mecca for runners, who could purchase truckloads of booze in nearby Minnesota and make a huge profit reselling it in Sioux Falls. *Author's collection.*

the morning to get his car, he was arrested. Among his possessions, police found an address book with names and addresses of several prominent Sioux Falls professional men, doctors, lawyers and others, with the amount and kind of booze to be delivered to them.

In November 1925, Peter Gunderson and John Nelson, both of Hudson, were happily homeward bound from Chatsworth, Iowa, with a load of illegal liquor stashed in their Ford automobile. Although it was not a good idea, but probably to avoid detection, the Ford's lights were doused. Unfortunately, a Sioux Falls to Sioux City bus heading south failed to see the little Ford rattling along in the opposite direction. There was a collision, and the Ford was badly damaged, although no one was injured. In the confusion, Gunderson and Nelson panicked and ran from the scene. The driver of the bus had, however, observed Nelson throw a gallon can into the weeds as he sprinted into the darkness.

The bus driver retrieved the can of alcohol and found another in the car. He notified Lincoln County sheriff M.T. Sundvold, and the sheriff and G.W. Rector, deputy state sheriff, were able to get the names of the car's driver and passenger. They soon arrested Nelson at his home in Hudson and then sought out Gunderson, who was also found in his home, sick in bed, the November 20, 1925 issue of the *Sioux Falls Argus Leader* reported. A doctor determined Gunderson was suffering from the effects of drinking rubbing alcohol, apparently to calm his nerves as he waited for the arrest he knew would eventually come.

Most of the vehicles confiscated by the law were in good condition and later sold at auction. A pristine Chrysler Imperial 80 used by Jack Davis, one of the leading illegal liquor dealers in Sioux Falls, was on Sheriff John H. Johnson's auction block in October 1931. Police had confiscated the car in July 1931 when it was found in the vicinity of Mount Pleasant Cemetery with twenty-three one-gallon cans of booze in the back seat, according to a report in the July 1931 *Sioux Falls Argus Leader*. The Imperial had a market value of $3,200. About fifty curious observers and a few potential buyers showed up at the auction. The bidding opened at $100 and went up to just $332. The sale was over, and the buyer had made a killing. Davis was later sentenced to sixty days in jail and fined $500.

A Willow Lake man, Ray Dworak, was caught with a load of liquor in December 1929. He later made South Dakota history by becoming the first person to repurchase his car at a police sale. He paid a fine of $250.00 plus $44.40 costs for his offenses and then attended the sheriff's auction and bought his car back for $360.00.

Every bootlegger and moonshiner had competitors, so they weren't always loyal to one another. Anonymous tips to law enforcement agencies often came from one bootlegger or liquor maker intent on putting another out of business. Wood Smith, a deputy state sheriff, speaking at the Mitchell Men's Twelve O'Clock Club in 1922, said the state sheriff's office regularly received information from a bootlegger or moonshiner hoping the state sheriff's office would investigate and arrest his competition, thus narrowing the field and creating new customers. "The information we receive is given by them so they can 'get even' with some member or members of the bootlegging gang, and it is usually authentic information," Woods said in a *Sioux Falls Argus Leader* story on June 21, 1921.

Bootleggers transporting large loads of illegal booze not only had to keep a sharp eye out for the law, but hijackers also found competing bootleggers' cars easy pickings. Robbing from one another was a nearly perfect crime because the theft would not ordinarily be reported to police, for obvious reasons. Minnehaha County sheriff George Broadman found a Ford coupe abandoned on the Valley Springs road in 1925. The sheriff detected a strong odor of alcohol in the car and noticed several counterfeit whiskey labels on the car floor. The *Sioux Falls Argus Leader* on March 20, 1925, said a broken windshield added to the officer's suspicion the car had been hijacked and the illegal content removed.

The lonely road could be a violent place. High-speed chases between bootleggers and law enforcement officials were common. Often, shots were exchanged, and in some instances, bootleggers were injured. Occasionally, death from gunshots resulted during some of these pursuits. Usually, however, bootleggers came to their senses and surrendered or were captured when their automobiles went out of control and crashed. Of course, these chases endangered innocent motorists, too.

One ploy that was occasionally used by dry undercover agents was mentioned in a speech in Sioux Falls in September 1932 by Tony Boyington, a federal Prohibition agent. He said bootleggers were complaining because agents often used bumper signs, then tied to car bumpers, that carried a wet message, such as "Repeal the 18th Amendment." Decorating dry cars with this anti-Prohibition message could be a free pass, allowing the vehicle to approach the unconcerned moonshiners and bootleggers. Boyington quoted one bootlegger who said, "You guys are not playing fair with us," the *Sioux Falls Argus Leader* reported on September 20, 1932.

Dempster was a little watch fob–sized town at an out-of-the-way wide spot between Castlewood and Estelline. Its population today is in the teens.

Even though it was off the beaten path in 1931, it had a thirsty and thriving population sufficient to keep five bootleggers from the Watertown area busy. In January 1931, Dempster mayor John G. DeWall placed his tongue firmly in cheek at a town meeting and appointed a committee to confer with the known bootleggers serving the town and then select one who would be given an exclusive Dempster bootlegging franchise. One evening, the mayor said, he counted the cars of five bootleggers making their rounds and came up with his franchise idea. Mayor DeWall believed having just one bootlegger in town would stabilize prices and enable at least one "legger" to make a decent living in the difficult economic times, according to a story in the *Sioux Falls Argus Leader* on January 14, 1931.

The press quickly picked up the story, and the Dempster mayor and town board decided to play along to give their little community some statewide notoriety. The committee, in making its report to the mayor, informed him of meetings with the five bootleggers. All the bootleggers indicated they were eager to serve the town, but the committee members were unable to agree which of the five would have exclusive Dempster rights, expressing disappointment that none of the bootleggers had submitted samples of their product. Negotiations with the traveling liquor dispensers would continue, the committee said.

In February, Mayor DeWall told the inquiring press the naming of an official bootlegger was still "up in the air." He joked, saying he had received four samples of "very good stock." The mayor had also received a letter from a Watertown bootlegger whom the mayor facetiously accused of attempting to bribe him and the town's bootlegger franchise committee. He read a portion of one of the bootleggers' letter: "If you wish me to appear at your next town meeting I am sure I could produce samples that would meet with your approval, as well as other members of the town board." The little joke made South Dakota headlines and gave newspaper readers a chuckle during the time of Dust Bowl adversity.

The innocent fun by Dempster officials not only illustrated the bootleggers' reach and acceptance in South Dakota communities but also conveyed the increasingly accepted wet philosophy of citizens who were beginning to step forward to expound upon and joke about the failure and ineffectiveness of Prohibition. Efforts at humor were also good medicine that took people's minds off the stifling heat of the record-breaking Dirty Thirties. In late June 1931, when Dempster considered a whiskey franchise, Pierre and Mitchell had recorded temperatures of 108 degrees. The next month, Pierre and Aberdeen both had temperatures on July 15 of 112 degrees. The stifling heat caused more than ninety deaths in the Midwest in 1931, according to a report in the July 15, 1931 *Sioux Falls Argus Leader.*

Competing with the frustration brought on by the heat was the periodic invasion of billions of grasshoppers thriving in the stifling weather, which seemed to spark their voracious appetites. A horde of hungry hoppers could strip fields of corn in minutes. Washday clothes on sagging outdoor clothes lines were a delicious dessert for them. They were also attracted to pitchfork and shovel handles saturated with perspiration, going after the salt-permeated handles worn smooth from use. Grasshoppers could swarm down on a small South Dakota town and strip the leaves from every shade tree in hours. No wonder some people drank. It was a hot, dusty, miserable time. A quaff of liquor and some humor helped it pass.

Of no laughing matter to many was a national law that became known as the Padlock Law. It was a little-used part of federal rules passed during Prohibition allowing for the locking up of the home or business of repeated violators of liquor laws. It was used sparingly in South Dakota. The first to be hit with a padlock order was the Sioux Falls Fraternal Order of Eagles home at 432 West Ninth Street, as recounted in the January 13, 1925 issue of the *Sioux Falls Argus Leader.* The complaint was that intoxicating liquors were "habitually" sold at the club.

One of the first main street businesses in South Dakota to experience the padlock rule, as ordered by the federal court in Sioux Falls, was the popular John Barringer Pool Hall in Tyndall in June 1925. A week after the hearing on why the place should not be padlocked, federal witnesses who had testified that they purchased and consumed alcohol in the pool hall were attacked and beaten in Tyndall by some pool hall regulars. Related to those beatings was a Saturday night near-riot in town on June 24, 1925. The *Sioux Falls Argus Leader* described it as a "wet orgy" as raucous drinkers expressed their displeasure with the closing of the pool hall. Federal and state officers were sent to the community to quell the defiant crowds.

The Tyndall drinking party continued through Saturday night and into Sunday morning. Dr. A.L. Cook, pastor of the Federated Church in Tyndall, preached a Sunday morning sermon on the situation. He told a reporter for the *Sioux Falls Argus Leader* on June 6, 1925, that the celebration near the Barringer Pool Hall was the "worst he'd ever seen." The *Sioux Falls Argus Leader* correspondent wrote this understatement in his story: "Tyndall has a reputation of having an element which is exceedingly wet."

Of course, simple logistics prevented bootleggers from hauling around all their booze in one basket and risking losing it all if arrested. Hip-pocket bootleggers and the big boys in fast cars hid their surplus stash until it was needed. Of course, they couldn't just rent a storehouse. Some secret place was arranged. Dry agents became quite proficient at finding these hidden treasure stashes. Trapdoors to small storage spaces beneath the floor of a home, hidden by rugs or linoleum, were ubiquitous and predictable.

Outside, postholes were one of the favorite stashes. Tools for digging postholes, in either a brilliant marketing strategy by manufacturers or an unbelievable coincidence, were designed and manufactured to make holes just slightly larger than the size of popular liquor jugs. The holes were usually dug along fence lines where livestock would be less apt to step in them and where the fence served as a good marker for their location. Farm machinery was also less likely to disturb the cool and secure fence line hiding places. Weeds grew around the holes, providing natural camouflage. Postholes were not limited to fence lines, however. They also provided hiding places in other unlikely spots.

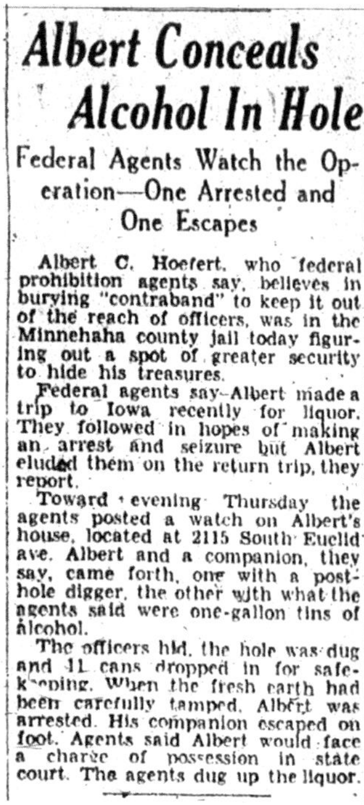
**Albert Conceals Alcohol In Hole**

**Federal Agents Watch the Operation—One Arrested and One Escapes**

Albert C. Hoefert, who federal prohibition agents say, believes in burying "contraband" to keep it out of the reach of officers, was in the Minnehaha county jail today figuring out a spot of greater security to hide his treasures.

Federal agents say Albert made a trip to Iowa recently for liquor. They followed in hopes of making an arrest and seizure but Albert eluded them on the return trip, they report.

Toward evening Thursday the agents posted a watch on Albert's house, located at 2115 South Euclid ave. Albert and a companion, they say, came forth, one with a post-hole digger, the other with what the agents said were one-gallon tins of alcohol.

The officers hid, the hole was dug and 11 cans dropped in for safe-keeping. When the fresh earth had been carefully tamped, Albert was arrested. His companion escaped on foot. Agents said Albert would face a charge of possession in state court. The agents dug up the liquor.

*Sioux Falls Argus Leader*, April 29, 1932. *Author's collection.*

J.G. Brown of rural Watertown was suspected of having liquor on his property. In a raid on March 22, 1921, according to the *Sioux Falls Argus Leader*, a search of the premises uncovered nothing. Officers rechecked outbuildings, including the henhouse, but again came up empty. Then an agent noticed a soft spot in the ground inside the chicken shed. They dug into the ground until they came upon a gallon jug of booze. Beneath it was another jug, and under it they found a third. After more searching, they located two other postholes. Each was layered with three one-gallon bottles of liquor. Brown was sentenced to thirty days in jail.

At the Herman Groneberg farm, two miles from Yankton, officers in August 1922 found three one-gallon jugs of liquor hidden in a posthole in the hog yard. Chris Sorenson of rural Lake County also had his farm checked out by the law. He used a posthole for a hidden cache, attaching a string to the neck of the bottles so he could easily haul them up from the cool depths. He'd also placed a board over the hole and shoveled dirt on it. His chickens ranged the area, and their scratches and pecks made the spot appear even more normal, according to the April 30, 1924 *Sioux Falls Argus Leader*. In 1932, the mother of all postholes was found in the backyard of the Albert C. Hoefert home at 2115 South Euclid Avenue in Sioux Falls. Officers said eleven one-gallon tins of whiskey were buried in one large double posthole in Hoefert's yard.

At the Roy Smith place in Ashland Park, a suburb in north Huron, officers found forty-nine quarts of moonshine hidden in a threshing machine. Officers said the front chamber of the thresher was lined with bottles, according to a report in the September 23, 1921 *Sioux Falls Argus Leader*. In addition to a still and fifty gallons of rye mash found at the home of Carl Person in northern Yankton County, officers found a supply of liquor bottles in the oven of the Persons' kitchen range. Ed Miller of Chamberlain hid his stash of two gallons of moonshine and twenty-five gallons of mash in a straw pile. Miller denied ownership of the stash, telling officers it had probably been left there by some other person, according to a December 12, 1921 report in the *Sioux Falls Argus Leader*.

George Nunamaker of Kimball was reminded of the adage about trouble coming only in threes, except trouble came in twice that amount for him. Officers found trouble in six different locations on his farm. He had liquor hidden in his cellar; two gallons of moonshine hidden under a haphazardly stacked pile of sun-bleached, weather-beaten boards in a cow pasture; one quart tucked away in an oat bin in the barn; a second quart hidden on Nunamaker's person; plus a still in a straw pile, said the *Sioux Falls Argus Leader* in its December 1, 1921 issue.

James Buell of Sioux Falls probably wasn't even a hip-pocket bootlegger, but he may have just spent time with one when Night Captain Hayes ran into him on Phillips Avenue. Hayes became suspicious of Buell when he spotted him carrying a live duck under his arm. The policeman approached Buell to inquire about the duck and concluded the serene duck was a decoy to hide a bottle of booze, also held under the same arm, but partially hidden by the duck. Buell was further flustered when he threw the bottle into the street, assuming it would break and destroy the evidence. However, the road at Tenth Street and Phillips Avenue was paved with creosoted wooden blocks, and the bottle survived the fall. He paid a fifteen-dollar fine, according to the *Sioux Falls Argus Leader*'s issue of June 27, 1922. The duck was not charged.

The same newspaper in December 1930 told about two Sioux City bootleggers who selected an isolated farm in Clay County near Vermillion as a place to hide their liquor supply until it was needed. During one delivery run in the area, they brought along a friend from Vermillion. When they stopped at the farm hiding place to pick up some of their supply, the Vermillion friend was astounded. He knew the farm. It belonged to the Clay County sheriff.

In June 1922, police in Miller stopped Louis Kaelin. They found a bottle of booze hidden in an automobile tire in Kaelin's rear seat. He was charged with transporting liquor and held for trial in circuit court, where he was found guilty, fined $100 and sentenced to thirty days in the hoosegow, the *Sioux Falls Argus Leader* reported on June 16, 1922.

A tire shop in Carthage was used more as a blind pig than for repairing flat tires, dry agents learned after raiding Gus Recknegle's place three days before Christmas in 1923. They found a dozen men playing cards. The liquor supply to fill the quaffing glasses on the card table was finally located in a toolbox under the counter, empty except for the whiskey bottle, according to the *Argus Leader* on December 22, 1923.

Raiders at the Earl Mabie home at 127½ North Phillips Avenue in Sioux Falls could have used a toolbox when they entered the home on May 15, 1935. They heard Mrs. Mabie emptying a pitcher of alcohol into her kitchen sink, destroying the evidence. One of the deputy sheriffs grabbed a pair of pliers from the kitchen table and removed the U joint on the drain beneath the sink. Some booze was captured and poured into a milk bottle for the court to see. The *Sioux Falls Argus Leader* noted the raid took place after federal and state Prohibition laws had been repealed, but Mabie was charged with possession of liquor in a container without a tax stamp on it.

An unidentified man stored his potatoes in the basement of the vacant Methodist church on South Main Avenue in Sioux Falls. As it turned out, he stored something more there, too. He appeared at the police station on April 14, 1922, the *Sioux Falls Argus Leader* said, to tell officers about some boys who broke into the church basement and, in digging around in the potato pile, found four pint bottles and three half pints of moonshine, each nicely wrapped in tissue paper. He told suspicious police officers he had no idea how the whiskey got mixed in with his spuds. The police desk sergeant, an eye asquint, asked patrolmen to check it out. They learned the man rented the empty church basement as storage for his potatoes and that he apparently also used the pile for his liquor stash for his hip-pocket bootlegging business. The boys did find his stash, but the bootlegger apparently reasoned that if he reported a theft to the police before the boys or their parents got to police, he could avoid any charges. From a legal evidence standpoint, his ploy must have worked, because he was not charged. But police were still highly suspicious and also amused by the potato pile caper.

In Clay County near Wakonda, federal, county and state officers arrested Milton and Leffert Schooley. As officers arrived at the Schooley place, the brothers grabbed hammers and started beating the daylights out of the inside of their horse-drawn seeder. Officers placed a pail under the seeder and saved enough liquid evidence for the Schooleys' day in court, the *Sioux Falls Argus Leader* reported on August 29, 1923.

This headline in the *Sioux Falls Argus Leader* the day before Christmas 1924 probably caught readers' eyes: "Sheriff Finds Jugs of 'Moon' in Load of Hogs." Hog farmer J.W. Gordon of Montrose didn't actually keep a jug in with the hogs he was hauling to Sioux Falls market. His two gallons of booze were in the cab under the seat.

Officers looked high and low for illegal booze in the home of E.J. Thraen of 1006 West Eighteenth Street in Sioux Falls but found nothing. This was probably music to the homeowner's ears. Then officers looked in Thraen's music box and found three pints of liquor in the record player. Another domestic hiding place was found at the Al Dagle home in Jefferson when officers uncovered a cache of booze in the family's sewing machine cabinet in October 1929.

William Ward was fishing when he was arrested. Officers caught the suspected Sioux Falls resident on the banks of the Big Sioux River. They found two pints of whiskey tied together with string hanging around his neck and hidden by his coat. Assuming there were half-pint bottles in his hip pockets, the frisking had been from the waist down, so they missed the fisherman's unusual necklace on the first try. There were also instances where liquor bottles tied to fish line were stored out of sight in reeds and brush along the riverbank to be reeled in cool and fresh when needed, according to the April 25, 1925 *Sioux Falls Argus Leader*.

When federal agents raided the farm of William G. Duncan near Spencer in late January 1925, they looked everywhere and finally found a still but, surprisingly, no white mule. However, in a corner of the barn where they were searching a bulldog was penned in a makeshift kennel that protected the goods. Hidden beneath the straw on the kennel floor were two quarts of liquor.

Teenager Oscar Steen of Brookings, along with a buddy, heard rumors about a bootlegger who was using a particular grave marker at Greenwood Cemetery as a drop point. Once the bootlegger made his sale in a Brookings pool hall, he would tell the buyer to go to a certain place in the cemetery, tip the waist-high metal obelisk at a certain grave site, reach in and the stash would be there.

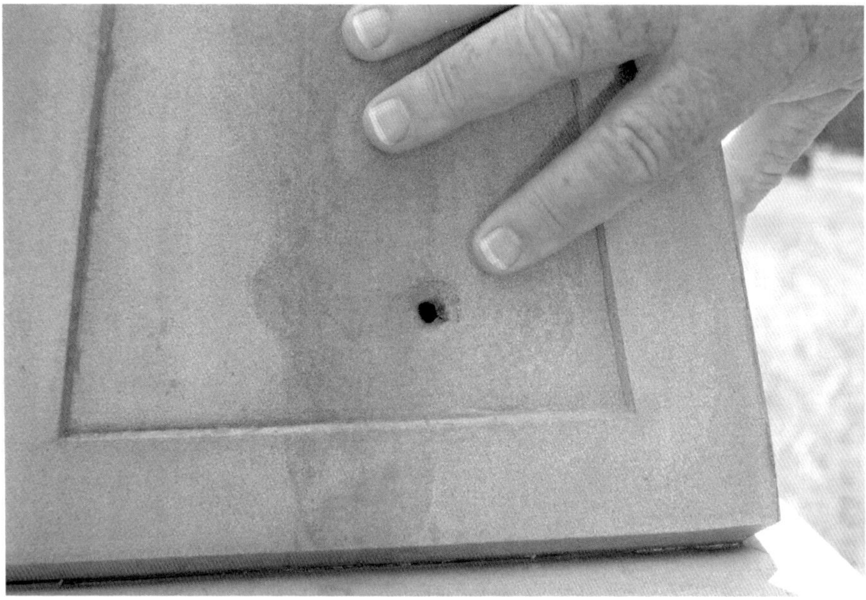

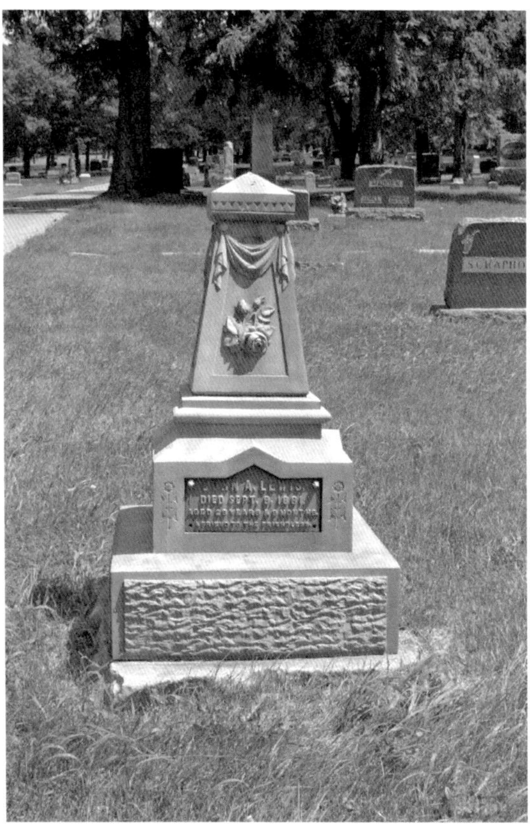

*Above*: A bullet hole in a Greenwood Cemetery grave marker after a bootlegger placed a warning shot for someone inspecting his liquor drop. *Author's collection.*

*Left*: A bootlegger tipped up this Greenwood Cemetery grave marker in Brookings to place liquor that would be picked up later by a buyer who made previous arrangements for the sale. *Author's collection.*

One afternoon, young Steen and his friend went to Greenwood and found the grave marker about twenty yards from the roadway along the north side of the cemetery. Curious, they tipped the marker slightly to look under it. As they did, a shot rang out. A .22-caliber slug missed the boys, probably on purpose, and pinged into the pewter grave marker, holing it. The warning shot did the trick. The youths never again had any desire to check out the bootlegger's drop point. The damaged grave marker can still be seen today. A similar metal grave marker in the Aurora cemetery a few miles east of Brookings was also used as a drop point. Another handy drop point for bootleggers was highway culverts, but skunks like the dank tunnels, too.

The all-time state champion imaginative bootlegger drop site is the one discovered by accident on a lonely graveled township road six miles west of Bruce in Brookings County. Road crews were grading the lonely road, something they seldom did on the little-used stretch. But weeds were creeping out onto the roadway and becoming unwanted snow fences, catching winter drifts.

A county road grader was sent out in November 1927 to reclaim the road and peel back the weeds. The grader blade was lowered and went to work. Shortly, it smashed into something. On investigation, county workers discovered it was a glass jug of moonshine buried among the weeds along the side of the road. Crews noticed a small piece of cloth tied to the fence exactly opposite where the bottle was buried.

Further inspection in the area revealed other knotted cloth pieces tied to the fence a short distance away, with others down the fence line at varying intervals. In the weed-infested roadside gravel exactly opposite each cloth signal, they found a gallon jug of booze buried with only a few inches of the bottle's top above ground, hidden by the weeds. At the end of the day, they had dug up seventeen one-gallon jugs, plus the damaged jug the grader had broken open, according to a report in the *Brookings Register* on November 11, 1927.

While liquor was often hidden away in unlikely places, it was readily displayed at the speakeasies and blind pigs that became popular watering holes in many South Dakota communities.

Chapter 9

# Panthers and Pigs

During Prohibition, most of the illegal alcohol, whiskey, wine, gin, vodka, beer and other spirits was tippled along with friendly conversation and kibitzing in barns, on isolated gravel roads, in haystack shade, at food-laden holiday dining room tables and in joyous reminiscences with rocking chair neighbors on cool back porches. Some entrepreneurs took the chance of providing more public quaffing grounds, operating what were known as blind pigs and speakeasies.

The eye-catching nomenclature "blind pig" was invented after illicit saloon operators made their places legal in their minds and the minds of their customers by enticing, for a fee, people into their establishment by promising a display of an animal, such as a sightless hog. While waiting for the animal to appear, although it never did, a complimentary alcoholic libation was served. Blind pigs gradually morphed into plain old-fashioned illegal saloons.

Speakeasies were similar but were intended for the more cosmopolitan customers who politely mingled and quietly ordered their fancy gin fizz or Manhattan, speaking in soft voices, rather than the more boisterous calls for whiskey or foaming mugs of beer at the blind pig.

Speakeasies and blind pigs were most common in populated eastern cities. South Dakota was more a "blind pig" venue, and the state's version of the blind pig was usually just the town's old tobacco-smelling pool hall with a strategically placed potbellied stove drawing a rabble of "chawbaccy" chewers and expectorators. Such was the case in Joe Hill's Pool Hall in

Revillo, where in 1931, Grant County sheriff M.A. Carlson and his deputy found twenty-five pint bottles of whiskey hidden among the billiard balls, bowed-from-age pool cues and three-sided, equilateral snooker racks. Hill also had a pint sloshing in his back pocket, the March 19, 1931 *Sioux Falls Argus Leader* report said.

The blind pig hangouts, along with what dry agents called beer gardens, blossomed in South Dakota after the state's bone-dry law was passed in 1916, to be effective in 1917. Many pool hall and saloon proprietors, whose experience, livelihood and life's investment had been bartending, especially in the smaller towns and out-of-the-way places like Revillo, were determined to hang on and remain in business despite the sudden ban on booze and saloons. The concept of Prohibition was strange to them. They couldn't imagine fancy-pants legislators in Pierre really being serious about shutting them down just for selling a little booze. So they took a chance. Lieutenant Governor Hans Ustrud, writing in Chapter 7 of his 1933 manuscript, *Behind the Scenes*, said despite its illegality in South Dakota, "beer was freely sold all over the state without any regulations or any revenue for the State Treasury."

The owner of one of the more unusual blind pigs, Roberts County farmer Michael Reiser, thought he'd found a surefire way to sell white mule and his other homemade, illegal alcoholic condiments. Reiser opened what he called a "sanitarium" specializing in the treatment of rheumatism, having gotten the idea because he himself found relief from the painful affliction after a few swigs of his version of John Barleycorn. He decided he could make a profit marketing his product to others in the area also suffering from the malady. Almost overnight, neighbors by the dozen unexpectedly became afflicted. It was a veritable area pandemic. Law enforcement officials said it wasn't long before practically all the farmers for miles around developed varying degrees of rheumatism and ambled over to the Reiser Sanitarium for treatment. Some days, patients stood in line for the medication, the September 3, 1921 *Sioux Falls Argus Leader* reported.

The sanitarium operator was arrested in September 1921, and in January 1922, Reiser was found guilty by a Sisseton jury. The judge fined him $100 and sent him to the county jail for sixty days. He was back in court in December of the same year charged with selling a deputy sheriff a liquid the officer claimed was alcohol. Reiser's attorney said the liquid was not liquor, and the jury accepted the argument.

J.W. "Cock-eyed" Smith of Mitchell owned a couple of mangy bloodhounds, and he advertised to rent them out to track down criminals. He had few takers, so they whiled away their time in the basement of his house on Wisconsin Street north of the Omaha Railroad track. Police raided his home a week before Christmas 1922 and found a well-appointed bar in an upstairs bedroom. Smith was away from the house when state deputy sheriffs and federal agents arrived, but his wife was home, throwing bottles of beer and booze out the bar's upstairs window to destroy the evidence. One missile nearly conked the head of an officer assigned to guard the back door.

In the basement of the home, officers came face to face with the two sad-eyed bloodhounds they described as "vicious." The "ferocious" dogs were guarding a still Smith had been using to manufacture his elixir for the upstairs blind pig and his delivery route, the *Argus Leader* reported in December 1922.

A year later, in the now-defunct town of Janousek in southwestern Yankton County on the Platte Line about sixteen miles north of Yankton, Deputy State Sheriffs Charles Peters and Wood Smith came upon a blind pig the two veteran lawmen described in a *Sioux Falls Argus Leader* article in November 1921 as a "real curiosity." It looked like a genuine vintage saloon, they said, with the bottles lined up in neat, straight rows on shelves and with jugs at the ready under the counter for home consumption sales. Operator A.O. Wagner's liquor inventory, the deputies said, consisted of moonshine and different kinds of booze, including scotch, bourbon, rye, port and several others, all in plain sight.

In early October 1924, Sioux Falls police led by Patrolman Fred Markham banged on the door of Ma's Place at 218½ South Phillips, to no avail. Entrance was refused. So the cops broke down the door, searched the place and found the whiskey they expected would be there. The elderly proprietors of Ma's Place, Pa and Ma John Early, had been selling it for a quarter a throw.

Dance halls were not the full-blooded traditional "blind pig" species but quasi–blind pigs with dances as the main attraction and drinking available as secondary entertainment. In 1925, Minnehaha County judge Lewis Larson, who had seen his share of lawbreakers, attributed the majority of cases of juvenile delinquency in South Dakota to "automobiles, moonshine and public dances," according to a December 8, 1925 article in the *Sioux Falls Argus Leader*. "I find that it is the girl who goes to the public dance halls who is usually the one who is brought to my court," he said.

In 1929, the Reverend H.W. Blackburn, pastor of the Wessington Springs Methodist Church, also expounded on public dancing. He questioned those who considered tripping the light fantastic as an innocent amusement.

He preached about it at an evening Bible-banging sermon to nearly eight hundred persons, telling them, "You take away the close contact between the sexes and you kill the dance. You pass a law making men dance with themselves and you've crushed the serpent's head. It's the liberties that the dance gives that makes it so attractive. Practice them on the street and you'd be arrested." His sermon was reviewed in an article in the *Sioux Falls Argus Leader*'s May 24, 1929 issue.

Prohibition during the fast-paced, anything-goes Roaring Twenties had a profound influence on the type and tempo of dance preferred by Americans. Flappers stunned the traditionalists and ruled during the '20s. As Prohibition ended and the fast pace of life subsided, the waltz and the tango returned to pre-Prohibition popularity by the mid-1930s. There was a preference for grace and rhythm in place of the bootleg-era frenzy for haste, hurry, shock and sensationalism on the dance floor as elsewhere, according to a survey of the nation's dance teachers in an *Argus Leader* story published on September 16, 1934.

Although liquor flowed at the Rowena Dance Club east of Sioux Falls, it was advertised as a dance hall. The *Sioux Falls Argus Leader*, in a November 14, 1924 story on a raid of the place for operating a public dance hall without a permit, described the place: "The second floor of what officials call a rickety old firetrap in Rowena recently has been swaying under the weight of scores of wriggling forms; its walls have been re-echoing with ribald laughter; its bare rafters almost obscured by a haze of cigaret [*sic*] smoke, have been trembling from the clamor of a jazz orchestra."

During the raid, members of the Minnehaha Sheriff's Department and county probation officer Clarence M. Satnan arrested three of the club's officers: John Brady, Fred Ritter and Clell Ritter. The other dance hall officer, Floyd Flatt, was apprehended later. Probation officer Satnan had heard rumors of improper conduct at the club's biweekly dances. He was given a dance membership card that carried on it a guarantee of a good time and listed the four club officers. Satnan decided to see for himself. He said his first impression on entering the hall that evening was the abundance of "members," and most were "hardly more than children." He told of bow-tied orchestra members going through the "gyrations of a contortionist" to which couples were dancing a variety of "shuffles and wiggles." He got the impression nearly everyone was "more or less" under the influence, drinking unabashedly from bottles when not shuffling and wiggling, he said in a November 14, 1924 article in the *Sioux Falls Argus Leader*.

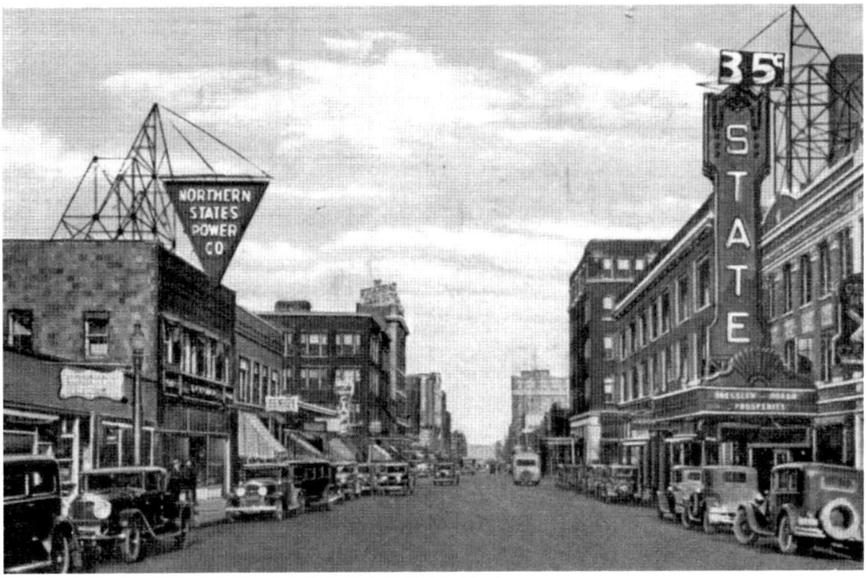


Although Chicago's Al Capone's influence on the flow of illegal liquor in Sioux Falls, the state's largest city, could never been proven, local and state police believed his agents were at work in town. *Author's collection.*

In the summer of 1927, Minnehaha County sheriff George Broadman grew weary of being called to calm unruly crowds at dances. He announced he was "declaring war" on country dances after arresting eight persons at the Bernard Stockwell farm on an early Sunday morning about four miles from Brandon. Stockwell was charged with conducting a public dance without a license, the August 15, 1927 *Sioux Falls Argus Leader* reported.

In Huron in 1927, it got so bad that a city ordinance was passed requiring a special policeman be on duty at all public dances. The policeman was to help "deny" intoxicated persons from entering the dance hall. As part of the new ordinance, to prevent bootleggers from plying their trade in the parking lot, anyone leaving the dance hall had to purchase another ticket to reenter, the *Sioux Falls Argus Leader* reported on February 25, 1927.

In Armour in the summer of 1929, the Douglas County commissioners denied a dance license for an applicant because the venerable commissioners said they simply did not believe in dancing. A circuit court judge didn't think a personal dislike of dancing was a valid reason and reversed the commissioners' action. In Parkston in 1931, after a fight broke out at a public dance and police had to be called, local authorities "declared war" on "young men from neighboring towns who attend dances in Parkston and become drunk and disorderly," a Parkston official was quoted as saying in an April 1931 *Sioux Falls Argus Leader*.

A delegation of about fifty people appeared before the Sioux Falls City Commission after word got out in 1934 regarding a commission plan to "liberalize" the city's dance ordinance. Attorney John C. Mundt was the spokesman for the protesting group. He denounced what he termed the "evils of dancing." In an October 1934 issue of the *Argus Leader*, Mundt claimed his angry contingent represented the feelings of 77 percent of Sioux Falls residents. The provision of the new Sioux Falls ordinance that sent the protestors into apoplexy was the setting of closing times for dances at 2:00 a.m. Mundt's group wanted dances to end at midnight. They also requested names of police dance matrons be submitted in advance to the City Federation of Women's Clubs for its approval.

In 1922, the Minnehaha County commissioners revoked the license of H. Fox for the dance hall he managed at Wall Lake. Officials said the dance pavilion was "run in a disorderly manner, and intoxicating liquor was being used on the premises, and immoral and indecent practices had been carried on in and about the place," reported the September 8, 1922 *Sioux Falls Argus Leader*.

A canvas-walled blind pig in the rear of a second-floor dance hall over a Garretson store was raided in 1927. Officers said a piece of canvas covering an interior window in the wall between a small rear room and the dance hall had a slit cut in it large enough to allow a man's hand and arm to be poked into the room from the dance hall side. Behind the canvas window, police found alcohol tins and arrested J.C. Allenbaugh, Alex Jordahl, Albert and Fritz Holzapael, A.C. Rudd and E.O. Quamen.

In 1931 in Sturgis, federal agents led by the incomparable E.L. Senn, head of the federal Prohibition effort in the state, raided a blind pig with the unusual moniker "Old Paper Alice's." They arrested Hulda Land on a charge of selling liquor, reported the February 1, 1931 *Sioux Falls Argus Leader*.

The saloon's creative title was an alliteration of the name of a local character and bootlegger, Poker Alice (Tubbs), a celebrated Black Hills free spirit who had died a year before the raid. In her old age, Poker Alice became entangled in the state Prohibition law. In 1928, when she was seventy-five, her Sturgis home was raided and she was arrested for possessing liquor and operating a house of ill repute. Her sentence was six months in the Sioux Falls Penitentiary. As she was preparing to spend 180 days in a jail cell far from home, hundreds of her Black Hills friends signed a petition that they

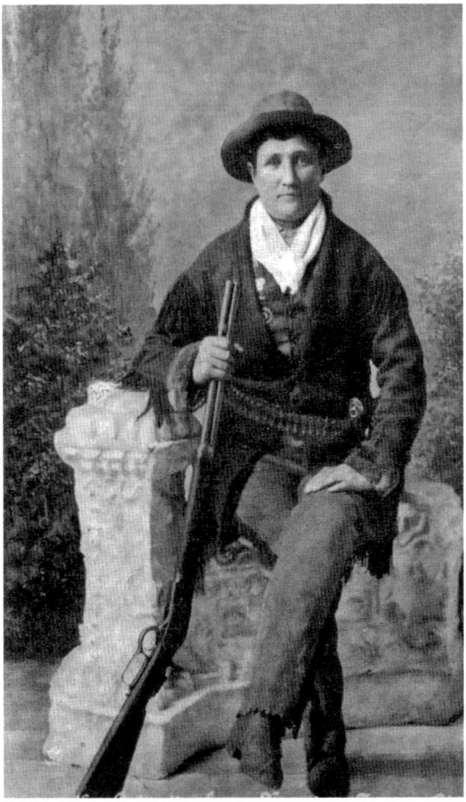

*Left*: The Black Hills' hard-drinking Calamity Jane. *Author's collection.*

*Below*: The Rapid City Methodist Hospital once occupied a spot on today's now paved Mount Rushmore Road. *Author's collection.*

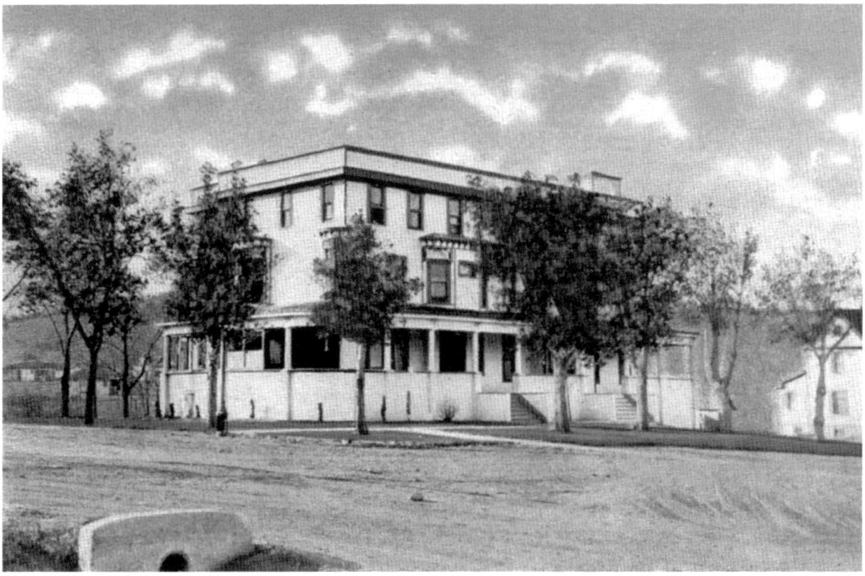

then presented to Governor William Bulow urging him to pardon her. The petition claimed her frail health and her altruistic involvement in Black Hills charity work in recent years were reasons enough to forgive her past transgressions. On December 20, 1928, as reported in the *Sioux Falls Argus Leader*, Governor Bulow pardoned Alice Tubbs. She died on February 27, 1930, after a gallbladder operation in a Rapid City hospital.

In 1932, an unlikely, low-budget blind pig operating in the Hines Battery Shop in Madison was raided, and a quantity of illegal booze, often humorously referred to as battery acid, was seized.

Beer gardens were the targets of a big raid in Aberdeen in July 1932. The *Sioux Falls Argus Leader*'s lead paragraph on the story on July 23, 1932, said, "Aberdeen thirsts again, for beer, not water." Federal and state dry officers and Brown County officials stopped at eight beer gardens and left with a cargo of 539 illegal pints of beer and nearly one hundred gallons of beer mash.

Especially at dances, the drink of choice was a mixture of alcohol and soda pop. After the illegal booze had been poured and mixed with Coca-Cola, 7-Up or another favorite brand in the bottle, carrying the mixed drink around seemed innocent enough and would not as easily pique the interest of always-suspicious agents who might be in attendance at these social affairs. After Prohibition ended, South Dakota soda pop manufacturers took stock and claimed Prohibition had changed forever the way their product was consumed and where it was consumed. Prohibition was also responsible for the largest loss of pop bottles ever in the state to that time, they claimed.

Soda pop was once a rare treat consumed at the place where it was purchased because there was a bottle deposit charge if taken from the premises. During Prohibition, citizens were more apt to take the bottle with them so they could use its contents as an alcohol mix and the bottle as a handy container. After the mixture was consumed, the bottle was discarded, perhaps thrown in a roadside ditch or a garbage pile. Many were broken, of course, lost from the inventory forever. Surviving bottles lived another recycled life.

Collecting discarded bottles to recover deposits became an industry for youngsters who plied the roadside ditches, dance hall parking lots and out-of-the-way places, collecting the valuable treasure. Not only were pop bottles of value for their deposit, but there was also a market among bootleggers for empty pint and half-pint whiskey bottles and beer bottles. The bottles were cleaned—often by sloshing shotgun shell pellets, soap and water in them—and then sold to moonshiners, bootleggers or junk dealer middlemen, who were regularly visited by moonshiners looking for containers. A visit to a dance hall parking lot the morning after a dance could be quite lucrative for a youngster in quest of empty pop and booze bottles. A young person on his roadside ditch or dance hall parking lot search could earn from six to eight dollars a day, according to information in an *Argus Leader* story on June 13, 1925.

Incidentally, the recycled whiskey bottles were often resold with counterfeit label facsimiles of the better whiskey brands pasted on them. Whiskey from Canada, such as Seagrams, always trumped the locally manufactured concoctions.

Mixing soda pop and liquor was expanded upon at blind pigs and private parties, where any number of extracts and flavors could be added to become the forerunners of today's panoply of mixed drinks.

In 1929, the government's thirty-four-year liquor tester from Minneapolis, Sari J. West, was in Sioux Falls as an expert witness at a trial. While there, he was interviewed by an *Argus Leader* reporter. West said he and two other Prohibition laboratory chemists were kept busy with samples sent in for analysis, processing about fifty samples a day from a three-state area. West said moonshine made in 1929 had an alcohol content of about 40 to 45 percent, which translated into eighty to ninety proof. Most of it was made from raw corn, but some of the more artistic and adventurous moonshiners had special additions for various flavors. West said illicit distillers could make moonshine out of just about anything. He'd even tested moonshine made from clover he described as "just as potent with as much quality as any other type or kind of booze."

A somewhat unusual vegetable for making wine was discovered during an August raid by federal officers in 1922 on the Rosebud Indian Reservation. At the David Deutsch ranch south of White River, officers found two gallons of what Deutsch said was parsnip wine. In Deadwood, businessman Thomas Burchell was arrested and fined $147.50 for selling a concoction made from orange peelings. Officers said it had more "kick" in it than any moonshine they had yet sampled. They also classified its taste as "something awful." They arrested the maker after he sold what the newspaper called the "deadly, brain-deadening booze" to several young men whose crazed actions resulted in the investigation leading to arrest, the *Argus Leader* reported on May 26, 1922.

Extracts of just about anything contained too much alcohol to be legal in bone-dry South Dakota. Officers arrested Peter Ellenbecker, a Sioux Falls North Main Street grocer, for selling almond extract found to be 80 percent alcohol. Another Sioux Falls man, Albert Monsor, was taken into custody for selling vanilla extract. In some polite social circles, to avoid saying "liquor," moonshine was often called "vanilla extract," according to the *Sioux Falls Argus Leader*'s February 27, 1920 issue. In Parker, the local creamery was burglarized and three gallons of lemon extract intended for ice cream flavoring was stolen. In Miller on May 27, 1922, William Edge was fined for purchasing a bottle of lemon extract and a bottle of orange pop and mixing the two. Arresting officers told the *Sioux Falls Argus Leader* that his condition when arrested was "one of the worst" cases of intoxication they'd ever seen in town.

In Sioux Falls in 1923, a large quantity of vanilla extract was seized from the O.J. Moore Grocery Store after an examination indicated there was both liquor and water in the containers labeled as vanilla. The state alleged 187 cases of the Three Star brand vanilla extract was adulterated and mislabeled. An order was issued for the seizure of seventy-seven dozen one-ounce bottles and eighty two-ounce bottles. When agents arrived to seize the cases, however, they also discovered thirty more cases not listed in the court order, according to an *Argus Leader* account.

Obtaining a bottle of lemon extract was apparently a powerful incentive for some. In late November 1928, the proprietor of a store in Rosholt refused to sell Arthur Neumann a bottle of the extract. Neumann became enraged, stomped out of the store, picked up a rock and chucked it through the store's plate-glass window. He was sentenced to nine months in jail after pleading guilty in Circuit Court in Sisseton, the October 18, 1923 *Sioux Falls Argus Leader* reported.

As with anything, the cost of illegal booze smuggled into the state from Canada and from surrounding states and moonshine manufactured locally depended on supply and demand. When supply exceeded demand, price wars among bootleggers often erupted.

An 1889 diary uncovered in a Sioux Falls basement and reported on in the *Argus Leader* in February 1926 listed prices for whiskey at about thirty cents a half pint. In 1920, a gallon of alcohol was sold in Colton for $40. A quart of booze in 1922 in Woonsocket was selling for $20. In Sisseton in 1922, Helmuth Klaatz was arrested after he tried to sell a gallon of moonshine to Deputy Sheriff Minder for the bargain basement price of just $6. He was fined $250, according to the July 24, 1922 *Sioux Falls Argus Leader*. A bootlegger in 1925 told a curious judge in Sioux Falls Municipal Court that he bought alcohol for $16 a gallon, watered it down and made twenty-two pints from it that would reap him a $28 profit per gallon of alcohol bought. On a good day, he said, he sold enough half pints of whiskey to require him to buy two gallons of alcohol to dilute with water. He was fined a total of $250 for selling booze, an amount about what the bootlegger could acquire and sell in half pints from a little more than nine gallons' worth of alcohol—hardly a month's business for him, the *Argus Leader* reported on October 10, 1925.

A moonshiner near Chamberlain in 1921 told the court he could make $1,000 from a fifty-gallon crock of peach mash. In Sioux Falls in 1921, booze was selling for $25 a quart. In Sturgis in 1922, a bootlegger bought ten gallons of moonshine for $50. By comparison, the cost of a quart of milk in Sioux Falls in 1923 was twelve cents, and gasoline was selling for twelve and a half cents a gallon. By 1927, customers were paying bootleggers in the Sioux Falls area $15 for a pint of booze. One bootlegger in Sioux Falls in 1926 bought moonshine for $6 a gallon from a distiller and sold it on the street for $15.

Leona Pietz, in her book *Memories of a Bootlegger's Daughter*, wrote about her father, Adolph Schelske of rural Parkston. He used his own homegrown rye or oats for mash, and his cost for enough mash to make a gallon of moonshine was $0.35. He then sold the gallon of liquor for $1.50.

Some temperance leaders often called moonshine snake oil, but it was much cheaper than real snake oil by far. In fact, a new industry was developed in Texas in 1926 to collect what the press called "rattlesnake oil" for medicinal purposes. The Texas company paid $100 a gallon for the venomous snake oil, the *Argus Leader* reported on March 1, 1926.

Hank Widdoss, a well-known ranchman in the Redwater District of the Black Hills, must have thought he'd been "snake bit" while on a vacation in California in 1923. The drink prices in nearby Tijuana, Mexico, so astounded him that he decided to swear off drinking. In the Mexican border town just south of San Diego, Widdoss and two friends were at a Tijuana bar, and Widdoss offered to buy his friends a shot of whiskey. He laid a dollar bill on the bar to pay for the treats. The bartender asked for another fifty cents. Widdoss told a Deadwood-based reporter for the *Argus Leader* in Sioux Falls on April 27, 1923, that he was "shocked" to have to pay fifty cents for a shot of whiskey. "We don't need any more laws to make me a prohibitionist," he said. "I'm one now."

Related somewhat to the cost of booze during Prohibition was the cost of Prohibition law enforcement. In 1930, the federal budget for Prohibition law enforcement nationally was more than $7.5 million. The cost for enforcement of federal dry laws in South Dakota in 1930 averaged six cents for every South Dakotan. In 1932, violators of federal Prohibition laws were sentenced to a jail terms averaging 178 days.

Despite all the glamour flickering on the nation's movie screens and described in novels and newspapers, bootlegging could be a tough, hard, competitive business. Aside from an element of danger and the possibility of fines and incarceration, the competition was fierce. In a 1930 *Brookings Register* interview with a bootlegger from across the South Dakota–Minnesota border, a dealer painted a sour picture. "Bootlegging isn't what it used to be," he said. "I used to buy alcohol at $7.50 a gallon and could sell all I could get at $25 a gallon and no questions asked. Cars would drive to my farm every day in large numbers and would take all the alcohol I could get and pay spot cash." He said in 1930 he paid the same for moonshine, $7.50 a gallon, but got only $12.00 for it. "I think I will have to quit the business to keep from going broke," he told the *Register* reporter.

Some state citizens could easily and legally obtain the elixir of joy. Alcohol for medicinal and scientific purposes and for religious uses was allowed under both state and federal Prohibition laws. In 1929, 298 ministers in South Dakota had permits for sacramental wine. Enough wine was issued to them to average out at a gallon a month for each minister. "Scientific purposes" allowed research universities and other entities engaged in science-related inquiry the use of alcohol in the pursuit of new knowledge.

Physicians were authorized to have a supply of alcohol at their homes, offices, clinics or hospitals. Some probably even carried liquor around in their little black bags, although as a group, most of the state's doctors did not believe alcohol was a necessary medicinal therapeutic. Doctors could also write prescriptions for alcohol that registered druggists could fill. The law limited the quantity of drugstore prescription liquor to a pint every ten days for a single patient for medicinal purposes. In 1929, according to the annual report of the state sheriff who, in concert with federal officials, approved and supervised these special uses, fifty-eight South Dakota druggists were registered to fill alcohol prescriptions. For the year, their combined stock was 1,193 gallons of alcohol, 172 gallons of brandy, 83 gallons of wine and, remarkably, 3,063 gallons of whiskey. In the event physicians prescribed another form of booze, the druggists also had on hand during the same year 6 gallons of rum, 2.5 gallons of gin and, curiously, 1.5 gallons of champagne, according to the 1929 state sheriff's report.

Medical doctors issuing alcohol directly to patients without writing prescriptions were not limited to the amount of liquor a patient could receive. Because each patient's needs were different, the law merely stated,

"No more liquor shall be prescribed than is necessary for such sickness." A report by State Sheriff Bruce Barnes in late 1931 listed that 5,600 gallons of alcohol for medicinal, scientific and sacramental purposes was approved in South Dakota. This was 1,700 gallons less than was approved for the same purposes the previous year, the December 17, 1931 *Sioux Falls Argus Leader* reported.

Sheriff Barnes's report showed 4,718 gallons of alcohol, brandy, whiskey, rum, gin, champagne and wine were issued in 1930 for the purposes the law stipulated. In those cases, whiskey was the most popular medicinal beverage, with alcohol, brandy and wine as the second, third and fourth choices. Sheriff Barnes estimated 1,038 gallons of wine were used for sacramental purposes during the year.

His report contained the names of 49 drugstores in the state with permits to dispense liquor from prescriptions written by physicians. Their permits were issued "for life," and Barnes reported that the 247 physicians' permits in existence in 1930 grew by 21 in 1931. In 1918, there were 373 druggists in South Dakota, according to the 1918 state sheriff's report. By 1933, just 60 South Dakota druggists requested permits to fill prescriptions ordered by physician prescriptions.

A national survey of physicians by the *Journal of the American Medical Association* in 1922 showed that of the 214 of the 658 physicians practicing in South Dakota receiving the questionnaire, doctors responded by a two-to-one margin against writing prescriptions for alcohol. To the question if the physician regarded whiskey as a necessary therapeutic agent in the practice of medicine, 80 respondents said yes and 120 said no. On the same question regarding the use of beer for patients, 44 said yes and 157 said no. In 1922, physicians who held liquor permits practiced in only eleven of South Dakota's sixty-four counties, the January 16, 1922 *Sioux Falls Argus Leader* reported.

In 1923, a farmer near Milltown was arrested in Mitchell for having liquor in his possession. He claimed it was obtained with a physician's prescription as medication for his nine-year-old son, who had injured his knee in an accident, but this turned out not to be the case.

For years, the membership of the American Dental Association had worked for the same rights as medical doctors regarding the use of liquor in the practice of dentistry. In 1930, meeting in Denver, Colorado, the organization's membership approved a resolution saying whiskey and brandy were just as necessary in the practice of dentistry as in the practice of medicine. The passage culminated years of effort within the organization by those who believed they were being discriminated against, according to an Associated Press report of July 25, 1930. By 1935, dentists qualified for the use of alcohol in their practices, but by then, Prohibition had passed from the scene.

By far the most difficulty in enforcement of Prohibition laws for medicinal, scientific and sacramental purposes was at the drugstore, where myriad other over-the-counter products contained alcohol in excess of what the state's bone-dry law allowed. This included everything from the ubiquitous prepackaged patent medicines to furniture polish, shaving lotions and just about every liquid cosmetic known to womankind. The list even included toilet water. These items could be sold legally, provided they were not advertised as beverages or identified by the pharmacist as being beverages.

Until 1927, drugstores in South Dakota were the only outlets for the sale of the prepackaged, alcohol-laced patent medicines then so common. In Mitchell on May 20, 1926, non-pharmacist P.E. Wood was arrested for selling these proprietary medicines, of which there were literally thousands of types and brands. Wood argued the laws governing the pharmacists of South Dakota should not forbid the sale of proprietary medicine by any person not a pharmacist when the product is in the original manufacturer's package. Judge William Herbert agreed, and the state, on behalf of South Dakota pharmacists, appealed to the South Dakota Supreme Court.

Wood's contention in the suit had the enthusiastic backing of a national association of proprietary medicine manufacturers, which stood to gain thousands of new retail outlets if it was ruled anyone could sell its products. In October 1927, the South Dakota Supreme Court ruled against the state and the pharmacists, saying pharmacists did not have exclusive rights to sell patent and proprietary medicines since the medications came prepackaged and the pharmacists' expertise was not necessary in the selling of those packaged items. According to the Supreme Court ruling reported on in the *Sioux Falls Argus Leader* on October 11, 1927, "If one had a doctor's prescription filled at a drug store, he buys not the medicine alone, but the druggist's knowledge and skill in dispensing it. But if he were to buy Watkins Painoliem at the drug store what more would he buy if he bought elsewhere?"

Another interesting rule emerged in South Dakota in 1931, when the state said druggists with permits to dispense alcoholic liquor could place signs announcing they "fill liquor prescriptions." In Sioux Falls at the time, only six of the twenty-three drugstores in the city had permits to fill whiskey prescriptions.

Druggists could not sell sacramental wines unless they were considered "importers" of wine. No druggist in the state qualified as an importer, so it remained for churches to order their sacramental supplies from out-of-state firms.

As previously mentioned, grape juice sales by California growers grew by 400 percent during Prohibition.

CHAPTER 10

# Prohibition Potpourri

In 1935, residents of Colton, a Minnehaha County village northwest of Sioux Falls, had to choose between liquor or a park. They got booze by a vote of 101 to 56 and lost their city park.

Back in 1905, seven years after the town was platted, J.E. and Paulina Colton had deeded for one dollar several city lots for a community park. A clause in the transfer to the city stated the land would remain a city park in perpetuity unless intoxicating liquor was ever allowed in town. If it were, the land would revert to the benefactors or their survivors. Because of this clause, Colton for a time in the 1920s was nationally known as America's driest town, according to an August 14, 1933 report in the *Sioux Falls Argus Leader*. The town was dry for nearly three decades, and the park and its $2,000 pavilion were popular recreational retreats for holidays and weekend outings.

Along came legalization of low-point beer by congressional decree in 1933 and, several months later, acceptance of beer in South Dakota. Several citizens applied to the Colton City Council for a license to sell 3.2 percent beer. To abide by the park land agreement, council members set the applications aside. Three of the applicants—A.C. Thompson, Winifred Pederson and Nels J. Dale—joined in a friendly circuit court action seeking a writ of mandamus for the city council to reconsider.

In August 1933, circuit court judge Lucius J. Wall signed a writ directing the Colton City Council to take action on the beer license applications. Further, the judge said since Congress and the state did not consider low-point beer intoxicating, the city would not be in violation of its agreement regarding intoxicating liquor with the Colton family. Also, the city council could only approve or disapprove the license application. The power to actually issue the beer license was the province of the state. Colton leaders, on advice from their attorney Verne Jennings, believed if ordered by the court and forced to issue beer licenses, it would probably not violate the city park land agreement and the town could allow beer.

Two years later, in 1935, with federal Prohibition in the history books and South Dakota's bone-dry Prohibition laws in jeopardy, Colman city leaders assumed that when state Prohibition ended, it would be confronted with a similar challenge regarding applications to sell hard liquor. As expected, when applications for hard liquor sales in town were presented to the city council, it twice declined requests submitted by A.C. Thompson and Nels Dale. Concurrently, some citizens who wanted the city to share in a part of the cash flow that anticipated liquor sales would bring to the city's coffers circulated a petition asking for an election to allow the municipal sale of liquor. At the city election on June 28, 1935, Colton residents, by a vote of 101 to 56, approved a city municipal liquor store, and the city council applied to the state for a license to do so.

At about this time, the J.E. and Paulina Colton's family initiated proceedings to reclaim the park property. It was a lengthy process, and in 1939, the city council again retained the services of attorney Verne Jennings to represent it in discussions with Colton family members, according to the 1939 Colton City Council minutes. The minutes contain scant information about the northwest parkland negotiations with Colton family representatives, but in April 1940, there is a hint that negotiations were not going well for the city. The minutes briefly mention an appropriation by city leaders of $300 for "trees for East Side Park." Apparently the city was developing a new park area to replace the lost Colton park lots. Today, the city has a spacious park on the southeast side of town known as Redway Park. The former Colton City Park is a park no longer and remains in private hands.

Colman's adventure with liquor legalization did not end with development of a new park. In 1941, citizens against city liquor sales tried to shut down the very profitable city liquor store. In its first month of operation in 1939, the store made a profit of $102.36. The net profit increased by $50.00 during the second month's operation, according to Colton City Council minutes. The vote to close the city liquor store failed 148 to 140. The city now leases its profitable municipal liquor store to a private party, and as of 2009, Colton was receiving approximately $1,500.00 a month as its share of the store's profits, according to Colton's city clerk.

Members of the Rapid City Chamber of Commerce and Black Hills tourist promoters, apparently dizzy from the altitude, intoxicated with the Black Hills beauty and Banana Belt weather and despondent none of these appealing qualities were receiving national attention, reached out to Chicago in 1930 for aid and comfort—but mostly for free national publicity. The organization invited bootleg king and gangster Al "Scarface" Capone to relocate his nefarious operations to Rapid City and to bring his criminal cronies with him. It was a rather crude publicity stunt.

Asked about the invitation, dour and proper governor William J. Bulow was unmoved and unsympathetic. "We don't want Capone or any of his kind in South Dakota," he emphatically told the *Sioux Falls Argus Leader* on March 28, 1930. State Sheriff Fred Minier of Brookings rolled his eyes and called the invitation "foolish publicity." Even Deadwood, hardly a bastion of the virtuous and law abiding, rudely yanked in the latchstring for Capone and exhibited a new, less raucous side. "We citizens of Deadwood are noted for our true western hospitality, but also for our quick action in dealing with criminals and outlaws," said Mayor F.W. Howe. "Our desperadoes died with their boots on fifty years ago. Our city has outgrown its wild past and we intend to keep it that way."

Rapid City mayor Theodore B. Werner was running for Congress at the time. He immediately sought to put distance between his candidacy, the invitation and the national publicity the Rapid City business group sought. He advised Capone and his cohorts not to take the invitation seriously. "It neither represents the attitude nor carries the approval of the people," he said, adding that the gangster's "ill-gotten wealth cannot buy him happiness here." Rapid City ministers also condemned the idea. The rest of the astounded folks in South Dakota just shook their heads in disbelief.

Pennington County sheriff William P. Baken boldly offered to take the underworld king on a "fishing trip if he came to town." His deputy, George Lenbecker, boasted that Rapid City could deal with Scarface. "We've reformed tougher guys," he said, "and we'll make him look like a college boy."

The day after the invitation was issued, Capone responded. The *Chicago Tribune* quoted him as saying he appreciated the invitation but that he had "no desire to live in the Black Hills."

The nonsensical invitation wasn't the only wild idea the Rapid City Chamber of Commerce ever tried in efforts to garner publicity for the area. Eight years earlier, in 1922, the organization had invited Pope Pius

XI to relocate the Vatican to the Black Hills. The Pope never responded. In November 1944, as World War II was ending, the chamber proposed the United Nations establish its world headquarters in or near Rapid City, safe from an atomic attack at the time because of bomber aircraft range. In 1950, Rapid City business and professional groups urged the United States Congress to move the nation's capital to Rapid City. But nothing ever surpassed the cockamamie offer issued to Capone, who did move to Palm Island in Miami, Florida, for a time. He later moved back to the Windy City before his longer stay behind bars for tax evasion.

The trials and tribulations of the little city of Colton and the Capone caper were just two of hundreds of often strange, eye-catching, sometimes ridiculous and very unusual circumstances during the helter-skelter Roaring Twenties in South Dakota that carried over into the sluggish, worrisome '30s.

The Reverend John Hamstra of the Elkton Baptist Church a few miles from the western border of Minnesota was helping members of the church ladies' aid serve lunches at the end of an annual daylong city celebration on October 3, 1922. He noticed a nearly constant parade of women passing by carrying brown paper packages and heading toward the local dance hall, but he didn't recognize the ladies. Curious, Pastor Hamstra followed along. At the dance, he watched as the brown paper bags were handed to several of the men, who dutifully dug into their pockets for their coin purses.

He followed the now emptyhanded women when they left the dance hall and hurried to the eastern edge of town and the Elkton Park. The women joined several men there who were there imbibing moonshine. It was about midnight. Reverend Hamstra marched boldly into the midst of the small gathering, tipped over their stash of about fifteen gallons of booze and gave the celebrants five minutes to leave town. They hurried to their cars and departed Elkton in a cloud of dust, headed back toward Lake Benton just beyond the state line in Minnesota. But they would return.

According to the August 23, 1923 *Brookings Register*, eleven months after Pastor Hamstra's midnight park lecture, unidentified bootleggers delivered a gift to the Baptist minister. On Saturday morning, August 18, 1923, on the porch of his home, Reverend Hamstra found several bottles of beer and a note: "From your Lake Benton friends."

After nearly two decades of bootleggers depositing illegal booze at various and sundry hidden locations, or "drops," some of the stash was bound to remain hidden away, forgotten and abandoned. A rumor circulated in the town of Veblen ten miles from the North Dakota border in Marshall County that the water-filled cistern in the town's hotel was to be drained for cleaning.

Local lore said it had been a hiding and cooling place for homemade beer the hotel sold on the sly to selected customers.

When word got around about the hotel owner needing help in cleaning the cistern in May 1922, volunteers with visions of free, cool lager beer rushed to sign up. A pump was primed, and volunteers got in line to work its levered mechanism. It was laughingly said that so constant and vigorous was the pumping that one man had to be assigned the job of pouring water over the pump mechanism to keep it from overheating. At last, the cistern was emptied, but only the remains of a few of the town's missing cats were found at the bottom. There was no beer, according to a *Sioux Falls Argus Leader* story published on May 18, 1922.

In Redfield in March 1921, workers were tearing down a venerable livery barn. They found three bottles of Hamm's Peerless beer entwined in cobwebs and covered with dust from long storage under the rickety floor, probably forgotten by a long-ago stable keeper. Some of the workers, the press reported, became so enamored with the find after a swig or two of Peerless that they forgot to quit work for the day when the town's six o'clock whistle blew, the *Sioux Falls Argus Leader* reported.

In Gregory, a gang of workmen in April 1923 was excavating for the foundation of the new Commercial State Bank building planned on the site of an old saloon. Workers were spurred to more rapid digging when one of them uncovered a quart bottle of liquor with the cork seal intact. Someone in the crew remembered the saloon, before Prohibition, had kept its liquor supply in an underground dugout beneath the building. Perhaps, workmen thought, the dugout had caved in, burying hundreds of well-aged bottles of whiskey. Digging was intense, but to no avail. Only the lone bottle was uncovered, according to the *Sioux Falls Argus Leader*'s April 11, 1923 edition.

During the excavation for a new creamery at the site of the old Sioux Falls Brewery building in October 1925, workers shoveling out an abandoned cellar found a dozen bottles of old beer. How long the pre–Volstead Act exhilarator had been buried wasn't known, but workers did their part in doing away with the evidence the old-fashioned way before lawmen arrived to confiscate their finds, the *Argus Leader* reported.

In May 1921, a man with the famous name of Frank Leahy of Tripp County was bound over to court under $800 bond for "having intoxicating liquor in a public place." Notre Dame coach Frank Leahy grew up in the Tripp County town of Winner, where he was an outstanding athlete for Winner High School. But future coach Frank Leahy was born in 1908. This Frank Leahy arrest was in 1921, when young Coach Leahy was only thirteen, so there must have been another, older Frank Leahy in the county at the time. That bootlegging Frank Leahy had also been charged the same month with having a "cream can with false bottom containing a faucet." Coincidentally, Notre Dame's Frank Leahy and his father shared the same first name...

At the height of the Depression, the Red Cross purchased wheat it provided to the needy to use as livestock feed. Fred Sturzenbecker of rural Huron found another use for his endowed Red Cross wheat allocation. In 1932, Beadle County sheriff Leo A. Temmey charged Sturzenbecker with making moonshine with it. Raiding parties at the Sturzenbecker farm found a still, some mash and five gallons of Red Cross booze, according to the May 17, 1932 *Sioux Falls Argus Leader*.

In 1934, Elk Point city historian and treasurer E.E. Wenner had research that revealed 295 steamboat wrecks on the Missouri River between 1819 and 1897. He was particularly intrigued by one wreck, the *Leadora*, which went down on May 21, 1866, with one hundred barrels of whiskey and other merchandise on board. During his explorations in 1911, he claimed to have found the boat's old, rusting safe. Thus inspired, by 1934, he was looking for someone to put up $2,000 to finance the raising of the boat from its burial beneath twenty-five feet of silt and sand. An issue of the January 1934 *Sioux Falls Argus Leader* said the investor would equally share in the sale of the boat's cargo. The boat was by then under dry land a quarter of a mile from the river's old channel. Wenner was certain the water and sand had preserved the whiskey and had helped it age to perfection, making it worth a fortune. No one stepped forward with the money, so presumably, the old boat and its liquor cargo are still aging, waiting to be exhumed, according to the *Sioux Falls Argus Leader* on January 1, 1934. The boat and its cargo are apparently still locked in the Missouri mud.

Even Evenson of rural Brookings was serving time in the county jail after repeated liquor law violations. He was a notorious, often-arrested bootlegger but a model prisoner, and he soon earned trustee status with the run of the jail as long as he was in his unlocked cell at the appointed evening hour. The *Brookings Register* reported in its May 17, 1927 issue that a house in west Brookings had been raided the previous night. "In the house when officers entered," the *Register* reported, "were a group of people engaged in drinking, and much to the surprise of the officers, they found in the group Even Evenson, who is serving time in the county jail on bootlegging charges." Embarrassed county officers said their investigation revealed Evenson had often left the jail on unauthorized night leave, crawling out an upstairs jail window. The county sheriff's home was on the jail's first floor, but he never heard a thing as the model prisoner left for another night cavorting on the town.

Stories abound of Prohibition-era farm animals gaining access to homemade whiskey or the fermented alcohol mash. Pigs and chickens, and sometimes even fish in ponds and creeks near stills, were most fortunate because moonshine-making equipment was usually hidden in the less desirous of places to discourage searches by Prohibition agents. Pigpens, hog houses and henhouses were not exactly the neatest and cleanest of places, so they were the obvious hiding places.

The fermented mash, once most of the alcohol had been wrung from it, had to be disposed of to make room for a new batch. It was usually just dumped on the ground. Hogs and chickens were attracted to this worthless byproduct. Others let the mash drain into lakes and streams.

Leona Pietz of Parker, in her book *Memories of a Bootlegger's Daughter*, remembered her father, Adolph Schelske's, excellent distillery work. He strained his used mash and then drained it away through a hose to a nearby creek. "The fish loved it," she wrote. "That area where the mash was dumped became a good feeding ground for them, and a good fishing hole for us."

Agents uncovered a still near the hog yard on the W. Cross farm, north of Pukwana, a few days before Thanksgiving Day 1921. In the mash barrels, lawmen found fermenting barley and rye, which farmer Cross and another man, Joe Dusseau, claimed was hog feed. Some of the used mash had indeed been used for hog and chicken feed, the defendants told the court. When agents arrived at his farm to search for illegal contraband, some of the chickens were "in bad shape," they said. They mentioned one particular rooster that had been too long in the cups and was strutting around trying to crow. Each time he stretched out his neck and tried, he lost his balance and tipped over, flapping wings akimbo, they said. Hogs were better able to handle the discarded mash, although it wasn't unusual for a good hog fight to break out over territorial mash disputes, according to the *Sioux Falls Argus Leader* on November 21, 1921.

A posse of officers and federal Prohibition agents under the direction of N.J. Folsom of Sioux Falls, chief special officer of the law enforcement division of the Indian Service, raided a farm in June 1932 owned by Berg Cozad about five miles northeast of Greenfield. Cozad apparently got word of the impending raid. Wanting to destroy the evidence, he tipped over four barrels of fermenting mash before hurriedly departing. When agents arrived, a passel of pigs had most of the mash consumed, Folsom said. Officers joked with the *Argus Leader* reporter about finding plenty of "pickled pigs feet" and many "blind pigs" at the Cozad place.

Children at play often inadvertently found illegal stills or liquor stashes. During recess at the Box School in Yankton County in 1921, youngsters noticed newly turned ground near the school. Investigating, they found more than thirty gallons of home-brew buried in a grove of plum trees. The teacher, Mrs. Harry Box, called Sheriff A.P. Johnson. He identified the booze as whiskey, saying it was "good-looking and peppy-smelling."

On November 1, 1921, an eleven-year-old boy, son of I.A. Syverud, was beaten with tree branches and left bound by grapevine near the same Box School. Young Syverud had apparently left other students during recess to chase a pheasant into the tree grove near a good highway. The place was a known pick-up site for bootleggers, and for months it was observed by law enforcement officials because it was such an ideal rendezvous point for bootleggers. When the boy was found, he was more frightened than hurt. Word spread through the Box neighborhood, and a manhunt was organized, but to no avail. Officers believed the boy was in the wrong place at the wrong time. His assailant, probably a young bootlegger, may also have been motivated by revenge for having lost his earlier stash to the curious Box School kids.

In 1923 in Mitchell, two young boys found six gallons of alcohol buried north of town all wrapped up and ready for shipping. They could not carry it all to the police station, so they hid three gallons in a nearby shed. With the other three gallons in tow, the boys headed for the police station. On the way, they passed by the Mitchell Waterworks building. Fireman Ross Davidson was at the plant and saw the boys struggling with their heavy load. He hailed them and asked what they had in the tins. They told him, and he volunteered to take the heavy tins off their hands, put it in his car and deliver it to the police, the boys later testified.

The youngsters happened to see the police chief a few days after their discovery. They mentioned their find and the welcome help Davison gave them. The chief learned Davidson had never contacted his department about the contraband. He was arrested and charged with possession. Checking the shed where the boys had left the rest of the stash, police found that liquor supply missing, too. F.E. Goheen was arrested for that part in the heist, according to the *Sioux Falls Argus Leader* issue of December 6, 1923.

In late October 1926, Pi Kappa Delta National Forensic Association selected the topic of modification of the Volstead Act for the upcoming college debate season. The topic was officially stated as follows: "Resolved, that the Volstead Law be amended to permit sale of light wine and beer."

A week later, Dakota Wesleyan University president E.D. Kohlstedt objected to the subject. He said no Wesleyan debater would lift a voice in the affirmative. But he did offer a Dakota Wesleyan team to uphold the negative question against all comers. Northern State Teachers College also objected, declaring the subject "verges on repudiation of the Constitution." He said Northern "stands for law enforcement."

Pi Kappa Delta's national president, responding to Dakota Wesleyan's president Kohlstedt, said the national forensics group was in sympathy with Dakota Wesleyan's protest. In a letter to Kohlstedt, Alfred Westfall of Pi Kappa Delta said his organization "respects the attitude you and other college presidents have taken. We recognize colleges have a right to indicate what their students may debate publicly. I have regarded the selection of the light wines and beer question as unfortunate and most of the institutions have, though their provincial organizations, selected other subjects." South Dakota, Iowa, Minnesota and Colorado debate teams consequently selected other debate subjects, the *Sioux Falls Argus Leader* reported on November 27, 1926.

John Lutz of Tyler, Minnesota, picked the wrong day to drive his Velie touring car with Minnesota license plates to Brookings. Everyone in town was on high alert on Saturday, September 15, 1927, because of the much-anticipated arrival later in the day of a very special guest. Otherwise, no one in Brookings would have probably even known Lutz and his Velie were in town. But President Calvin Coolidge, returning to the White House from his Summer White House in the Black Hills, was to arrive and would be driven to the State College campus to dedicate a new library and symbolically mortar in a cornerstone at the school's new outdoor Sylvan Theater.

So a citizen's call about a strange car in town certainly piqued the interest of Brookings police. They located the car, searched it and were surprised to find twenty-one gallons of moonshine in a keg in the car's back seat, plus a few gallon jugs on the car's floor. Lutz initially told police he had no idea how the liquor got in his car. In fact, he was surprised it was there. He later changed his tune, according to a story in the *Brookings Register*. He told Judge W.W. Knight he was driving the booze to Huron in return for $100. It was to be delivered to a man whom he conveniently knew only as "John."

President Coolidge; his wife, Grace; and their son, John, spent more than an hour in Brookings and then continued on the long journey to Washington, D.C. Lutz remained in Brookings a few days longer, watching the world pass by through a window at the city jail, according to the August 15, 1927 issue of the *Brookings Register*.

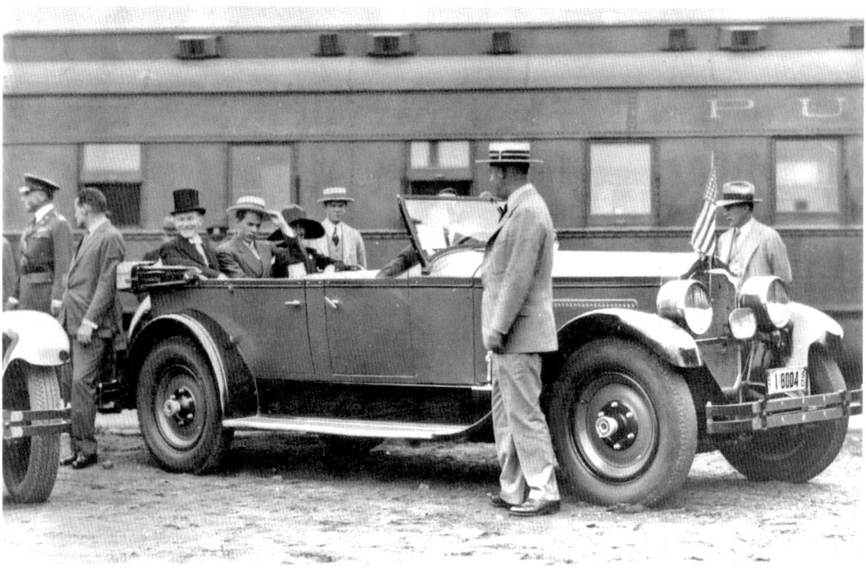

President Calvin Coolidge (in top hat); his son John, then twenty-one; and Grace Coolidge stopped by Brookings to dedicate South Dakota State University's new outdoor theater on September 10, 1927. *Author's collection.*

A year after Silent Cal visited Brookings, federal Prohibition agent Joseph Wilshire sped into Vermillion, another college town, with a man in his car whom he'd just arrested for having a supply of liquor on him. The man had identified a Beresford bootlegger as the source of the booze.

The agent was speeding to the Clay County Courthouse to obtain a search warrant before heading to nearby Beresford to arrest the bootlegger. As Wilshire entered town with his prisoner, who would help prove to the judge the reason for the search warrant request, Vermillion motorcycle cop Joseph Bliss spotted the speeding Wilshire car and gave chase. It ended at the Clay County Courthouse door, where Bliss arrested Wilshire. Taken before Justice W.A. Bauman, Wilshire explained he was an agent for the federal Prohibition office of South Dakota and related the reason for speeding. He declined to ask for leniency, so Judge Bauman quickly fined Wilshire five dollars, which he paid. The December 24, 1928 issue of the *Argus Leader* reported that a search warrant was issued, and Wilshire sped off at an appropriate speed to Beresford to make the arrest, according to the *Sioux Falls Argus Leader* issue of December 24, 1928.

This conversation took place in Sioux Falls Municipal Court in April 1929, between F.J. Pallanch and municipal judge Ransom Gibb:

*Your honor, I won't plead guilty because I was not drunk.*
*Had you been drinking?*
*Yes, sir, and I think that I was just a little, a slight bit, intoxicated.*
*Just how intoxicated were you?*
*I can't hardly say because I don't remember the exact date.*
*Don't you keep a diary?*
*Oh, yes, but I don't write about my drinking. I think, probably, though that I might have been slightly, a little bit intoxicated.*
*For the last month?*
*I imagine for the last month.*

"Well, the law does not provide for degrees of intoxication. It is the judgment of this court that you be sentenced to thirty days in jail," the *Sioux Falls Argus Leader* reported on April 8, 1929.

Later that year, somewhat similarly, W.A. Lorenzen, a farmer near Corson, told a judge he wasn't drunk, he was just intoxicated, during his trial in Sioux Falls. The judge fined him twenty-five dollars for being intoxicated, not drunk.

C.J. Delbridge, Sioux Falls judge pro-tem of municipal court, had to hide his face and fake a cough in his handkerchief when Lars Jensen of 131 South Lincoln Avenue, facing a liquor charge, said the liquor police found at his home wasn't intended to be used for drinking. As Jensen was quoted in the September 1, 1932 issue of the *Sioux Falls Argus Leader*: "I had the liquor in the house to bathe my kids feet with."

One product not in the sights of dry agents was the plumbing pipes and fixtures used in most homes. Joseph G. Hildebrand, director of the regional Management Conferences of the Plumbing and Heating Industries Bureau, said the Volstead Act and the resulting Prohibition laws had a positive effect on the sale of plumbing fixtures.

"Illicit thirst," he said during a stop in Sioux Falls, "caused thoughts of the nation to turn towards the basement, and the old cellar graduated into a club room, rathskeller and chamber of conviviality." He cited the extraordinary demand for copper tubes for stills and the coiled copper tubing (the worm), which the vapors of alcohol passed through and condensed into a clear liquid after wafting up from the heated vats of mash.

An unintended consequence of Prohibition was a sudden overcrowding in jails or the need to build a hoosegow in communities where a place for incarceration hadn't been needed before. Ree Heights, in its forty-third year of existence, had never before felt the need to have a city jail. In 1925, thanks to John Barleycorn, an overabundance of area residents arrested for liquor violations required a jail be built, the *Argus Leader* reported in December 1925.

In Lemmon, after a raid by federal agents in 1930, seven men were arrested for various liquor violations. Space in the Lemmon jail was by then squeezed to capacity because of the success of the federal lawmen. Only six of the prisoners could be incarcerated in Lemmon. A cell in a nearby town helped fill the order for the seventh man, according to the *Sioux Falls Argus Leader* of January 28, 1930.

A year later, the Lemmon jail had difficulty even holding long-sought northwestern South Dakota bootlegger D. McPherson. After his arrest, he was lodged in the Lemmon jail but escaped within a few hours. He was recaptured and returned to the same Lemmon jail. This time, as a precaution, he was also chained to one of the cell bars. The next morning, however, he was gone. Officers located him asleep on the banks of a creek a few miles from town and this time reconsidered using the Lemmon jail to house their elusive prisoner once more. The September 3, 1931 issue of the *Sioux Falls Argus Leader* said authorities took him to the less porous Perkins County Jail in Bison.

In August 1922, Presho police wondered why they were receiving an inordinate number of calls and visits from housewives who said they were missing the barrels used to catch and store the naturally soft rainwater that drained off the roof and was captured in the barrels for household uses. Then police found a still on the Sam Dolly farm six miles northwest of town. In the brewing shack they also found a small army of former rain barrels now filled with bubbling mash, according to a report in the August 8, 1922 *Sioux Falls Argus Leader*.

The USS *Yankton* started out in 1893 as the yacht *Penelope* in Leith, Scotland. It was acquired in 1898 as a United States gunboat in the Spanish-American War, renamed the USS *Yankton* after the South Dakota county and sent to Cuba. After that conflict, it did coastal duties for the navy and in 1907 was added as one of the ships composing the Great White Fleet for its famous around-the-world cruise as a symbol of America's strength.

The ship became a tender in World War I and in 1918, on escort duty, fired on a German submarine, forcing it to flee the area. At one time, Yankton residents were so proud of their city's namesake that they contributed a set of silverware for the captain's cabin.

The proud USS *Yankton* was decommissioned in 1920 and then sold the following year. The new owners converted it to a merchant ship. When stopped on the high seas and boarded by the coast guard in the West Indies some months later, during Prohibition, the former USS *Yankton* was found to be loaded with about half a million dollars of rum headed for the United States. It was confiscated and later sold for scrap in 1930, according to the *Sioux Falls Argus Leader* of June 26, 1923.

Prohibition dry agents and other officers of the law in South Dakota became immune to the excuses they constantly heard during raids and arrests of Prohibition lawbreakers. Officers found two barrels of mash in the kitchen of bachelor Gregory County farmer Oliver Anderson. The *Sioux Falls Argus Leader* reported that police asked Anderson what it was. "Pig feed," he replied. In Watertown, A.J. Struckman was arrested in July 1921 on a charge of manufacturing intoxicating liquor. He told the judge it wasn't liquor but "carburetor cutter."

Mitchell-area farmer Henry Peters—after a 1921 raid on his farm where deputy state sheriffs found a barrel of moonshine in a haystack, another barrel in a straw stack, a number of bottles of booze in his car and carefully packed jugs in his farm wagon and more in a wheat bin—swore to officers he had no knowledge of the stashes and was as surprised to learn about the contraband as they were.

Herbert Muckow of Sioux Falls was arrested driving around town with a large tin of alcohol between his feet on the floor of his car. He told officers he didn't know the can was there, according to a report of the incident in the January 25, 1927 issue of the *Argus Leader*. Ole Olson of Pumpkin Center was brought before Sioux Falls judge Ransom Gibbs for intoxication. He told the judge he drank for medical reasons. "A doctor told me several years ago it would be better to drink alcohol while I was working in the fields in the sun than to drink ice water," he said.

Lake Andes clothing store owner Seb Homolka had a visit by federal Prohibition agents in early 1922. They found more than twelve gallons of moonshine on his store building's second floor. Homolka explained the drinking water in Lake Andres was so bad he couldn't drink it; therefore, he made the whiskey to whet his dry whistle.

August Holter, who farmed thirteen miles northwest of Madison, had a similar bad water problem. The October 30, 1922 issue of the *Sioux Falls Argus Leader* said he pleaded guilty after officers found two stills and more than fifty quart bottles of moonshine on his place. "We have nothing but alkali water to use here and I wanted to distill some of that," he said, then added, "a little later I thought I might as well make a little something else to drink, too."

Although the reach of Chicago bootlegging czar Al "Scarface" Capone was vast and surely extended into South Dakota during Prohibition years, no definite tie between the gangster and the Sunshine State was ever established. Except one.

In the spring of 1927, reports surfaced about a famous Prohibition enforcement officer for the Cheyenne Indian Reservation, known far and wide as "Two Gun Hart," being killed. But in a May 10 report in the *Sioux Falls Argus Leader*, the death was discounted by Rosebud Reservation rancher Frank Yancey, who had painful proof Two Gun was alive and very well.

Hart and three deputies were tracking down the source of a considerable supply of liquor on the reservation and went to the Yancey Ranch. Frank Yancey was not at home but had left two hired men in charge. Two Gun and his deputies found a one-hundred-gallon still and a quantity of moonshine. While Two Gun was still at the ranch, Yancey arrived and wasn't happy to find federal agents on his property. The press report quoted the rancher as saying to Two Gun: "If you were not protected by the other officers I would give you a good licking."

Two Gun told Yancey to "just forget they are here" and waved the other officers back. Two Gun then threw his guns off to the side and invited Yancey to "go ahead." Yancey did manage to throw a landing punch on Two Gun's chin, and he then picked up an iron bar and swung it at the lawman. Two Gun dodged the sweeps of the rod and sailed into the rancher. He pummeled him severely, the *Argus Leader* report said. Yancey was so badly injured that he had to be taken to the Rosebud Agency Hospital for treatment.

It turns out Two Gun Hart was actually James Vincenzo Capone, oldest of the six brothers of gangster Al Capone. Two Gun was born in Italy in 1892 and came with the then-small Capone family to New York around the turn of the century. The family settled in Brooklyn. At age sixteen, James Capone left home and joined a circus. His travels took him to Nebraska, and he found the state to his liking. He was fascinated with guns and spent hours shooting at targets, becoming an expert marksman.

During World War I, Hart enlisted in the infantry and served in France, rising to the rank of lieutenant. After the war, he settled in Homer, Nebraska, and changed his name to Richard James Hart, partly in honor of his favorite cowboy movie star, William S. Hart. He married in Homer and, in 1919, became a federal Prohibition agent.

After making several liquor raids while wearing a holstered gun on each hip, he got the nickname "Two Gun," and it stuck. By 1924, his efforts to hide his relationship with the Chicago Capones were uncovered. The revelation caused Hart and his family to leave Homer, according to *The Brothers Capone* by Allan May.

Another account claims Hart's identity came to light in 1951 in Chicago, where a grand jury was investigating an alleged $96,679 income tax evasion charge against another brother, Ralph "Bottles" Capone. Unknown to Two Gun, his name was on the deed to property that Bottles owned, according to *Law Enforcement: The SD Experience* by Alan Clem and James Rumbolz.

Hart's Nebraska career during Prohibition took him to South Dakota in 1927 during President Calvin Coolidge's vacation in the Black Hills. Hart was one of the president's bodyguards. He was also at one time assigned to Prohibition work operating out of Timber Lake and Mobridge in South Dakota.

While working in the Timber Lake area, Hart became famous for averaging one liquor raid a day. He was the scourge of bootleggers, and as one North Dakota attorney said, "He was a good officer although his tactics sometimes were on the rough order." In 1931, Hart returned to Homer, Nebraska, and continued in Prohibition work until it ended in 1933. He then became a justice of the peace in Homer, but the pay was low and he was soon nearly destitute. He swallowed his pride and asked for help from his gangster relatives.

Two Gun Hart, or James Vincenzo Capone, died an honorable man in Homer, Nebraska, on October 1, 1952, at the age of sixty, having outlived his younger brother Scarface by five years.

A month after South Dakota erased all its Prohibition laws, a chain letter began showing up in mailboxes around the state. Recipients were instructed to "within three drinks, make five copies of this letter and deliver them and one pint to five friends who are experiencing the drough [*sic*]." The letter promised good returns. Each respondent would receive, in return for the five pints, a total of 15,625 pints, or nearly two thousand gallons, which the letter writer claimed would be "almost a year's supply," an article in the May 10, 1935 *Sioux Falls Argus Leader* said. The writer also urged everyone to send "good liquor."

CHAPTER 11

# Barnyard Ambush

Temporarily hired to make a liquor buy in Redfield, he was now at the wheel of federal Prohibition agent R.A. Labrie's roadster, with Labrie hunkered down out of sight in the cramped rear compartment. Hours before, the buyer, new to the Redfield area, had met up with forty-year-old farmer Walt Chrisman in a Redfield pool hall, where a deal was struck for fifteen gallons of home-brewed whiskey from Chrisman's farm still.

Chrisman was known as a moody, quick-tempered moonshiner who loathed lawmen. He'd already served time for making illegal booze. Four years earlier, in 1923, agents found his illegal still, and he was convicted. But he was back in the illegal liquor business almost as soon as he was released from jail. Now, Chrisman was being set up for another arrest.

With the unidentified buyer at the wheel of Labrie's roadster on May 4, 1927, the deal was about to go down at an agreed-upon spot on the dusty highway east of Redfield.

The nervous driver soon alerted Labrie of Chrisman's vehicle parked on the road ahead. Labrie's car pulled to the side of the road and stopped about fifty feet in front of the Chrisman vehicle.

"You got it?" the buyer called out as he stepped from the hidden agent's roadster. "Yeah," Chrisman replied, poking his head out the driver's side window. "I'll meet you halfway." Chrisman stepped out and opened the door to the rear seat of his car, reached in and unloaded three big, shiny five-gallon tins of booze. He then reached back in and pulled out a shotgun. The buyer, now some distance from Labrie's roadster, had no way of warning the hidden agent of this shocking, unexpected surprise.

Leaving one tin near his car, Chrisman carried one of the big tins in each hand and cradled the shotgun under one arm. He walked toward the agent's car, stopping a short distance from the vehicle. "Now," he said, putting the cans on the road and holding out his hand, "let's see your money."

The unarmed, undercover buyer walked toward Chrisman as calmly as he could under the circumstances. As he did, Agent Labrie carefully adjusted the canvas covering under which he was hiding. "Here it is," Labrie heard the buyer say. It was the previously agreed-upon response indicating the booze sale had been consummated. Labrie, still unaware Chrisman was armed, threw back the canvas cover and jumped down from the car with pistol in hand, informing Chrisman he was under arrest.

In an instant, a surprised and startled Chrisman raised his shotgun. Shooting from the hip without aiming, he fired from almost point-blank range. The blast slammed into Labrie, throwing him back. His left arm had been nearly shot away. The buyer near Chrisman, fearing he would be next, dashed back toward Labrie's car, intent on getting behind it before Chrisman could fire again. It proved to be a good move.

Sprinting down the road behind the car, the buyer was briefly visible again as he angled off to reach a field. He waited for another shotgun blast but none came. Chrisman was too focused on the downed agent. The fleeing man sprinted into the field and was quickly out of sight, heading back to Redfield to find help. Meanwhile, Chrisman fired another poorly aimed round in Labrie's direction. It missed.

Labrie, bleeding profusely, then heard the ugly sound of Chrisman racking another shell into the gun's chamber. He assumed these were his last moments on earth. Chrisman approached to administer the coup de grâce, Labrie thought. But Chrisman must have assumed the bloodied Labrie was already dead or was dying. He yelled out, "There, I've been trying to get you and now I have you." He then leveled his gun at the driver's side tire of Labrie's car and flattened it, also blasting the radiator with the close-quartered shotgun blast. Another car was approaching the scene from the east. Chrisman hurried back to his car, threw the five-gallon tins of booze into the rear seat and sped off before the car arrived. Labrie weakly signaled the wide-eyed driver of the approaching vehicle. He identified himself and asked to be driven to the Redfield Hospital.

At the hospital, the doctor treated the ugly wound as best he could. His prognosis was guarded. The shredded arm would have to be amputated at the shoulder. First, however, Labrie needed to be stabilized and then transferred to a better-equipped hospital in nearby Huron.

The horrible shooting incident at Redfield on May 4, 1927, was followed by a murderous ambush nine days later in Chrisman's barn, resulting in the death of two agents and the suicide of the shooter. The incident, which will be detailed later in this chapter, shocked the citizens of the state and seemed to mark the apex to the troubling times in the history of Prohibition in South Dakota. People were beginning to see that the movement intended to rid society of the ugliness brought on by liquor was failing in South Dakota and nationally.

Most violators of Prohibition law were amateurs, harmless, easily caught and peacefully escorted to jail. On a few occasions in South Dakota, death resulted, either for the arresting officer or a moonshiner or bootleggers. There were other South Dakota shootouts during the Prohibition years where injury occurred and even noisier incidents where no shot found its mark.

During the nearly eighteen years of Prohibition in the state, law enforcement officials were not only shot at but also pushed from speeding cars or run down by careening vehicles. They dodged thrown hammers, bottles, stones and lumps of coal. One officer even had to jump out of the path of a fish spear. That was when federal Prohibition agent William J. Ahern and Roberts County deputy sheriff John L. Minder raided a moonshine still on Big Stone Island on Big Stone Lake on July 20, 1923. They found a 40-gallon still, 150 gallons of mash and 2 gallons of finished moonshine at Sol Knight's place. The irate moonshiner attacked Deputy Minder with a barbed fish spear but was overpowered before any serious spearing could be done, according to an article in the July 21, 1933 *Sioux Falls Argus Leader*.

State deputy sheriff Ed Glau and Brown County state's attorney George Crane visited the Nick Reiter place south of Bath and found two stills and three jugs of liquor. As Glau was carrying out a big jug on each shoulder to load in his car as evidence, Reiter, in disgust, threw a hammer at Glau. Fortunately, it hit the jug and not the back of Glau's head, reported the *Sioux Falls Argus Leader* in May 1923. The contents of the container thoroughly perfumed Glau and his clothing.

Lumps of coal were the weapons of choice of a livid Aberdeen woman, Mrs. Fred Lawson. As officers carried out two jugs of booze from the pool hall owned by her husband, she reached into a coal bucket next to the pot-bellied stove and heaved a hunk of lignite at the officer. The clunker missed the agent but hit one of the jugs, breaking it. Mrs. Lawson flung another chunk as the drenched officer headed for the pool hall door. The missile missed, and the surviving evidence was saved, the January 21, 1925 *Sioux Falls Argus Leader* reported.

An unidentified federal Prohibition agent and other Deadwood area law enforcement officials raided the home of John Basso in the nearby town of Trojan. Basso was suspected of being one of the biggest suppliers of illegal booze in the Black Hills. His place had been raided many times before, but he had always managed to "clean house" before the raid, and no evidence was ever found. This time, lawmen located some fermenting mash in the man's outhouse. The agent who made the discovery paused at the outhouse door to look around inside so he knew what he was getting himself into. He noticed one of the floor planks had been sawed halfway through. Any weight on it would have caused it to break. The outdoor "necessarium" was sited over an eighty-foot shaft of the old Trojan Gold Mine. The agent's caution and good eyesight probably saved his life.

At a July dance in Stickney, Town Marshal E.S. Carter was patrolling a dark parking lot when he observed suspicious activities at one particular vehicle. He determined the young couple in the car was selling moonshine, so he moved in to make an arrest. The man in the driver's seat started the car and took off with Carter standing on the running board, holding on for dear life. As the car picked up speed and headed for the parking lot exit, the marshal decided discretion was the better part of valor and jumped off, badly bruising his arm. The couple was later arrested, according to the July 31, 1923 issue of the *Sioux Falls Argus Leader*.

Several agents from E.L. Senn's federal Prohibition office were helping fellow agents from Minnesota on a big raid at Winona, Minnesota, in August 1929. The contingent of thirty-five federal agents rode in a bus, stopping at one white mule quaffing place after another, loading up prisoners and evidence as they went along. Down the line, customers at the other parlors were alerted. Well fortified with white mule, they gathered at the east end of Winona. When the bus pulled up at their favorite evening watering hole, several of them threw stones as the agents stepped from the bus. The rock barrage stopped when the agents waded in and arrested one member of the angry, tipsy crowd, the *Argus Leader* reported.

On Canton's main street, Sheriff Charles Kundert approached a car belonging to bootleggers and brothers Edward Viken of Canton and Olaf Viken of Chicago. The Vikens saw him coming, jumped in their car and started to leave town, the *Sioux Falls Argus Leader* reported on June 27, 1922. As it sped off, Kundert leapt onto the Essex running board and got a firm grip on the door handle. When the car hit about forty miles an hour, the door handle he was holding broke off, and he fell from his perch.

A group of Canton citizens had witnessed the incident and rushed to the fallen sheriff's aid. He was not seriously injured. Meanwhile, Canton's mayor Rowe and county judge Herbert Rudolph saw it all, too. They confiscated a nearby car and took off after the booze runners. Other cars joined the chase. Unfortunately for the bootleggers, a bearing in their Essex burned out, and the car stalled a few miles from Canton on the King of Trails Highway. The brothers dumped out all the liquor in their vehicle but forgot three one-gallon cans in the trunk and then fled into a nearby field. But with all the help the sheriff had by then, they were soon apprehended five miles north of town.

There was no arrest on a Kimball farm, but one of its big pigs didn't fare too well. The young farmer was operating an illicit still on his farm in 1920 when a reporter for the *Sioux Falls Argus Leader*, on the promise of anonymity, interviewed him. He told the reporter if any "blankety-blank dry agent" ever came to close down his still, "I'd have no mercy." Then, the cocky young braggart raised his pistol and sighted in on a rusty pail partially buried in the hog yard muck. His shot missed the pail, but a big Hampshire hog nosing in the ooze nearby dropped dead.

Turner County sheriff Olaf Karp approached two men as they arrived in Marion by car about 11:00 p.m. on a cold January Monday night in 1920 and eased into a parking space on Main Street. Sheriff Karp found two suitcases in the car, each packed with bottles of whiskey. As the two men struggled with the sheriff to prevent him from removing the suitcases from the car, one of them, John Heintz, pulled out his revolver and started shooting at Sheriff Karp, who was about fifteen feet away. The sheriff drew his gun but had difficulty releasing the pistol's safety mechanism. He was hit twice, in his right leg and his right forearm.

Heintz and John Blumhardt, both of Marion, started to make their getaway, but the sheriff finally got his gun working. Despite his painful wounds, he fired as the two men drove away, causing them to stop and surrender. Sheriff Karp had just returned home unscathed from service in Europe in World War I. His homeland baptism of fire and combat wounds happened just two days after the town board had appointed him to the job.

Unknown to Sioux Falls bootlegger Clarence Kendall and a companion, who were on a liquor-smuggling mission in October 1920, they were headed straight for a roadblock near Westhope, North Dakota. They stopped at the checkpoint, and as officers approached the Kendall car, the two South

Dakota men opened fire. In the mêlée, Kendall was killed, but his partner survived and was arrested for transporting liquor.

A few days before Halloween in 1927, officers in Belle Fourche were alerted by telephone of two Wyoming bootleggers headed their way from across the border. The two were later spotted in Belle Fourche and ordered to halt but refused. A running gun battle through the town ensued. One of the bootleggers, a man later identified as "Chausse," the driver, was hit and killed instantly. The car swerved and smashed into a sturdy support on the town's Red Water Bridge. During this noisy ruckus, the second man, William Francisco, was also shot in the knee. He was arrested at the crash scene and taken to the hospital for treatment of his minor wound. At the hospital, doctors discovered he had also suffered serious internal injuries in the car crash. But it was too late. He died of those injuries within minutes, according to the *Sioux Falls Argus Leader*'s October 27, 1924 edition.

In the early evening of July 12, 1928, Hand County sheriff A.H. Abbott observed someone hiding booze at a secluded drop point about a mile west of the Pleasant Valley Dance Hall, which was twenty-three miles southwest of Miller. The sheriff hid out near the liquor "plant" to await retrieval and make an arrest. Soon, a car carrying four young men stopped at the drop site, and James Heenan, seventeen, of Highmore, jumped out and ran to the location of the planted bottle, retrieving it.

Sheriff Abbott stood up and ordered him to stop, but the boy panicked. As he sprinted back toward the idling car, the sheriff drew his revolver, and it accidentally discharged, the sheriff later claimed. The bullet entered the upper part of the young man's right arm, severing the artery. Heenan's companions sped away without him. The sheriff applied a tourniquet to the boy's arm and drove him to the Miller hospital, the *Sioux Falls Argus Leader* of July 10, 1928, reported.

The boy was in critical condition for a time but eventually recuperated. Meanwhile, his parents filed charges against Sheriff Abbott. A circuit court trial was held in October 1928. After less than two hours' deliberation, the jury returned a verdict of not guilty

In Brookings County, state deputy sheriff Lon Minier, son of state sheriff Fred Minier, and deputy Paul Mershon, a feisty thirty-year-old former amateur boxer, staunch Democrat and close Brookings friend of State Sheriff Minier, got word of the antics of a known Flandreau bootlegger, Ira Dawson, who would be making his northern delivery rounds on the night of May 30, 1928. They knew Dawson's trip would take him first to Elkton and then through White in northeast Brookings County.

Earlier that year, the Moody County sheriff in Flandreau had written Governor William J. Bulow telling of Dawson's threats and bullying. Dawson had repeatedly publicly belittled the sheriff, had embarrassed him in front of friends by taking away his pistol and had also beaten a Flandreau policeman, according to an unpublished manuscript titled "A Long Lifespan in but a Fleeting Moment in Time" by Lon Minier.

Later in life, Deputy Minier wrote about Dawson in his memoirs:

> *Paul Mershon and I went to Flandreau and consulted with the sheriff. The bad actor was the same fellow Paul and I had arrested some months previously. He had gotten into the big time bootlegging, reportedly connected with Al Capone. No one locally wanted to prefer charges against the bad actor.*
>
> *Paul and I decided we would take our time in investigating his conduct and we were soon to learn he made two major trips weekly from Flandreau, one heading south and the other heading north on his runs delivering alcohol in a new Pontiac car he had acquired. Then we learned he had just made a trip south so we went north the next day and parked my car in a dark little park at the main intersection of White, parking late at night.*
>
> *About 2 a.m. we saw the lights of a car approaching from the south. We waited until it passed under the streetlight and were able to determine it was our man with a lady companion. We waited a minute before going in pursuit as we wanted to take him on the open road north of town. To our surprise, he suddenly turned into a side street and both occupants had jumped out of the car and gone into a house.*
>
> *I told Paul to take control of the Pontiac and I started up the steps on the porch when our man came out with a gun in his hand and fired one shot at my head; so close I thought I felt a pain in my shoulder, thinking I had been hit. Both Paul and I fired almost simultaneously, striking him in the stomach. He fell to the porch. We picked him up and placed him in my car, then routed out neighbors to drive his car to Brookings. Paul and I rushed him to a doctor in Brookings. He knew he was dying and said, "I should have moved from South Dakota after you fellows arrested me before." It was too late.*

A later search of Dawson's car revealed thirty-one gallons and one pint of alcohol. The shooting happened in the front yard of a family named Montgomery. The woman with Dawson was identified as Ethel Montgomery, daughter of the home's owners. An inquest determined Dawson, who was married and the father of two, had been hit in the stomach by a slug from

Minier's .45-caliber pistol and by a deadly pellet spray from Mershon's .410 shotgun/pistol. Before he died, Dawson denied to Mershon and Minier that he had fired the first shot. The Montgomery girl who was with Dawson swore she had heard only the two shots from Minier and Mershon, but a neighbor, J.D. Allison, testified he had heard three shots. This was verified at a coroner's inquest.

Later investigation revealed that when the two deputies had arrested Dawson earlier, in June 1927, Dawson swore to them he would never again be taken alive.

Ironically, another place also named White would be the site a few months later of a second dangerous altercation involving the same two Brookings-based agents. While policing the White Palace Dance Hall ten miles east of Pierre on October 1, 1928, an angry, drunken mob descended on the two deputies, and the confrontation almost reached a flash point. Mershon and Minier had seized four pints of booze and a .45-caliber gun from patrons only minutes before. The *Sioux Falls Argus Leader* of October 1, 1928, reported that in recounting the incident the next day before the Hughes County commissioners, Minier told them that if he "had attempted to make any arrests Friday night in the drunken condition of that crowd that was ready to mob us, we could not have done so without a shooting scrape. Rather than risk the killing of several persons as might have been the case had we had to shoot our way out, we turned over [to the crowd] half the liquor and gun."

Arthur Huebner of Pierre was found guilty of assaulting Deputy Minier as he and Mershon retreated from the White Palace Dance Hall. He was fined forty-five dollars and court costs. During his trial, witnesses testified that the angry crowd at the dance hall followed Minier and Mershon as they retreated to their vehicle. Near the deputy's car, Huebner attacked Minier and grabbed his vest, tearing it, as the deputy was about to get into the vehicle and drive away. A brief scuffle between the two men ensued until calmer, more sober heads in the crowd grabbed Huebner and hustled him away.

A week after the incident, young Minier decided he had his fill of law enforcement and announced his resignation. He said he intended to move his family from Fort Pierre to Watertown to work in an automobile supply company. He later purchased the Gamble Store in Rapid City that he operated for many years before moving to Minneapolis.

Mershon, a veteran of World War I, remained with the state sheriff's office until 1931. After working in several Brookings County and federal departments, he came home to farm on the southwest outskirts of

Brookings until 1958. For a time in the 1950s, he served as chairman of the Brookings County Democratic Party.

The most violent incident of the Prohibition years in South Dakota began with the shotgun injury to Agent Labrie near Redfield in May 1927. This precipitated an even more horrific encounter nine days later.

After the Labrie encounter on the Spink County road in 1927, the shooter, Chrisman, evaded search parties for more than a week. Officials were later unable to piece together his whereabouts during that time, but they believed he was hiding on his own property, perhaps in the fields and buildings he knew so well.

Law enforcement officers had always been wary of Chrisman, fearing he might commit some desperate act. C.J. Rufer of Sioux Falls, former federal Prohibition officer, told of several raids on the Chrisman farm. He said Chrisman took up the manufacturing and selling of liquor as a sideline, and he slowly got deeper and deeper into the illegal enterprise, according to the May 5, 1927 *Redfield Press*. Everyone knew Chrisman was high-strung and could be dangerous. Whenever officers raided his place, they were always on the alert and well prepared, keeping their guns out of sight but at the ready.

Rufer believed a jail sentence in Aberdeen and the death of Chrisman's young son had set him temporarily on a straight and narrow path. But his illegal activities soon caught the attention of federal officers again. Rufer remembered one particular visit to the Chrisman farm. After searching everywhere for illegal contraband that day, they finally found alcohol hidden in postholes, the *Sioux Falls Argus Leader* reported on May 13, 1927. On another raid, after nearly abandoning the search for Chrisman's still that officers were sure existed somewhere on the farm, they decided to search every inch of the place once more. One agent finally noticed a loose board on a stair step in Chrisman's house. Removing the board, they found an elaborate setup for distilling alcohol, including a well-designed exhaust system preventing fumes from wafting into the home.

Chrisman's early brushes with the law had finally led to the shooting near Redfield of Prohibition agent Labrie, and now he was on the loose.

On May 12, 1927, officers got a break with information that Chrisman had been seen at his home seven miles east of Redfield. When officers spoke with Chrisman's wife early that day about the sighting, they learned Chrisman had never been far from his home. In fact, his wife said he was expected to return that night, if he wasn't already somewhere on the premises. Based on Mrs. Chrisman's information, a stakeout was planned. Officers decided that rather than search for the armed man, they would wait until he made a move from his hiding place, perhaps entering his home for food, water or other supplies, and then move in. By now Chrisman had been on the run for nearly nine days since gunning down Labrie.

The stakeout was planned by Sheriff Bradley. He knew Chrisman and was familiar with the Chrisman farm. He decided he would lead a contingent of four men on the stakeout, with two men composing two stakeout teams.

Because they had been tested under fire, both in the world war and as lawmen, and because they also knew Chrisman by sight, having arrested him four years earlier, Sheriff Bradley selected federal Prohibition agent Charles Bintliff of Mitchell and state deputy sheriff Charles Halpin of Aberdeen as one team. Sheriff Bradley would work with John Uhre, an agent from the state sheriff's office in Rapid City whom he knew well, on the second team.

By pairing off as they did, the officers would know the sight of two men together on the dark night would be the other stakeout crew. Likewise, if a single man was encountered, it would probably be Chrisman. The four men drove to near the Chrisman place, arriving at about 11:00 p.m. on that fateful Friday the thirteenth. They quietly exited the sheriff's car and crept to preassigned locations that provided clear views of the farm home and its outbuildings. In doing so, they were mindful of the nearby home across the road from the Chrisman farm, where Mrs. Chrisman's mother and brother lived. The agents were under orders to not go in or near any farm buildings on either place. They would remain on watch until morning, when other officers arrived to relieve them should the sheriff decide to continue the watch.

Bintliff and Halpin took up surveillance at about 11:30 p.m. behind a small pile of dry thistles trapped in the fence corner about one hundred yards from the farm's barn. At some point during the next two hours, the two men, possibly to get out of the late-night chill, left their fence line outpost and entered the Chrisman barn. Their boss, E.L. Senn, who knew the two men well, later surmised they did so "to better perform the duty to which they had been assigned, guarding approaches to the house." Whatever reason, it proved fatal, because unknown to them, Chrisman was in the same barn, his loaded 16-gauge shotgun at his side.

He may have been in the barn all along, or maybe he crept into the building after an earlier police visit to the farm when lawmen, as a precaution, took Chrisman's brother, Dave, into custody. Those lawmen and Chrisman's brother had left the farm at about 10:30 p.m., about a half hour before the stakeout was set up. Chrisman may have entered the barn during the sliver of time between when those officers departed the place with Dave Chrisman and the arrival of the stakeout teams.

"Evidently Chrisman was already in the barn when Bintliff and Halpin arrived," Senn later guessed. This had been intimated by Chrisman's wife, Senn said. She admitted she'd seen him after the arresting officers left with Dave Chrisman. At that time, she said she pleaded with her husband to surrender. She told him she had told officers of his presence on the farm the night before. According to the May 17, 1927 *Sioux Falls Argus Leader*, Mrs. Chrisman said her husband then said to her: "So you have poached on me. Have you? You'd better go in the house or you may not live long."

Shortly after the two lawmen on stakeout entered the barn, Chrisman must have silently extricated himself from his hiding place and crept up on the unsuspecting agents. A small opening in an oat bin was the aperture through which Chrisman slowly and silently leveled his shotgun at Halpin, who was standing near the barn doorway looking out, giving Chrisman an easy, silhouetted target. With a shotgun from such close range, careful aim was hardly necessary. Without warning, Chrisman fired, and the scattershot hit Halpin full on in the chest above the heart. The blast nearly tore him in two. He died instantly. Immediately after the shot, Chrisman racked another shell into the chamber.

Agent Bintliff was on the other side of the barn when he heard the shot and the reload. In reconstructing the scene, Senn speculated Bintliff apparently ran out a side door and then dashed east around the barn. Sheriff Bradley remembered hearing Bintliff call "halt," and this was followed by two more shotgun blasts. Chrisman, after shooting Halpin, apparently ran through the barn and fired twice out a small barn side door as Bintliff ran by. Bintliff was hit in the stomach. He managed to call out, staggered about fifty feet and collapsed and died within minutes. The *Redfield Press* described the killings in its May 19, 1927 issue: "The cruel, gaping wounds both Halpin and Bintliff received by the gun in the hands of Chrisman bore striking evidence the officers could not have been but a few feet from him when shot."

At the sound of Chrisman's gunshots, Sheriff Bradley and Uhre rushed to the barn. As they did so, they saw a fleeting, shadowy figure running north across a plowed field, but they were unsure who it was so withheld fire. Then they noticed Halpin's body by the barn door. The fleeing figure was then beyond range, but they emptied their revolvers anyway, hoping for a lucky hit or possibly convincing Chrisman to give up. They followed Chrisman a short distance before returning to help the two downed agents. From the direction of the chase, officers believed Chrisman was headed for the James River and the heavily timbered bottomland a mile or so from the scene.

Sheriff Bradley's car was not equipped with a two-way radio, so he drove about a mile from the Chrisman farm and used a farmer's telephone to call deputy sheriff Grant Haggerty in Redfield. The town's riot call was sounded at about 2:00 a.m. Redfield citizens responded and were organized into search teams. Within hours, the countryside was swarming with armed men in search of the killer.

Law officers throughout the state were also alerted. As more men arrived, the massive search in the area was expanded. Officials from the state and federal Prohibition offices hurried to Redfield as soon as they were alerted. Helping coordinate the four-hundred-man search effort were district Prohibition administrator Glen A. Brunson; his assistant, J.C. Palmer of Sioux City, Iowa; and South Dakota federal Prohibition director E.L. Senn. Also involved were United States marshal Chet Leedom; United States district attorney Olaf Eidem and his assistant, Frank McCormick; state sheriff's department personnel; and local law enforcement officials.

At first light, for the first time for such an occasion, an airplane was flown to the area to aid in the search. Bloodhounds were arranged for but did not arrive in time to help. Even United States senator Peter Norbeck of Redfield, home from Washington, answered the call. His assignment was to help other men guarding a key bridge near Redfield in the event the assailant attempted to drive from the area, according to an account in the May 13, 1927 issue of the *Sioux Falls Argus Leader*. Within hours, the Spink County commissioners offered a $250 reward for information leading to fugitive Chrisman's capture, and Senn's federal office soon added to the reward amount.

No trace of Chrisman was found. The next day, officers got a break when two farmers sought out county sheriff Bradley. They asked if the sheriff would take Chrisman if he surrendered and how that would come about. One of the farmers, David Jones, said Chrisman had stopped at his farm about 4:00 a.m. on Saturday after he had shot the lawmen, and they talked about Chrisman surrendering. A distraught Chrisman agreed to do so. Jones and the other farmer set out to find the sheriff and inquire about surrender conditions, and Chrisman left to hide in a nearby straw stack on Jones's farm. It was agreed that when Jones returned from his conference with the sheriff, he would ride out to the straw stack on a white horse so Chrisman would know who was approaching.

Sheriff Bradley told the farmers he would accept the fugitive if he was disarmed and handcuffed with his hands over his head. Sheriff Bradley gave the men his pair of cuffs, and they left to get Chrisman and bring him back.

Jones got back to his farm about noon on May 13. He bridled his white horse and rode toward the straw stack, calling out to Chrisman as he neared. There was no response. He soon discovered why. Chrisman had turned his shotgun on himself.

Police found his bloody body partly buried in the straw. He'd removed a shoe and sock from one foot and laid back on the straw, using the shoe and the sock as a small pillow to raise his head slightly. He'd placed the muzzle of the gun to his forehead and pulled the trigger with his toe, the *Redfield Press* reported in its May 19, 1927 issue.

The worst incident of the eighteen years of Prohibition in South Dakota was over. Halpin and Bintliff were 2 of 55 federal Prohibition agents nationally who had been killed while performing their Prohibition duties up to that time. Also killed by law enforcement personnel nationally during the Prohibition years 1920 to 1929 were 125 criminals.

Deputy State Sheriff Halpin, who was twenty-nine, attended Notre Dame University and played on the Irish football team after graduating from high school at Germantown, Pennsylvania, in 1914. He joined the army in 1917 as a private in Company H of the 109th Infantry Regiment and spent two and a half years in the army, including service overseas from May to October 1918. He was wounded in France and twice cited for bravery, receiving the Distinguished Service Cross for gallantry. After the war, he joined America's Secret Service and was assigned to investigate drug smuggling along the California coast. Halpin was the father of two boys. Both his widow and his mother were invalids. His mother lived in Turton, South Dakota, and his wife in Aberdeen, where he had been stationed as a state deputy sheriff since being hired four months before his death. He played baseball for two seasons for the town team at Groton east of Aberdeen.

The other victim, federal agent Charles Bintliff, thirty, was the senior federal agent in the state, having started with the unit soon after Prohibition was enacted in early 1920. He and his wife lived in Mitchell. He was a student at Dakota Wesleyan University when the world war broke out and enlisted as a marine officer. Square-jawed, tall and muscular, with close-cropped hair, he looked every bit the tough marine.

Labrie, the agent who lost his left arm from Chrisman's shotgun blast at close range on May 4, recovered and remained with the federal Prohibition office in Huron. He had come to South Dakota with his parents when he was a boy, and the family homesteaded in Spink County in 1881. As a federal Prohibition agent, he was promoted in 1924 as chief of field forces for the department. Before joining the federal unit, Labrie had served two terms in the South Dakota House of Representatives in 1913 and 1915. He also served in the South Dakota Senate in 1917 and 1919, having been elected to the 1919 term while still serving with the Red Cross in France after being rejected by the army. He served six months with the Red Cross in Europe.

Labrie attended Redfield College, tried farming and then had a hardware and implement business in Doland, selling out when he went into the Red Cross service. Before joining the federal unit, he worked for a time as an insurance agent.

The loss of his arm did not hinder his career with the federal service. After federal Prohibition and his tenure with the Prohibition unit ended after twelve years of service, he became an inspector with the Bureau of Industrial Alcohol. The *Sioux Falls Argus Leader* reported his promotion in June 1935 from his South Dakota federal post to a similar assignment in St. Paul, Minnesota.

Chapter 12

# Drys Get Dunked

In 1927, after seven long years, a chink appeared in Prohibition's once impervious armor. The drys and the damps (those who were barely dry or barely wet) were asking questions. They wondered if Prohibition was spawning disrespect for the law and infringements on individual choices, rights and liberties. In South Dakota, the horrific Redfield ambush and the murder of two agents jarred citizens to the core and helped move the issue along. The bloody tragedy emboldened a few citizens to publicly suggest alternatives to the absolute bone-dry ban on liquor the legislature had bound up so tightly in South Dakota's law book more than a decade earlier.

In the 1927 legislature, something occurred that hadn't happened in more than ten years. A bill to slightly dampen the state's bone-dry edict was introduced by Senator Theodore J.P. Giedt. It proposed allowing beverages to contain not more than 1.5 percent alcohol. Giedt felt the bone-dry law made enforcement difficult. For one, it conflicted with federal Prohibition law, which allowed .05 percent alcohol in beverages.

That 1927 effort failed. But it was at least a slight breakthrough and must have provided a psychological shot in the arm for those who believed Prohibition represented a wrong-headed, unworkable ideology.

In the 1928 legislative session, Senator Giedt introduced a bill to bring the state's Prohibition laws into conformity with federal laws. Among other conditions, his bill would do away with "unnecessary red tape" required to obtain alcoholic beverages for religious, medicinal and scientific purposes. Giedt also introduced two resolutions, one calling for a referendum vote on the Eighteenth Amendment and another memorializing Congress to call a constitutional convention to propose Prohibition amendments.

Senator Giedt, a wet leader in the legislature, was a former member of the South Dakota House of Representatives, a lawyer, Eureka businessman and once a major in the South Dakota National Guard. He was also a lone voice in South Dakota's anti-Prohibition wilderness. The adventuresome Russian-born senator from the state's wheat capital displayed even more courage and conviction during his campaign for the 1931 legislative session. He announced his intention to again introduce laws and resolutions to bring state liquor laws he described as "too drastic" into conformity with federal temperance edicts. During the 1930 campaign for a 1931 legislative seat, most candidates for the legislature and for party leadership positions declined to take a stand on the volatile issue, other than taking the easy way out, favoring "strict law enforcement."

Senator Giedt considered the state's bone-dry law too inflexible. "The people of the state have not respected it," he said. Giedt didn't favor a return to the saloon system, however. "I would be the last to vote in favor of the old liquor traffic, yet I can't shut my eyes to existing conditions and the trend of public thought, which is changing rapidly to the idea of modification along lines that will preserve the good features of the end sought, and eliminate those parts which the public refuses to observe or respect."

Coincidentally, Giedt's bill and his two resolutions were introduced on the same day the Senate's Committee on Temperance unveiled two bills to strengthen the state's dry laws, according to the February 11, 1931 *Sioux Falls Argus Leader*. As expected, the powerful South Dakota Anti-Saloon League, the WCTU and other dry groups were as vocal in opposition to Giedt's approach as they were supportive of the temperance committee proposals.

Giedt's idea faced a difficult hurdle at the Committee on Temperance hearing. Its chairman was a minister, staid Senator J.S. Harkness of Mitchell, who was a staunch dry advocate. Within a week of Giedt's proposal arriving on the committee's table, it was given the expected unfavorable report by Chairman Harkness and his committee, and it suffered an expeditious demise, soundly buried without ceremony, thirty-eight to six. A disappointed Giedt told his fellow senators, "The country is dry in theory but wet in fact."

The argument accusing his fellow lawmakers of being wet but voting dry was often a part of Prohibition debates. During a House session in Pierre on February 19, 1925, when the body was debating Senate Bill 20, making a second violation of a liquor offense a felony, with confiscation of vehicles and penitentiary time as punishment, lawmakers enjoyed a moment of levity.

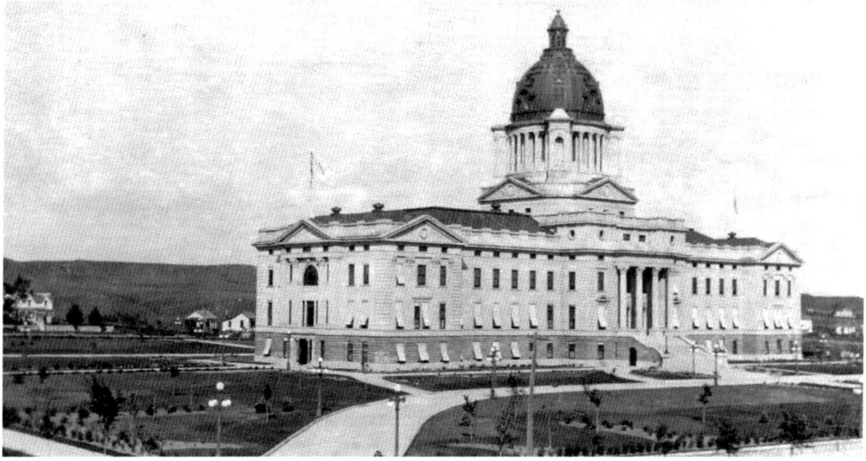

In 1910, this was how South Dakota's capitol in Pierre appeared. It would be the scene in the 1920s and early 1930s of bitter battles in efforts to repeal the state's 1917 bone-dry Prohibition law. *Author's collection.*

Sioux Falls representative William H. Lyon stood up to ask all members of the body who had never violated a Prohibition law to raise their hands. Nearly every member responded, and some mockingly raised both hands. "No, I want people that will tell the truth," Lyon said. "You don't take me seriously. But of course I realize I might as well be talking to herd of buffalo."

G.C. Blum of Codington County chided the bill's author, Representative Lyon, suggesting confiscation and time in the pen were light penalties. With tongue in check, he offered to amend the bill to allow either hanging or shooting at sunrise for offenders. W.W. Wumkes of Lennox said he supported Lyon's bill because he wanted to fill the books with "hypocritical stuff" that would eventually result in repeal of Prohibition. Despite the smiling exchanges, the bill passed sixty-four to thirty-three, the *Argus Leader* reported on February 19, 1925.

With the thumbs-down votes on those early forays advanced by wet candidates who perhaps realized their proposals were doomed but might at least kick-start some dialogue on Prohibition, it remained for the first efforts toward state repeal to begin at the national level. Congressional actions would finally help nudge South Dakota Prohibition repeal along. People were beginning to see that the paradox of national Prohibition was creating more problems than solutions. More intolerance of the law was encouraging more indulgence. There were also concerns with two more pressing and important national challenges: the Great Depression and the Dust Bowl. Newly elected president Franklin D. Roosevelt did not relish being encumbered with the very divisive and contentious issue of Prohibition.

The time for repeal was near because more citizens were beginning to realize Prohibition simply wasn't working. Barring more severe penalties, such as those in Representative Blum's facetious remark of hangings and firing squads for violators, total temperance had no chance of success. Alcohol, when difficult to obtain, seemed a magnet tempting otherwise law-abiding citizens to break the laws, not only in regard to access to liquor but on other fronts as well. A criminal element was gaining the upper hand.

National Prohibition arrived just as millions of America's young men and women were returning from war in Europe, battle tested, older and wiser. Prohibition stifled the jobs and opportunities many thought would be waiting for them, offering instead tempting work and opportunities in the illegal trade of whiskey, gambling and crime. Often, after a successful apprenticeship in bootlegging, young men migrated to other deleterious pursuits and temptations such as bank robbery and other exciting and nefarious endeavors attractive to those looking to move up in the criminal world with money in their pockets. Huge profits for gangsters and mobsters increased even more because no taxes were paid on the illegal profits from booze. Society was bereft not only of the jobs a legal liquor trade would provide but also of the fees and taxes legal liquor entrepreneurs would pay.

Repeal of Prohibition would most surely reduce crime, clear out prisons and help in rebuilding the country, not tear it down. Americans were beginning to realize people could be trusted to imbibe in moderation. Alcohol did not necessarily lead to moral corruption or inspire undesirable behavior. The nation was beginning to realize that morality could not be legislated.

The sense of self-righteousness, and a public "holier than thou" attitude so many in the temperance movement espoused, was beginning to ruffle wet supporters' feathers, and it did not sit well with those occupying the middle ground, either. The superintendent of the state's powerful Anti-Saloon League, H.E. Dawes of Mitchell, offered an example of this assumed righteousness: "More and more, the public opinion is being brought to bear. The man who had stocks of liquor in pre-prohibition days and is storing them, or the man who is purchasing now for his consumption and entertainment of others, is rightfully considered not at all a good citizen."

In 1930, a study of congressional attitudes by the American Federation of Labor's National Committee for Modification of the Volstead Act concluded only seventeen die-hard Prohibitionists were serving in the United States Senate, and there were just forty-three truly dry members in the House of

Representatives. However, protecting their jobs kept many congressional wet proponents in the dry column when voting. A joke in Congress was about fellow members planning pro-temperance speeches on the House and Senate floors fortifying their preparations with an ample shot of whiskey before stepping out on the floor and making their comments.

That same year, a national poll by *Literary Digest* magazine concluded that 40 percent of respondents favored repeal of the Volstead Act. Nearly 30 percent wanted a modification of the Prohibition laws. The remaining 31 percent thought strict enforcement of what was already on the books would correct the act's shortcoming. The survey found that teachers were among America's driest citizens and lawyers as a group one of America's wettest, the *Argus Leader* reported on May 1, 1930.

South Dakotans responding to the poll were much less enamored with Prohibition's repeal. Of the 23,336 responding, only 6,680 favored repeal. The largest number of South Dakotans, 9,155, wanted the law to remain as it was, with the caveat that it be more rigorously enforced. South Dakotans who thought liquor laws should be modified nationally numbered 7,501.

By 1932, with Roosevelt carrying the Democratic Happy-Days-Are-Here-Again standard and the befuddled Republican president, Herbert Hoover, tone deaf to the Great Depression cries for help, the Democratic Party endorsed Prohibition's repeal, and the landslide election victory by Roosevelt emboldened quick congressional action. On February 20, 1933, by more than a two-thirds vote, Congress passed a resolution calling for a referendum in every state to consider repealing the Eighteenth Amendment, although that repeal would not prohibit the transportation of intoxicating beverages into any state where it would be in violation of the state's laws. So even if the national law disappeared, South Dakota's Prohibition laws remained alive and well.

Congress quickly followed its February 20 action with another stunning vote on March 13, 1933. Lawmakers decided to immediately legalize 3.2 percent beer in order to provide tax revenue and jobs as quickly as possible. The legalization of low-point beer was welcomed by many in South Dakota even though it conflicted with the state's bone-dry law. Federal legalization of beer at 3.2 percent alcohol by weight did, however, serve as a catalyst to help nudge the repeal wheels out of the South Dakota gumbo created in 1916.

With beer on its way in many states, citizens also watched as state after state voted for or against the Twenty-first Amendment that would cancel out the Eighteenth Amendment and legalize hard liquor. It was a slow process, unlike the accelerated federal decision to legalize beer. Ratification to make hard liquor legal required state conventions rather than votes by legislatures.

During 1933, thirty-eight states held delegate elections to provide a direct expression of popular opinion. In states having delegate elections, 73 percent of the twenty-one million voters cast ballots for candidates who favored an end to Prohibition. Only South Carolina voters rejected repeal. Victory came as an early Christmas gift for wets on December 5, 1933, when Pennsylvania, Ohio and, finally, Utah, voted for repeal candidates. National Prohibition, which many felt had been a futile policy from the beginning, came to an end. The Twenty-first Amendment was the first and only one ever to repeal another.

With national passage of the amendment, and with the legalization of 3.2 percent beer nationally, South Dakota and its political parties found themselves stranded on a lonely, bone-dry island. North Dakota voters had repealed their state's Prohibition clause in 1932. Nebraska, Minnesota and Iowa had ditched the concept, too. So South Dakota politicians faced a huge task dealing with the state's law, now in conflict with neighboring states and national laws.

On February 3, 1933, Marshall County's state senator, Otto L. Kaas of Britton, picked up the cudgel Senator Giedt had brandished two years earlier. Kaas introduced a resolution calling for a statewide vote in the 1934 general election on repeal of the state constitution's Prohibition amendment.

A judiciary committee hearing on the proposal was held, and wets and drys argued their cases. Speaking against the Kaas resolution, labeling it as "un-American," were the expected voices of dry advocates, the WTCU, the Anti-Saloon League and practically every church group in the state. Flora Mitchell of Brookings, the state WCTU president, presented a petition at the Pierre hearing. Mitchell represented the WCTU at every regular and special session of the legislature from 1917 to 1939, leading the organization for twenty-four years. The petition she presented was signed by more than ten thousand South Dakota members who were against repeal. Among others testifying was Charles E. Wilcox of Huron, superintendent of the Huron-Pierre District of the Methodist Episcopal Church, who said Methodists wanted a dry state.

Only Senator Kaas argued for a repeal vote, saying the only opposition he had encountered was from a bootlegger in his area who berated him for trying to put him out of business. Late in the day, the committee sent the resolution out for a full vote, but with an attached "without recommendation," according to the February 3, 1933 *Sioux Falls Argus Leader*.

A few days after the Kaas resolution was sent out for a vote, Gladys Pyle of Huron, who had been an unsuccessful candidate for governor on the Republican ticket in 1930 and in 1938 would be appointed to fill the term of deceased United States senator Peter Norbeck, wrote a commentary for the *Sioux Falls Argus Leader*. Pyle's father, incidentally, was a Huron lawyer who served as South Dakota's attorney general from 1899 to 1902, when he died in office, the first state constitutional officer to do so. He was elected attorney general while serving as president of the state Anti-Saloon League, according to *Law Enforcement: The SD Experiment* by Alan Clem and James Rambolz.

Ms. Pyle reviewed the approaching South Dakota vote on the Kaas bill in her role as a special correspondent for the newspaper. Because her comments capture the tenor of those tumultuous times and the essence of the impending historic vote, the February 6, 1933 article is reprinted:

> *Today the Senate will decide whether they will submit to the voters of South Dakota the question of repeal of the 24th amendment, namely the prohibition amendment, which was written into the fundamental law of the state by the voters at the 1916 general election, more than two years previous to the ratification of the federal prohibition amendment by the 1918 special session of the Legislature.*
>
> *It is difficult to find any subject upon which legislators or people at large have stronger feelings than upon this question that will be discussed with the same strong convictions for and against which were evident in the sessions of twenty years ago when submission was discussed heatedly at each biennial session.*
>
> *The argument has frequently been advanced during the past decade that there is much more liquor consumed in this country under prohibition than during the years previous. Figures are advanced showing the increased consumption of intoxicants over that under the old order of things. Figures of course are not available since the business is an illicit one and accuracy cannot be guaranteed. However, the opponents of prohibition have not hesitated to use the statement.*
>
> *Within the past two months the* Chicago Journal of Commerce, *an outspoken opponent of prohibition, carried a leading article under the headline, "Beer Shortage Indicated If Legalization Is Quick." The article at some length goes into the entire detail of the tremendous shortage which would face the country and in speaking of the possible high price of the beverage incident to this shortage concludes "as the opinion of a man closely*

*connected with the industry this will not be the case as existing brewers will endeavor to encourage consumption through moderate prices."*

*Another argument advanced during the discussion regarding the committee reference of the joint senate resolution under the terms of which the South Dakota prohibition law would be referred to the people for reenactment or repeal was that this should be referred to the voters because of the large number of service men who were in France and unable to vote when the question was previously determined.*

*It should be borne in mind that South Dakota passed her state prohibition amendment several years before the United States entered the World War. It should also be borne in mind that while many men were in the army in France when federal prohibition was ratified, this was not done by the voters of the state but by the legislature in special session. Had the question been determined by popular vote more than half of the soldiers were too young to vote. It was ratified by the legislature so the soldiers could not have voted thereon had they been at home.*

*In determining one's position regarding prohibition it is also well to know that the organization for prohibition repeal has been principally financed by half a hundred millionaires who are outspoken in their position as wishing beer, so there will be a commodity to tax to relive them of the income taxes they now pay. It is questionable wisdom to shift the burden of the liquor traffic onto the laboring man to relieve the income tax burden of the wealthy.*

*South Dakota will probably vote upon the prohibition amendment at the November election of 1934. It is predicted that she will retain her law in its present form.*

In addition to the Kaas repeal bill in the Senate, the House also had before it a measure to repeal state laws governing the dispensing of intoxicating liquor by South Dakota druggists and doctors. It was defeated by eight votes. On February 8, 1933, however, in a historic, dumbfounding surprise, the state senate voted twenty-five to sixteen in favor of the Kaas bill calling for a state referendum on the question of repeal of the state's liquor amendment. It marked the first successful official move to tamper with the Prohibition machinery in South Dakota since the state became bone-dry on July 1, 1917.

As the Kaas bill made its way to the House of Representatives, two members of that body came up with a creative suggestion, albeit impractical at the time. They proposed the nation's former private liquor distilleries be reactivated to make alcohol under federal supervision and require the alcohol produced be diluted into all gasoline intended for internal combustion engines. Representatives W.E. Bartholow of Spencer and Robert E. Coyne of Ethan envisioned this use of alcohol as a fuel additive as a market for the state's and the nation's surplus of corn, wheat and rice, according to the February 10, 1933 issue of the *Sioux Falls Argus Leader*. The making of alcohol then was done in the same way it is today in the nation's giant ethanol plants except on a much smaller scale. The resulting product was called "ethyl" alcohol in the 1930s, when newspapers were first reporting the possibility of corn being distilled to fuel motor vehicles. Prohibition undoubtedly stifled the development of ethanol research in this country.

The ethyl idea didn't catch on, and neither did the South Dakota House of Representatives approve the Kaas bill for repeal. It fell by the wayside, sixty-eight against to thirty-three in favor. Trying once more, the South Dakota House of Representatives, on February 25, 1933, five days after the federal mandate making 3.2 percent beer a legal beverage, approved House Bill 197, defining intoxicating liquors in the state as containing not more than 3.2 percent of alcohol. This, of course, conflicted with the state constitution's mandate of 0 percentage of alcohol in beverages. So if passed, House Bill 197 would surely face a court test. The South Dakota Senate saved it a court date, defeating the beer bill by three votes.

The score at the end of the 1933 legislative session wasn't encouraging to South Dakota's wets. Because the legislature met every other year, it appeared it would be at least two years before any change could again be launched into the legislative gristmill. Some still held out hope that something could be done to at least legalize beer. The call for a special session to consider the question simmered but never boiled over. By interesting happenstance, one bill that passed the 1933 session, the controversial gross income tax bill, would have a role in what was to follow in the quest to legalize beer.

Governor Tom Berry was adamant that he would not consider calling legislators back for another vote on a beer bill. South Dakota lieutenant governor H.A. Ustrud of Huron, however, favored holding a special session to consider "legalization of beer for revenue and a limited sales tax on such articles as tobacco, soft drinks, chewing gum, and cosmetics, coupled with a graduated net income tax with low exemptions." That statement was eating around the edges of the gross income tax passed just months before, during the regular 1933 legislature. Ustrud had never been a fan of the gross income tax bill. He called it "the most all-inclusive, unjust and inequitable tax system that was ever placed on the statute books of any state in the Union."

Lieutenant Governor Ustrud, born and reared on a farm in Minnehaha County, had taught school in Wisconsin, and while there, he became a fan and admirer of Wisconsin Republican and progressive Robert LaFollette. Later, when Ustrud, a Republican, returned to South Dakota, he was first elected Minnehaha County superintendent of schools and then became state superintendent of public instruction. Frustrated with an increasingly conservative state, Ustrud switched parties to serve as Democratic governor William Bulow's director of taxation from 1927 to 1931 and was elected lieutenant governor in 1933.

Ustrud favored a special beer session because of the possibility that legislators would also take the opportunity to amend or repeal Governor Berry's gross income tax. The gross income tax bill would, proponents argued, help make up for legislatively created rural credit losses and provide cash-strapped schools with additional funds. Because of the economic depression, especially on the farm, a net income tax was considered to be a better idea. A farmer might sell eggs for a dime a dozen, which would be taxed on a gross basis without any consideration that the farmer's expense to produce that ten cents' worth of eggs came to twelve cents.

While other states were voting for or against Prohibition repeal during most of 1933, beer began to flow and foam again, except in South Dakota. This presented a special challenge for South Dakota. A good share of South Dakota's population lived within easy driving distance of towns and taverns in other states, particularly Minnesota, where beer would soon freely flow. It would be naïve to expect South Dakotans to stand at the state's borders with their tongues hanging out watching the joyous quaffing of cool glasses only miles away in Minnesota.

Meanwhile, communities in Minnesota were joyously passing local ordinances clearing the way so businesses could sell beer when it became legal on the magical day of April 7, 1933. Businesses and organizations in South Dakota, concerned with the loss of revenue, vigorously lobbied the governor and others to take steps to allow them to join in this anticipated golden largess. The South Dakota Automobile Club worried the unavailability of beer in South Dakota would slash tourist numbers headed for the Black Hills. The South Dakota Restaurant Association adopted a resolution in favor of 3.2 beer and sent it to the beleaguered governor on April 20, 1933.

Chambers of commerce from every large city joined in mutual hand-wringing, reminding everyone that South Dakota would soon be surrounded by "wet territories." Speakers at a gathering of businessmen and professionals in Sioux Falls argued it was not a question of beer but of business and taxes. Those at the Sioux Falls meeting were told the loss of income to local businesses the first year would be about $100,000, the *Argus Leader* reported on March 30, 1933.

Sale of beer in states contiguous to South Dakota presented other problems, as well. Word was soon passed on by the state sheriff's office, the Sioux Falls Police Department and the Minnehaha County Sheriff's Department regarding illegal smuggling of beer. There would be no attempt to stop the expected stream of beer-laden automobiles crossing the state line from Minnesota back into South Dakota because nipping the smuggling bug in the bud would be too difficult to enforce. A few cases of beer in the rear seat of a car would be acceptable, but truckloads intended for resale in the state would not be allowed. Sioux Falls police put a positive spin on the impending Minnesota beer sales. It would, they said, dry up the illegal making and selling of home-brew in the Sioux Falls area, since Minnesota beer would retail for about the same price as the illegal product in South Dakota, reported the *Sioux Falls Argus Leader* on March 31, 1933.

Minnesota towns gleefully rubbed their hands, gearing up for the sales bonanza headed their way. In Beaver Creek, Minnesota, twenty-two miles east of Sioux Falls, the town board set a sales license fee of fifty dollars for beer dealers and decided beer could not be sold after midnight on Saturdays or on the Sabbath.

In Luverne, Minnesota, thirty miles east of Sioux Falls, prospective beer sales turned the otherwise tranquil community into a beehive of activity. Luverne's governing board set license fees at twenty dollars a year and limited beer sales to an eight-block downtown area.

In Worthington, Minnesota, forty-five miles from Sioux Falls, businessmen envisioned the city becoming the center for beer distribution for all of southwestern Minnesota. Four brewing companies were said to have intentions of opening warehouses there, the *Argus Leader* reported.

Three Sioux Falls beer wholesalers, whose trade territories covered a part of southwestern Minnesota, placed an initial order of 5,700 cases of beer for communities they served just across the Minnesota line. Ironically, many of those cases would end up being purchased by South Dakotans and hauled back to the South Dakota dry side.

In anticipation of the demand for beer in Minnesota, St. Paul breweries cranked up production and were bottling beer at the rate of seven hundred to one thousand cases an hour, providing jobs for hundreds of unemployed. The price of a case of twenty-four bottles of Minnesota beer at that time was $3.40, with a $1.00 rebate on a case of empty bottles, making it a $2.40

net. A keg sold for $16.00. Glasses of beer over the bar were $0.15 for a pint-sized glass and a smaller glass for $0.10.

A week before the start of 3.2 percent beer sales in Minnesota, the *Sioux Falls Argus Leader* editorialized on March 31, 1933, on what it considered "three lively controversies":

> *The South Dakota air is fairly seething these days about 3.2 beer, a special session of the Legislature and the gross income tax.*
>
> *Demands are being made from some quarters that Governor Berry summon the solons to Pierre while others advise him not to do so. The friends of a special session are made up of two primary groups, those who favor 3.2 beer and those who oppose the gross income tax. Opponents of the session are principally the objectors to 3.2 beer.*
>
> *A lively argument, it seems, is in prospect.*
>
> *Enemies of 3.2 beer maintain that it should not be allowed in South Dakota. They contend that it is intoxicating, and undesirable, and furthermore assert that any action to permit 3.2 beer in South Dakota would be unconstitutional. Friends of 3.2 beer believe that it is non-intoxicating and that the Legislature could authorize its manufacture and sale in South Dakota without violating the State Constitution. They assert, too, that South Dakota will sustain a considerable economic disadvantage with the sale of beer allowed in adjoining states. They point to the tax income that can be derived from beer, and emphasize the large amount of money that would slip from this State into other states under conditions as they now stand. Another argument they advance is that the legal sale of 3.2 beer is preferable to the admittedly common though illegal, sale of much stronger beverages.*
>
> *Those who dislike the gross income tax contend that the Legislature erred mightily in endorsing this measure. They give the solons credit for the best intentions in the world, but explain that many flaws in the proposal were not brought out in the perfunctory considering allowed in the regular legislative assembly. Both farmers and businessmen, they say, consider the measure vicious and undesirable. Already it is asserted numerous legal actions over disputed points in the law are in prospect. It is emphasized also that the bill was approved at a time when more money was absolutely essential to maintaining the State's credit. Since passage of the bill, however, the State has obtained a loan from the Reconstruction Finance Corporation that has done much to alter the picture.*
>
> *On the other side of the gross income tax bill, little is heard. Apparently its friends are not numerous either in the cities or on the farms.*

*A natural question arises: Just what can the Legislature do if it is convened? No action by the people is required. If that is done, the law will not go into effect on July 1 as now scheduled.*

*The beer proposition, however, invites some questions. The prohibition clause in the South Dakota Constitution specifies that intoxicating liquor cannot be manufactured or sold in South Dakota. It does not define intoxicating liquor, though, and in this respect is somewhat similar to the 18th amendment to the United States Constitution. Congress has held that 3.2 beer is not in conflict with the federal Constitution. This, it seems, is a rather good authority for the assumption that 3.2 beer would not be contrary to the South Dakota Constitution.*

*The sale and manufacture of 3.2 beer in South Dakota is expressly prohibited under the state bone dry law. The Legislature cannot change the Constitution but it can change the bone dry law.*

*From some quarters comes the suggestion that the Legislature submit immediately to the people an amendment repealing the liquor clause in the South Dakota Constitution. As things now stand, such an amendment is to be acted upon at the general election in 1934. There is grave doubt that it could be considered at any other time. The Constitution provides rather specifically that such amendments must be voted upon at a "general election."*

*Costs of such a special session of the Legislature are also brought into the limelight. A rough guess would place the expenditure for a gathering lasting about a fortnight at $20,000. This in itself does not constitute a valid argument against a session. Tax revenues from beer as well as the economic advantages through purchase of beer at home are sufficient to offset this several times over.*

On April 6, 1933, a day before Minnesota and eighteen other states unlatched the swinging bar door for beer sales, the *Brookings Register* commented: "The American habit of overdoing things, from all indications, will reach its zenith in beer-dispensing emporiums in Minnesota tomorrow.… If agitators for beer will now be satisfied, everything will be lovely. It's up to them to maintain order and decency. They are now 'on the spot.'"

At midnight plus one minute on April 7, 1933, beer began gushing from the spigots in most Minnesota towns. The response was titanic. It was estimated between six and seven hundred strangers were in Luverne, Minnesota, to imbibe and then load up their cars for the return trip to South Dakota. Two trucks of beer to replenish supplies for Luverne bars were hijacked along the way.

At Beaver Creek, the beer supply was sold out by afternoon. Another truckload arrived, and its contents were gone in two hours. In less than three months, the little town of Beaver Creek had sold $42,611 worth of beer, the *Sioux Falls Argus Leader* reported in its July 27, 1933 issue.

Nationally, millions of the more than seventy million people living in nineteen states where beer sales were legal were bellying up to the bar. Jubilee and jollity were widespread. Estimates of national consumption during the first twenty-four hours of legal beer sales were from one to one and a half million barrels, with each barrel containing thirty-six gallons.

Breweries were careful to make beer that was well within the federal 3.2 percent standard. Better to err on the side of caution. A federal study of alcoholic content of newly manufactured beer showed it usually had less than the 3.2 percent by weight legal limit. Beer with the lowest alcoholic content by weight came in at 2.48 percent. The highest was 3.18 percent.

With South Dakota beer aficionados and businesses drooling jealously over the successes in Minnesota and elsewhere, yet another petition asked Governor Berry to call a special legislative session for "the sole purpose" of considering a measure making it possible to sell beer in the state. The petition preparers, aware of the governor's gross income tax concern, promised no other issue would be brought forward during the session. Of course, legislative warhorses knew once the gavel sounded in Pierre there were no guarantees of what might transpire. The governor, too, remained cautious about opening the way for opponents of the gross income tax to reconnoiter in Pierre. Not surprisingly, his feelings were reinforced by concerned and influential drys in the state, according to a report in the *Brookings Register* on April 11, 1933.

Meanwhile, there was a temptation among some bootleggers to make a quick buck. Some opportunists broke into the Dakota Diamond T Truck Company at 315 North Dakota Avenue in Sioux Falls on April 17, 1933, and drove away with a Dalton Bottling Works truck loaded with thirty-six cases of soda pop and near beer. Police found the innocent "bone-dry" cargo dumped unceremoniously in rural Sioux Falls. A few days later, the truck was found, abandoned near a coal yard on 120 West Second Street. Sheriff Melvin Sells speculated it had been used to smuggle a load of Minnesota beer into the state. The news report said the truck smelled of "Pilsener," a popular brand of lager beer, the *Argus Leader* reported.

Meanwhile, the wait was on for a special legislative session in Pierre to put the state on equal footing with its neighbors.

CHAPTER 13

# The Beer Bill Session

With beer being sold and swilled in surrounding states and hard liquor on the way in most states, it was business as usual, or the lack thereof, for South Dakota's bootleggers, as Governor Tom Berry continued to hold the line on calling a special session. Wrote V.W. Pratt, editor of the *Brookings Register*, on April 18, 1933:

> *Governor Berry is standing pat on his decision not to call the Legislature into special session in spite of the huge pile of mail on his desk asking that he do so. There has been such widespread dissatisfaction over the gross income tax measure, and it is thought many who want beer are behind the move to get rid of the tax law. The administration has been so solidly behind the tax bill there will be danger of party disintegration should a special session be called for beer and it later develops the new tax bill be repealed.*

The next day, Governor Berry departed from his prepared speech in Yankton. "Now I suppose you are all expecting me to say something about a special session to act upon a measure legalizing beer," he told the crowd at a meeting where he was to discuss his campaign promise for government economy and tax reform. "Having spent most of my life out on the range where it is impossible to dodge anything, I am not in the habit of trying to evade any issue. Our Constitution contains a provision prohibiting the sale of any intoxicating beverage containing the slightest percentage of alcohol. This constitutional amendment was placed in our Constitution by the majority of the people and can only be repealed by the same method," he said.

In early May, members of the State Hotel and Restaurant Association met with the governor, presenting him with 150 petitions calling for a special session signed by more than ten thousand citizens, which coincidentally matched the WCTU petition signing number. The association's spokesman assured the governor his organization had received indications from a majority of legislators promising they would consider only the beer legalization issue should a special session be called.

One aspect of allowing the sale of beer in South Dakota that the governor must have seriously considered was the economic benefit to the state. He was aware that coffers in thirty-three state treasuries were $4.5 million richer as a result of beer taxes collected since legalization. The combination of the Great Depression, the Dust Bowl and the serious grasshopper infestations was causing severe financial difficulties for nearly all citizens. South Dakota's coffers could use the extra cash that beer licenses, fees and other related income would provide.

South Dakota attorney general Walter Conway assured the governor the state could legalize beer because Congress had decreed 3.2 percent beer as "non-intoxicating." This would, therefore, not violate the state's Prohibition amendment, Conway said. A survey by Conway estimated 4,335 establishments in South Dakota would sell 3.2 percent beer. Governor Berry seemed to bend slightly, but the gross income tax bugaboo and a potentially out-of-control legislature still worried him.

Dry forces were not sitting idly by, either. In early May 1933, representatives of all the temperance organizations met in Mitchell to pool their ideas and money and to plan the fight against legalizing beer and hard liquor repeal, if necessary. About twenty different groups were represented at the big Mitchell summit. Delegates elected an executive board composed of C.M. Granskou

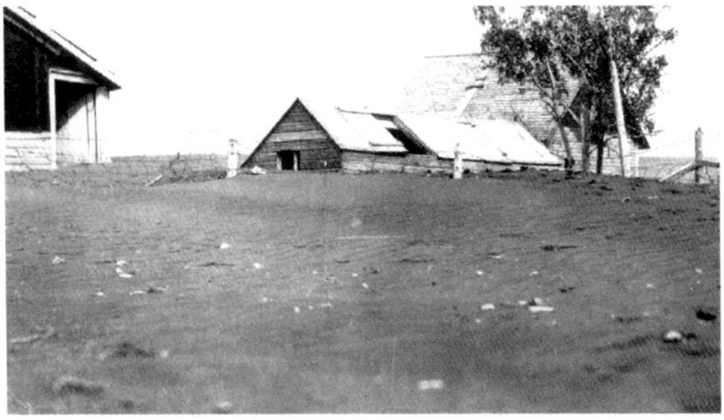

The Dust Bowl years of the early 1930s contributed to the misery of South Dakotans and drove many to join in the manufacture and delivery of illegal liquor. *Author's collection.*

of Sioux Falls; L.W. Robinson, Mitchell; D.K. Loucks, Watertown; Mrs. Alvin Waggoner, Phillip; James E. Kirk Jr., Avon; H.C. Halverson, Sinai; C.A. Wilson, Hot Springs; Mrs. Walter Shuck, Aberdeen; and Mrs. H.M. Minish, Winner. Alternates were S.B. Nissen of Sioux Falls; C.D. Erskine, Sturgis; Frank R. Fisher, Miller; Mrs. Lucy Borneman, Sioux Falls; George Kunkle, Yanton; Mrs. W.I. Kohl, Aberdeen; William Potts, Mobridge; J.E. Washburn, Highmore; and A.M. Clark, Brookings.

Governor Berry was apparently beginning to recognize the potential economic benefit beer sales would bring to his struggling state. So he devised a strategy he hoped might dull the rancorous scolding he expected from drys if he broke ranks and called for a "beer" session. The governor proposed all taxes and fees from beer sales be assigned to the state as relief funds. He wrote to every legislator asking them to assure him of his or her support of this beer issue–only approach should he call a special session, the *Sioux Falls Argus Leader* reported on June 26, 1933. Few legislators responded.

Despite legislative assurances, and after a nearly three-month hiatus, Governor Berry relented. On July 15, 1933, he called a special session. Legislators were to report to Pierre on July 31 "to legalize beer for relief revenue." It would be only the sixth special session ever called in South Dakota.

With the good news, and anticipating quick approval of a beer bill, communities across the state commenced passing laws and rules allowing and controlling beer sales. Chamberlain gained notoriety as the first to pass enabling laws. Dell Rapids, Carthage and Pukwana had letters in the mail the same day asking for copies of the Chamberlain ordinances, the *Argus Leader* reported. City officials in Huron, once considered the epicenter in South Dakota for making and distributing illegal booze, announced that if the legislature legalized beer, it would be for sale in Huron within nine days.

The special legislative session of the Twenty-third Legislature was gaveled to order at 10:30 a.m. on July 31, 1933. Governor Berry made brief comments, saying he called the session out of his concern for the state's faltering economy, not for his concern for beer sales. "It has become my duty as governor of South Dakota officially to call to your attention a calamitous condition existing in this state," he said. He reviewed the devastation from widespread drought made worse by the grasshopper plague. "A source of revenue is open to us without imposing hardship on any citizen. A law should be passed legalizing the manufacture and sale of non-intoxicating beer and wine, as defined by federal law, imposing a

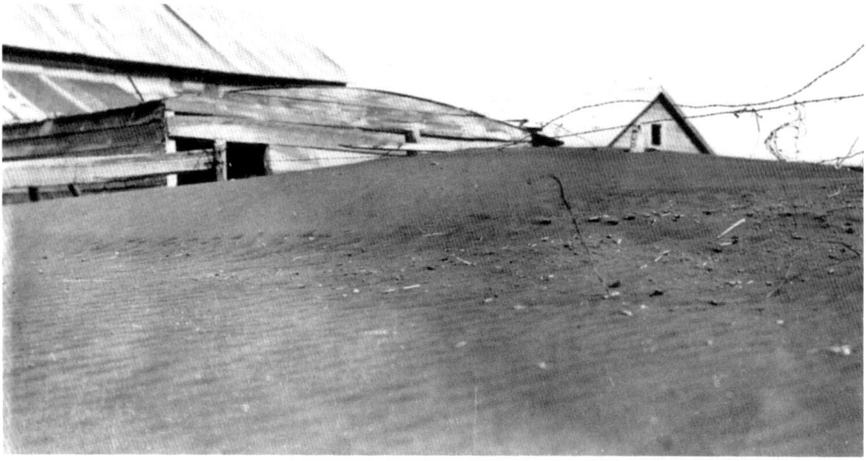

The financial hardships of farmers in South Dakota in the 1930s because of the Great Depression and the dust storms helped politicians to end the state's bone-dry Prohibition. *Author's collection.*

proper license and tax thereon, appropriating the proceeds to the relief of destitution and poverty." He added that such legislation should be the "only" legislation for the special session.

On the opening day, resolutions were introduced in both chambers to comply with the governor's mandate to limit discussions to only beer. The House voted on whether to comply, and with the speaker voting in the affirmative to limit the scope of the session, it ended in a tie, meaning the motion to limit the session to only beer failed. On reconsideration later, however, both the House and the Senate agreed it would be "hands off" the controversial gross income tax bill passed earlier in the year. The Senate vote sheltering the income tax matter was thirty-one to twelve, and the House followed with a fifty-nine to thirty-nine count, according to the Proceedings of the South Dakota House and Senate Special Session, 1933.

Within hours of the start of the session on August 1, 1933, five bills, including two having to do with legalizing beer, were introduced. Before the session ended a week later, fifty-nine bills had been introduced, thirty-seven in the House and twenty-two in the Senate, according to an article, "Democratic Party Politics," in *South Dakota History Quarterly* 26, nos. 2 and 3.

Forty-eight hours after the session started, the Senate approved a beer bill, Senate Bill Five, but only after members had amended it seventeen times from what the governor requested, according to Lieutenant Governor Urstad's *Behind the Scenes*. The Senate vote, which provided a local option should communities or counties decide to ban beer sales, was forty-two to one, with the lone dissenter being Sinai farmer H.C. Halvorson of temperate Brookings County. Senator Halvorson, who was an active member of his county's Consolidated Drys, said he believed the bill violated the dry amendment in the state constitution.

Governor Berry wanted all of the income generated from beer licenses and other related taxes reverted to the state for relief help, but senators changed the formula, splitting the money evenly between the counties and the state. Each entity, however, would earmark the income for poor relief purposes. In the case of counties, senators decided county relief should be used for "indigent hospitalization."

The Senate also revised the governor's requested fee structure, setting a $250.00 license for brewers and $200.00 for distributors. Off-sale retailers would pay a $25.00 fee and on-sale retailers $75.00. They also created a beverage tax and an inspection fee totaling $1.25 for each thirty-six-gallon barrel of beer, the *Brookings Register* reported on August 3, 1933. A paragraph in the bill said no malt beverage could be sold in the state unless two-thirds of the grain used in its manufacture was "barley malt."

Senate Bill Five's passage in the Senate did not come without some political intrigue. The bill did not have its final reading and passage until after 9:00 p.m. on the second meeting day. Lieutenant Governor Ustrud, the Senate's presiding officer, claimed later that he did not know the House had remained in session that evening, expecting Senate Bill Five to be sent to it so the House could give it a first and second reading the same evening. The House leadership plan was to have the third and final reading and passage the next morning and then adjourn, thereby avoiding having to vote on other pending bills.

Lieutenant Governor Ustrud said that when he learned the impatient House was still in session waiting for the passed Senate Bill Five, he conferred with Senate Engrossing and Enrolling director Agnes Johnson. Her staff, by that late hour, was not at full strength, and she estimated the time to prepare the bill for transfer to the House would take more than six hours, Ustrud wrote in his *Behind the Scenes* manuscript.

Lieutenant Governor Ustrud, the avowed supporter of changes in the gross income tax measure, said he made the decision not to call the full Engrossing and Enrolling staff back to the capitol building that night. Instead, he tucked the bill in his pocket and retired to his room for a good night's rest. He later said his plan was for the bill to be worked on for transfer to the House the next morning. This delay raised the hackles of Governor Berry and legislators, who suspected the lieutenant governor was tinkering with the process to provide time for a possible assault on the gross income tax bill. They cried foul and called in the press to explain the reason for their unhappiness.

Ustrud, in his published recollection of events that evening, claimed "The Berries," as he called the governor's staff and loyal advocates, raided the desks and files of Senate offices and those in the office of Engrossing and Engraving, looking for Senate Bill Five so the House could consider it.

The next day, after six hours of preparation, the House finally got Senate Bill Five at exactly 2:30 p.m. It arrived in the House one half hour before the body had admonished the lieutenant governor, censuring him for the delay and demanding the bill be sent to the House immediately, although it was already there by the time the censure vote was taken, according to *Behind the Scenes*. During the House debate, members flexed their muscles and amended the Senate's seventy-five-dollar fee for on-sale licenses, lowering it to forty dollars, and then passed the beer bill the next day, Saturday, August 5, 1933. Wine was also included in the legalization so long as it did not exceed the 3.2 percent alcohol content. The vote was ninety-one to ten.

House members voting against the beer bill were J.M. Bergan, South Shore; Edward Bogue, Canton; W.J. Eggert, Rockham; Lewis Ellefson, Sherman; Fred Hampton, Sturgis; Paul Lunder, Canton; A.S. Mitchell, Brookings; Ole S. Quammen, Lemmon; George Rice, Flandreau; and Peter Sorenson of Toronto, according to Proceedings of the House and Senate Special Session, 1933.

Governor Berry had earlier threatened to veto all bills if more than the beer bill was considered or passed, but he relented and signed Senate Bill Five on Saturday afternoon at 5:30 p.m., at which time it became effective. He also signed other bills approved during the special session. A columnist for the dry *Brookings Register*, Arthur M. Clark, wrote a six-word, one-sentence paragraph about the passage of the beer bill: "Well, doesn't beer rhyme with Pierre?"

Almost immediately after its passage, Herbert Ford of Mitchell, secretary of the state's disappointed dry contingent, announced plans to seek a state supreme court ruling on Senate Bill Five's constitutionality, since it ran counter to the state constitution's bone-dry amendment. Attorney Lauritz Miller of Mitchell was retained as counsel. Coincidentally, he was the author of the state constitution's Prohibition amendment in 1917. The threat of a lawsuit was short-lived, however, because the dry camp changed its mind and decided against a challenge, the *Argus Leader* reported. Some speculated the decision to not seek a ruling was to save the dollars in their dwindling war chest for use in the big battle ahead on the bone-dry restrictions that would usher in hard liquor.

Within days after the beer bill became law, companies announced intentions to enter the beer-manufacturing business and file incorporation papers with state officials. One, the General Beverage Company of Yankton, was incorporated with $25,000. The firm's intention was to manufacture "lager" beer and sell it wholesale. Incorporators were Henry S. Tammen and Henry Tammen, both of Yankton, and W.A. McGiffen of Detroit, Michigan.

The old Yankton brewery Schwenk-Barth Company indicated it would make beer again. It planned to have its Rosebud beer, famous and once in demand from coast to coast before Prohibition, on the market by November. The Yankton brewery would produce sixty thousand barrels of beer annually, according to the August 6, 1933 issue of the *Sioux Falls Argus Leader.*

The South Dakota Distributors Company of Mitchell was incorporated with $20,000 in capital stock to be a wholesale and jobbing business in beer and other beverages. Officers were A.C. Cohrt and David M. Rogers of Mitchell and Howard C. Turnley of Sioux City.

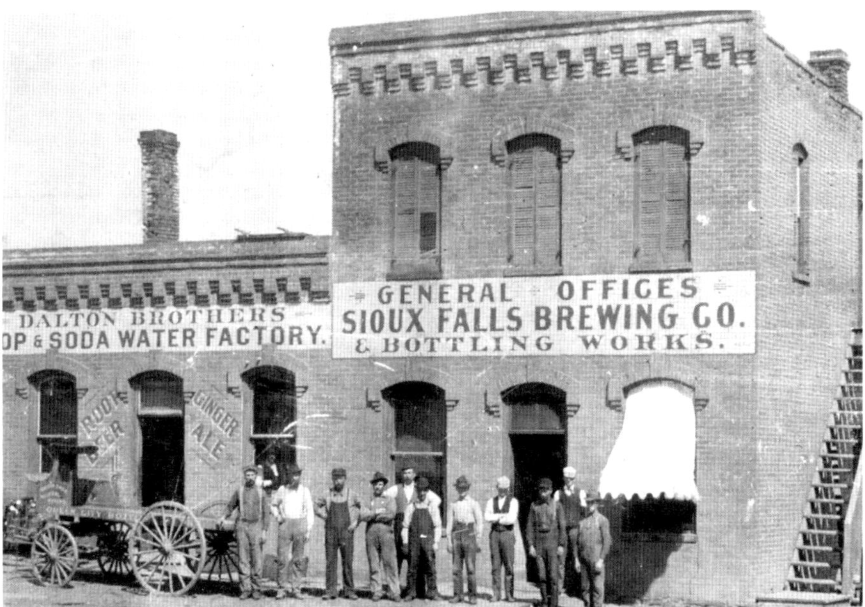


Sioux Falls Brewing Company was established after the Prohibition law was repealed. *Author's collection.*

Other plans for breweries in the state were forthcoming. The Sioux Chief Brewing Company of Sioux Falls announced it would make from 100,000 to 150,000 barrels of beer yearly in the old Jones Seed Company building on North Phillips Avenue. The plant would employ seventy-five people with a $100,000 a year payroll. The Henry Carlson Company was in charge of plant remodeling. The company brought five experienced beer makers and their families to Sioux Falls from Milwaukee, Wisconsin, including George W. Walgerle, who had worked in the beer industry in Germany, the *Argus Leader* reported on August 6, 1933.

In September 1933, five Sioux Falls men filed articles of incorporation for the Dakota Brewing Company of Huron, capitalized at $100,000. Incorporators were F.P. Hall, W.R. Laird, R. Dubel, C.J. Delbridge and J. Maher. John G. Dorsey of St. Paul, Minnesota, was the brewmeister. By April 1934, the plant was producing 1,244 gallons of beer a day. Dorsey said production capacity would be increased in the months ahead. To celebrate the opening, the public was invited to tour the plant with the offer of free beer.

In October 1933, the Minnehaha Brewing and Malting Company was incorporated for $500,000. F.W. Luedtke of Hutchinson, Minnesota, was president. Also on the board of directors were M.A. Clark, Minneapolis; and C.F. Whitehouse, R.W. Dickenson and J.M. Haggardt, all of Sioux Falls.

In the spring of 1935, the Old Town Beverage Company at 424 and 430 North Main Avenue in Sioux Falls went into operation as the city's first "liquor rectifying and manufacturing plant." Joseph K. Lorenz of Dubuque, Iowa, president of the firm, explained "rectifying" to the citizens of Sioux Falls this way, according to the *Argus Leader* of April 24, 1935: "Nobody would take tobacco as it is grown in the field and smoke or chew it, but that it is necessary to process it before it can be used. In a similar manner it is necessary to take distilled liquors and remove impurities, blend it for proper taste and proof, as many spirits in their original form are entirely too strong to be used for beverage purposes."

Even before the beer bill was approved nationally or in the state, the Sioux Brewing Corporation of Pierre had filed organization papers in anticipation of what might take place. To hedge its bet, the company indicated in its filing papers plans to begin manufacturing of near beer and other beverages. If beer was legalized, an amendment to its articles of incorporation indicated the word "near" would be deleted from its purposes. Directors were H.C. Stinchfield of Minneapolis, A.J. Fernald of Chicago and R. Mullen of Sioux Falls, according to the *Sioux Falls Argus Leader*.

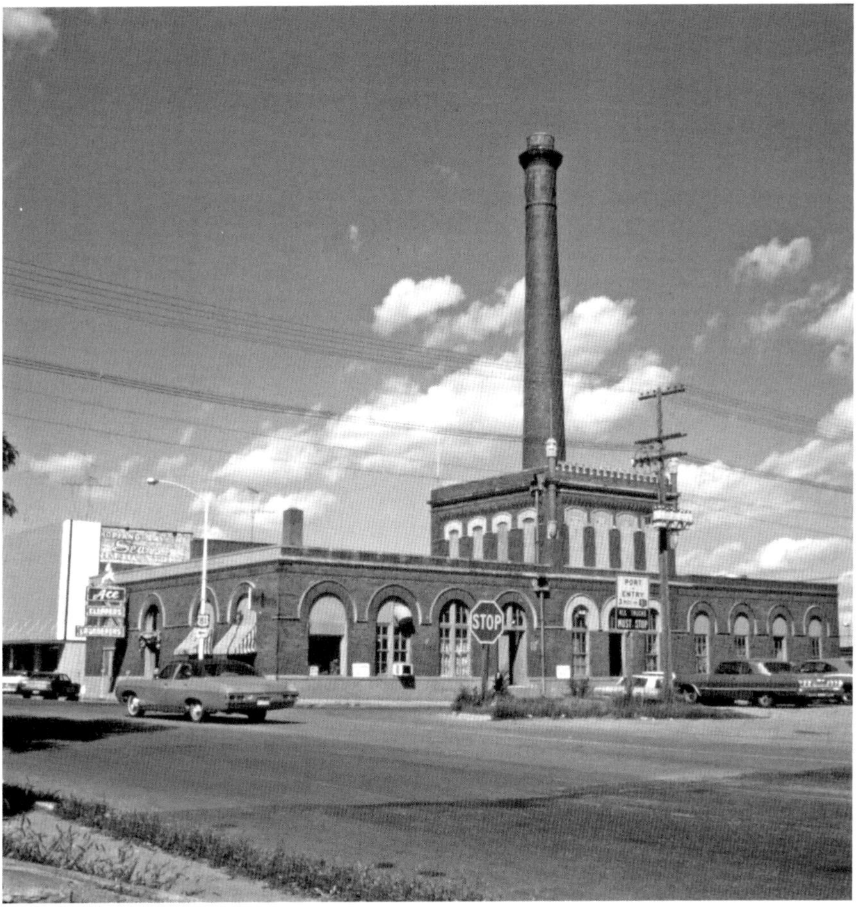


The former Schwenk-Barth Brewery building in Yankton. *Author's collection.*

In September 1934, the Rushmore Brewing Company of Deadwood filed incorporation papers to capitalize at $153,000. Incorporators were F.R. Barthold of Bridger, Louis Johnsen of Pierre and A.H. Markert of Sioux Falls.

Bars and saloons were also lining up for licenses. Within ten days of the beer law's passage, the City of Yankton led the list for the number of retail licenses issued, with thirteen. Huron had by then approved twelve retail licenses; Mitchell, seven; Aberdeen, five; and Lead and Rapid City, just one retail license each. Statewide, nineteen distributor's licenses had been issued by August 10, 1933, going to H.E. Neeley Company, Sioux Falls; Fenn Brothers, Inc., Sioux Falls; Stanley W. Barnett, Winner; Pierre Bottling Works,

Pierre; Rosebud Distributors, Winner; Haley-Neeley Company branches at Mitchell, Aberdeen, Huron and Pierre; Canton Creamery Company, Canton; J. Holm, Winner Bottling Works, Winner; Lee and Riveness, Faulkton; Binder Brothers, Inc., Yankton; Huron Grocery Company, Huron; B. DeMersseman, Rapid City; Vernon Vanderhule, Yankton; L.B. Albright and Company, Pierre; Crescent Creamery Company, Sioux Falls; and Henry S. Tammen, Yankton. The first Sioux Falls retailer to file for a beer license was William Chamley.

Within a week of Governor Berry's beer bill signing, the revenue from beer licenses and fees was already calculated at $28,000, more than enough to cover the approximate $20,000 cost of the special legislative session.

The State Agriculture Department was responsible for administering the law, and during the five working days after bill passage, the department approved licenses for 359 retailers, 51 distributors and 5 off-sale dealers. In addition, 8 special "dining car" permits were issued for $10 each to the Milwaukee Railroad Company. By August 19, 1933, nearly $75,000 from more than 1,000 retailers had already been collected, of which half would be transferred to counties. By the summer of 1935, of the 566 hard liquor licenses issued, 435 were for off-sale, or package sale, and of the 131

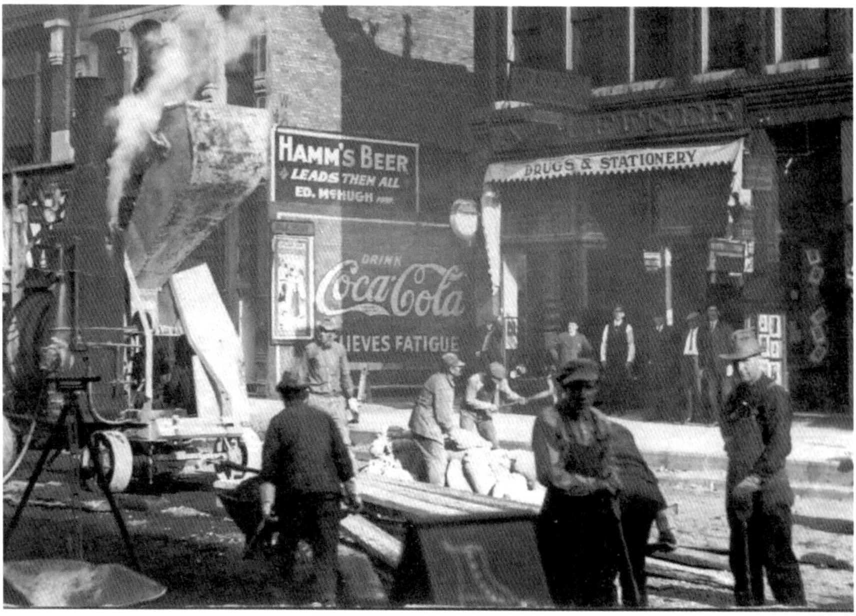


These thirsty post–Prohibition era road builders on Watertown's main street surely took heed of the Hamm's Beer and Ed McHugh's saloon sign beckoning over their shoulders. *Author's collection.*

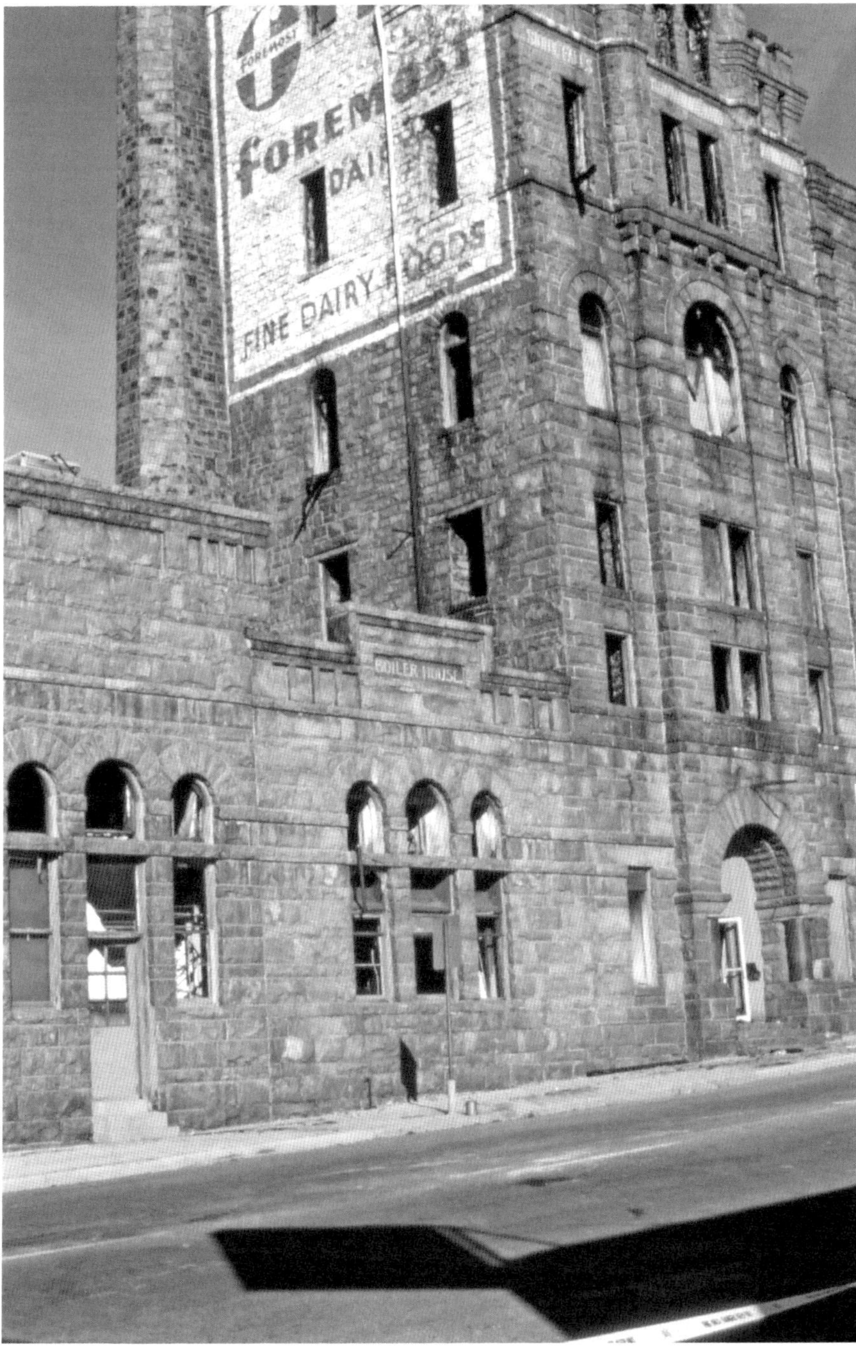


After serving its post-Prohibition days as the Sioux Falls Brewery, it became a creamery and then was abandoned. *Courtesy of South Dakota Historical Society.*

sale-by-drink licenses issued by the state, 61 were to first-class cities; 42 to communities of between five hundred and five thousand population; and 28 to towns with fewer than five hundred persons, the June 4, 1935 *Brookings Register* reported.

Perhaps because the beer bill was considered necessary by "The Berries" in those difficult times, but also for good public relations, rancher Governor Berry announced in late August 1933 the first use of the state's share of money from the sale of licenses. It was to purchase one thousand tons of hay for drought- and grasshopper-stricken areas. The hay was bought by the state for $6.50 a ton from N.J. Thompson of Presho. In making the announcement, Governor Berry noted that desperate farmers in many sections of the state were putting up Russian thistles for feed, according to the August 26, 1933 issue of the *Sioux Falls Argus Leader*. At the time, hardly any of the state's nearly eighty-five thousand farms were doing well.

By December 1933, South Dakota's Relief Administration's statistician, M.A. Kennedy, announced the state would discontinue using beer licenses and tax fees to purchase livestock feed because federal programs were now providing that funding. Kennedy said $15,025 of beer tax money bought hay and corn, leaving a balance in the fund of $47,608. Through December 12, 1933, Kennedy said 7,183 tons of hay was purchased, either from beer income or from federal funds, the *Argus Leader* reported in December 1933.

Although there was widespread belief that intoxication could not be induced by drinking 3.2 beer, the number of arrests for drunkenness increased in the state during the remainder of the summer of 1933. In August 1933 in Sioux Falls, for example, police reported intoxication arrests increased by more than 33 percent from the same month's averages of 1931 and 1932. Interestingly, driving while intoxicated, then called "drunken driving," declined by half during the same period. Until the January legislative session in 1927, by the way, there was no law in the state against drunk driving.

The increase in drunkenness attributed to drinking 3.2 beer in South Dakota motivated A.D. Aldrich, editor-publisher of the *Big Stone City Headlight*, to suggest a state beer-drinking contest to determine the efficacy of the oft-quoted "non-intoxicating" claim of 3.2 beer. He jokingly wrote that such a contest to determine who could consume the most 3.2 beer and remain sober would be a big attraction, "bigger than a corn eating contest." Aldrich proposed the scientist from New York who had devised a method of determining the extent of intoxication by drawing a few drops of blood from a fingertip be brought to South Dakota to help judges, the *Brookings Register* reported on September 21, 1933.

In 1934, the chairman of the physiology department of the University of Chicago conducted a four-month test of beer drinkers. He concluded a person could not "comfortably drink" enough 3.2 beer to become intoxicated. His subjects were from nineteen to sixty years old and weighed from 100 to 233 pounds. They drank from two to sixteen twelve-ounce bottles of beer over periods ranging from fifteen minutes to sixteen hours. Dr. Anton J. Carlson said people had to be forced to drink sufficient beer to exhibit the changes in behavior classed as intoxication, according to the *Huronite* of November 14, 1933.

Officials planning the 1933 state fair in Huron surprised citizens by announcing a ban on 3.2 beer at the fairgrounds, but for the 1934 state fair, secretary James G. Venables proudly trumpeted a new feature of the extravaganza. The old Machinery Hall would be remodeled into a beer garden with a motif patterned after the beer garden at the World's Fair in Chicago the previous year. Dancing would also be allowed in the garishly decorated garden. All this was a remarkable segue. The state fair beer garden came less than twenty years after beer had been banned in the state and only a few years after public dancing was condemned and ridiculed as "public hugging."

Now, with beer sales, dancing, cigarette smoking, beer gardens and perhaps a few selected curse words accepted at the South Dakota State Fair and in dance halls and main street pool halls in nearly every South Dakota town, Pandora's box finally sprang full open. In 1935, during the three-month period from April through June, the state treasurer reported consumption in the state averaged nearly three gallons of beer for every man, woman and child.

The next hurdle for the state was the vote on a complete packing away of what remained of the state's bone-dry Prohibition laws. Because beer was already plentiful, it would be somewhat anticlimactic, but many dry apostles had believed such a move toward hard liquor on call would never happen.

South Dakota's Anti-Saloon League member and officer, the Reverend John E. Booth of Big Stone City, was among those who were confident the state would never repeal its Prohibition amendment. But early in 1934, the approaching legalization of hard liquor in Minnesota, just as it had been with beer a year earlier, was about to happen.

The task of South Dakota's bootleggers finding a source of booze was about to become much, much easier. Even more worrisome, law-abiding citizens of the state would once again become engaged in the smuggling of liquor from other contiguous states onto the lonely, dry island of South Dakota.

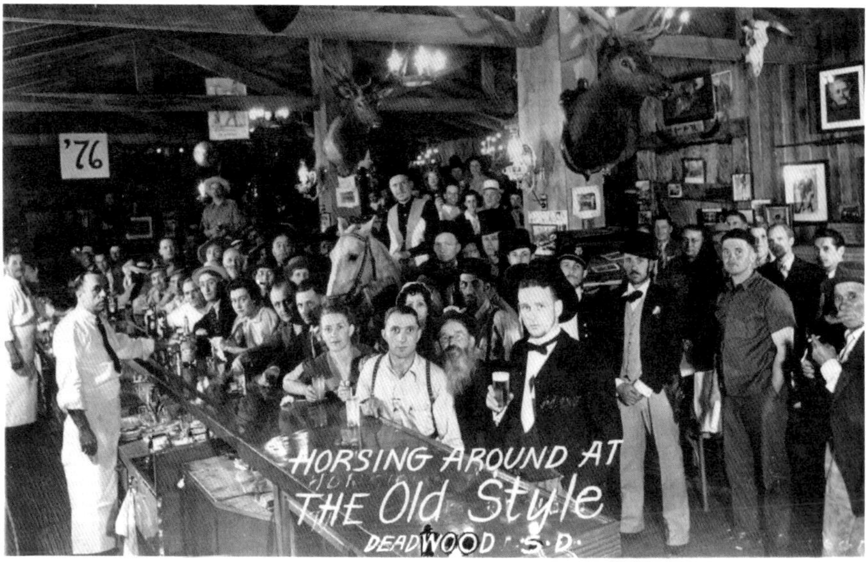


A raucous old-style saloon crowd in Deadwood join with a horse and rider to celebrate the end of the state's bone-dry Prohibition. *Author's collection.*

The statewide vote in South Dakota to change Prohibition laws would not take place until November 1934. Minnesota and other surrounding states could begin selling booze of all types ten months earlier, in late January 1934. In an editorial, the *Sioux Falls Argus Leader* saw one advantage to the state's late start. South Dakota would learn from the mistakes of Minnesota and Iowa, the newspaper said.

Finally, on November 5, 1934, South Dakota voters approved repeal of the state's Prohibition section in its constitution by a wide margin. Prohibition was out by more than 34,000 votes, 142,853 to 108,64, according to secretary of state election records. It was a record turnout.

Many of the dry proponents were shocked. H.R. Carpenter, publisher of the *Beresford Republic*, summed it up in a November 8, 1934 editorial: "Incredible as it seems after the campaign by the prohibitionists to prevent repeal, the state seems to have gone 'wet.' The decisions of the voters to again legalize the sale of hard liquor should be the signal for the 'wets' and 'drys' to bury the hatchet and join forces in the very important task of seeing that laws are enacted which will make good liquor easier to get."

After the vote, legal hard liquor went on sale in South Dakota on April 5, 1935, for the first time since February 21, 1917. The next day, the first license permitting legal sale of liquor by the drink in South Dakota was issued to Roy B. Heygood of Aberdeen, with early licenses also issued to the Widman Hotel Company and H.G. Scharnweber, both of Mitchell, and Pudwill and Stellflug of Herried. By 2010, retail liquor licenses in South Dakota numbered more than 880, issued in 263 South Dakota communities, according to Clare V. Charlson, senior research analyst at the South Dakota Research Council.

At last, South Dakotans, after nearly two decades, had hitched to the snubbing post the ornery, kicking white mule they'd been astride for so many dry, contentious years.

# Appendix

## National Prohibition Amendment

## October 19, 1919

*Resolved by the Senate and House of Representatives of the United States of America in Congress assembled (two-thirds of each house concurring therein), that the following amendment to the Constitution be, and hereby is, proposed to the states, to become valid as a part of the Constitution when ratified by the legislatures of the several states as provided by the Constitution.*

*Section 1. After one year from ratification of this article, the manufacture, sale, or transportation of intoxicating liquors within, the importation thereof into, or the exportation thereof from the United States and all territory subject to the jurisdiction thereof, for beverages purposes is hereby prohibited.*

*Section 2. The Congress and the several states shall have concurrent power to enforce this article by appropriate legislation.*

*Section 3. This article shall be inoperative unless it shall have been ratified as an amendment to the Constitution by the legislatures of the several states, as provided in the Constitution within seven years from the date of submission hereof to the states by the Congress.*

## "Stand Up for Temperance"
## (to the tune of "Stand Up for Jesus")

*Stand up! Stand up for temp'rance!*
*Ye writers bold and strong;*
*Proclaim its blessed teachings,*
*And help the cause along.*
*From country unto country*
*The story must be told,*
*'Till every mind is captured*
*And rum no more is sold.*

*Stand up! Stand up for temp'rance!*
*Ye tradesman of the state;*
*Dakota's golden morning*
*Has to us come though late.*
*Now rise and do your duty,*
*The liquor fiend help smite;*
*Then o'er our boundless prairies*
*Shall towns be clean and bright.*

*Stand up! Stand up for temp'rance!*
*Ye men who till the land*
*Be true to home and country,*
*And raise for God a hand.*
*Tell to the whiskey seller*
*That his dark reign must end;*
*So you and yours forever,*
*Your days in peace may spend.*

*Stand up! Stand up for temp'rance*
*Ye mothers and ye wives,*
*Display your wanted patience,*
*But ask for brighter lives;*
*With husbands, sons and brothers,*
*Plead earnestly and long;*
*And give to prohibition*
*Your strength, your time and song.*

—Reverend William Fielder

From *The Constitutional Prohibition Songster for South Dakota* (Constitutional Prohibition Organization, Aberdeen Daily News Company, 1889)

## Federal and State Prohibition Timeline

**1889**: State constitution is adopted. The vote on Prohibition amendment number twenty-four passes 40,234 to 34,510.

**1890**: First South Dakota Legislative Session adopts dry laws to put the 1889 vote on the books effective May 1, 1890.

**1895**: Question of Prohibition submitted by South Dakota legislature to the voters

**1896**: Dry amendment number twenty-four is voted out, 31,901 to 23,910. The state goes wet.

**1898**: Constitutional amendment number twenty-seven for state control of manufacture and sale of liquor is approved, 22,170 to 20,755.

**1900**: Prohibition amendment number twenty-seven is repealed, 48,673 to 33,927.

**1915**: Legislature resubmits the Prohibition question to voters.

**1916**: People vote 65,334 to 53,380; South Dakota is again dry.

**1917**: Legislature writes a state dry law among the most rigid in the nation, effective July 1.

**1918**: South Dakotans vote March 20 to ratify national Prohibition, the tenth state to do so.

**1920**: National Prohibition begins on January 16.

**1933**: Beer is made legal in South Dakota in August.

**1935**: Liquor is made legal in South Dakota on April 15.

## Repeal Votes

| County | Yes | No |
|---|---|---|
| Aurora | 1,356 | 1,213 |
| Beadle | 4,999 | 2,659 |
| Bennett | 610 | 672 |
| Bon Homme | 2,751 | 2,008 |
| Brookings | 2,462 | 3,645 |
| Brown | 7,373 | 4,042 |
| Brule | 1,685 | 1,120 |
| Buffalo | 370 | 316 |
| Butte | 1,660 | 1,135 |
| Campbell | 1,081 | 776 |

| County | Yes | No |
|---|---|---|
| Charles Mix | 3,613 | 2,150 |
| Clark | 1,817 | 2,039 |
| Clay | 1,743 | 2,058 |
| Codington | 4,389 | 2,367 |
| Corson | 1,797 | 959 |
| Custer | 1,360 | 692 |
| Davidson | 3,681 | 2,889 |
| Day | 2,933 | 2,745 |
| Deuel | 1,497 | 1,497 |
| Dewey | 1,377 | 720 |
| Douglas | 1,302 | 1,319 |
| Edmunds | 2,165 | 1,445 |
| Fall River | 2,145 | 967 |
| Faulk | 1,396 | 1,177 |
| Grant | 2,049 | 2,031 |
| Gregory | 2,186 | 1,532 |
| Haakon | 1,055 | 925 |
| Hamlin | 1,601 | 1,394 |
| Hand | 1,749 | 1,674 |
| Hanson | 1,176 | 1,158 |
| Harding | 645 | 720 |
| Hughes | 1,701 | 1,325 |
| Hutchinson | 3,177 | 1,620 |
| Hyde | 740 | 743 |
| Jackson | 629 | 466 |
| Jerauld | 1,009 | 1,371 |
| Jones | 594 | 666 |
| Kingsbury | 2,061 | 2,518 |
| Lake | 2,574 | 2,341 |
| Lawrence | 4,685 | 1,643 |
| Lincoln | 1,963 | 2,936 |
| Lyman | 1,368 | 1,109 |
| Marshall | 1,657 | 1,437 |

| COUNTY | YES | NO |
|---|---|---|
| McCook | 2,258 | 1,719 |
| McPherson | 2,435 | 720 |
| Meade | 2,270 | 1,915 |
| Mellette | 861 | 662 |
| Miner | 1,587 | 1,291 |
| Minnehaha | 11,649 | 7,622 |
| Moody | 2,009 | 1,467 |
| Pennington | 4,913 | 2,817 |
| Perkins | 1,575 | 1,631 |
| Potter | 1,364 | 977 |
| Roberts | 2,710 | 2,874 |
| Sanborn | 1,489 | 1,404 |
| Spink | 2,910 | 2,673 |
| Stanley | 654 | 566 |
| Sully | 615 | 689 |
| Tripp | 2,324 | 1,614 |
| Turner | 2,271 | 2,860 |
| Union | 2,013 | 1,941 |
| Walworth | 2,042 | 947 |
| Yankton | 4,042 | 2,146 |
| Ziebach | 717 | 545 |
| | | |
| **Unorganized counties** | | |
| Armstrong | | |
| Shannon | 375 | 269 |
| Todd | 1,038 | 657 |
| Washabaugh | 323 | 264 |
| Washington | 228 | 159 |
| | | |
| **Totals** | 142,853 | 108,648 |

Source: South Dakota Secretary of State's Office

# Index

## C

## D

## E



## F



## G



## H

# I



# J



# K

**Q**



**R**



**S**

## T



## U



## V

# About the Author

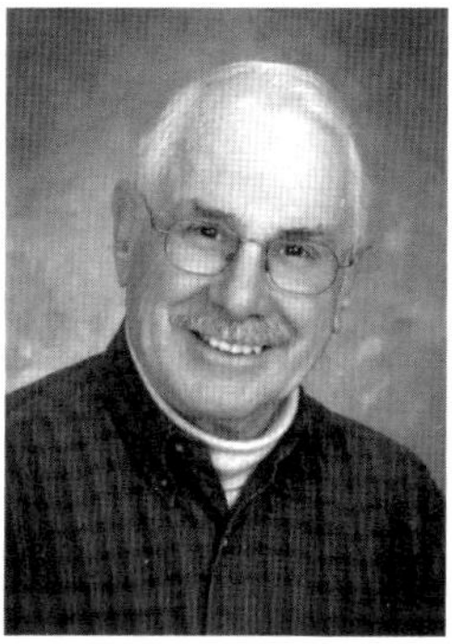

Chuck Cecil was born and spent his early years in Wessington Springs. He graduated from Rapid City High School, was an aerial photographer in the Korean War and graduated from South Dakota State University with a degree in journalism. Between his junior and senior years, he was successful gubernatorial candidate Ralph Herseth's campaign manager.

He was a reporter/photographer for the *Watertown Public Opinion* in the 1960s.

Now a retired university administrator and newspaper editor/publisher of eleven weekly newspapers, he is a freelance writer concentrating mostly on history for articles for local, state and national publications. He writes a prize-winning weekly column in the *Brookings Register* newspaper and has a short program on all of the Brookings radio stations.

He has written and published twenty-one books. This book on Prohibition in South Dakota is the only one ever written about that eighteen-year South Dakota experience.